THE WHITMAN REVOLUTION

IOWA WHITMAN SERIES

Ed Folsom, series editor

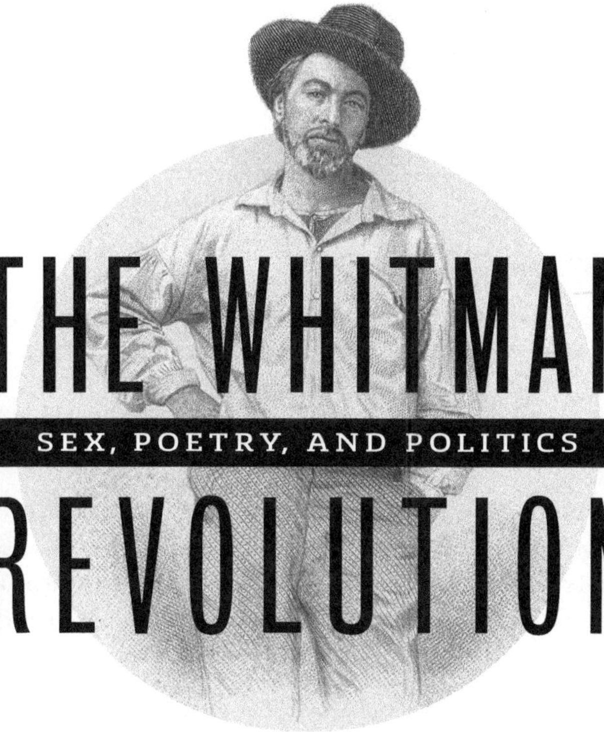

THE WHITMAN REVOLUTION

SEX, POETRY, AND POLITICS

Betsy Erkkila

UNIVERSITY OF IOWA PRESS, IOWA CITY

University of Iowa Press, Iowa City 52242

www.uipress.uiowa.edu

Printed in the United States of America

Design by April Leidig

Printed on acid-free paper

Library of Congress Cataloging-in-Publication Data
Names: Erkkila, Betsy, 1944– author.
Title: The Whitman Revolution: Sex, Poetry, and Politics / Betsy Erkkila.
Description: Iowa City: University of Iowa Press, [2020] | Series: Iowa Whitman Series | Includes bibliographical references and index. |
Identifiers: LCCN 2020020735 (print) | LCCN 2020020736 (ebook) |
ISBN 9781609387228 (paperback; acid-free paper) | ISBN 9781609387235 (ebook)
Subjects: LCSH: Whitman, Walt, 1819–1892—Political and social views. |
Whitman, Walt, 1819–1892—Criticism and interpretation. |
Democracy in literature.
Classification: LCC PS3242.P64 E737 2020 (print) |
LCC PS3242.P64 (ebook) | DDC 811/.3—dc23
LC record available at https://lccn.loc.gov/2020020735
LC ebook record available at https://lccn.loc.gov/2020020736

For Larry, with all my love

CONTENTS

Acknowledgments ix

Abbreviations xi

Introduction: The Whitman Revolution 1

PART ONE

Revolutionary Poetics

Chapter One
"The Federal Mother":
Whitman as Revolutionary Son
31

Chapter Two
Whitman and the Politics of Language
51

PART TWO

"In Paths Untrodden"

Chapter Three
"Song of Myself" and the Politics of the Body Erotic
69

Chapter Four
Whitman and the Homosexual Republic
79

Chapter Five
Radical Imaginaries:
Crossing Over with Whitman and Dickinson
101

PART THREE

The Revolutionary Transatlantic

Chapter Six
Whitman, Marx, and the American 1848
123

Chapter Seven
Insurrection, the Paris Commune, and *Leaves of Grass*
145

PART FOUR

Democratic Vistas

Chapter Eight
Whitman, Melville, and the Tribulations of Democracy
163

Chapter Nine
Public Love: Whitman and Political Theory
201

Notes 225

Bibliography 245

Index 257

ACKNOWLEDGMENTS

I have been blessed over many years by an international and national community of Whitman scholars and friends from whom I have learned so much. I want to thank all of them. I am especially grateful to the Transatlantic Walt Whitman Association, which has put me in touch with so many scholars, students, and lovers of Whitman throughout the world since its foundation in Paris in 2007. In Germany, I would particularly like to thank Walter Grünzweig for his warm friendship, intellectual generosity, and vast knowledge of Whitman's reception in Germany and throughout the world; and Jeanne Cortiel and Christine Gerhardt for their consistently illuminating work on Whitman. In Italy, I want to thank Mario Corona, for his brilliance as a translator and reader of Whitman and for his comradely affection over many years; Marina Camboni, for her contribution to our understanding of Whitman in Italy and in the context of American and transatlantic modernism; and Caterina Bernardini, who was a graduate student when she attended the first Transatlantic Walt Whitman Association Seminar and Symposium in Germany in 2008 and has since emerged as one of the leading scholars of Whitman and Italian poetry in a transatlantic frame.

In France, I would especially like to thank my French "sister" Lolita Hagondokoff, whose love for poetry has continued to inspire me since we first met in Paris in 1972 when I was a Fulbright Scholar writing my dissertation on "Walt Whitman among the French." She also helped me find Bruno Braquehais's photograph of the *Voltaire Lenoir Commune de Paris*, 1871 (Figure 16), which was scanned by the Musée de l'Histoire Vivante in Montreuil, France. I want to thank French scholar Éric Athenot for his brilliance as a reader and translator of Whitman and for all the inspirational Whitman conferences he has sponsored in France since our first gathering in Paris to celebrate the sesquicentennial of the publication of *Leaves of Grass* in 2005. For friendship and intellectual inspiration, I also want to thank Maria Clara Paro in Brazil; my former graduate student at Northwestern, Patricia Anzini, in Portugal; Wynn Thomas in Wales; and Marta Skwara in Poland.

I owe a particular debt of gratitude to Ed Folsom for his immense knowledge of Whitman, his warm friendship and support over many years, and his invitation to write this book on Whitman for the University of Iowa Press. I am also grateful to Ken Price for the wisdom and care with which he read and suggested revisions to the original version of this study. I also want to thank both Ed Folsom and Ken Price for their work as editors of the wonderful gift of *The Walt Whitman Archive* which they have given to scholars and lovers of Whitman worldwide. I thank my friend Vivian Pollak for many years of intellectual and sisterly exchange, and Alan Trachtenberg and Jerry Loving for all that they have contributed to our understanding of Whitman's life and poetry. I am especially grateful to Robert K. Martin, Jay Grossman, Michael Warner, Michael Moon, Gary Schmidgall, and Charley Shively for their inspirational and pioneering work in the fields of sexuality and gender studies and queer theory. Chapter 9 is dedicated with affection to the memory of Robert K. Martin, in gratitude for his brave and pioneering work in these fields.

At Northwestern, I have been blessed with wonderful colleagues—John Alba Cutler, Nick Davis, Harris Feinsod, Christine Froula, Reg Gibbons, Susan Manning, Viv Soni, Helen Thompson, Ivy Wilson, and Kelly Wisecup—whose work and intellectual exchange have continued to inspire me. I would like to thank Scott Krafft, the curator of special collections at Northwestern University Library, who has assisted me in locating photographs and other materials crucial to my research. I am especially grateful to my dear friend, Julia Stern, for her wisdom, compassion, and treasured moments of affectionate friendship and inspiration. I also want to thank Kathy Daniels, the administrator of the English Department, for her friendship over many years and her generous help in formatting the footnotes to my manuscript. I would also like to thank Karin Horler for her excellent work as copyeditor, and Susan Hill Newton for her expert advice and guidance as managing editor.

During the time I have worked on this book, I have also been inspired in body and soul by my dance teachers at Arthur Murray, Stephen Closs and Diandra Guarnaccia, and the many extraordinary people I have met while learning to ballroom dance with my husband, Larry Stuelpnagel.

I want to thank my daughter, Suli, who just received her Master of Sound Arts degree at Northwestern, for her brilliance, love, and sense of humor; and La Rue, my four-year-old German shepherd, for affection and companionship while I was writing this book. This book is dedicated to my husband, Larry, my love, my heartbeat, and my favorite dance partner.

ABBREVIATIONS

BB Herman Melville, *Billy Budd, Sailor*, in *Billy Budd, Sailor and Other Uncompleted Writings*, ed. Harrison Hayford et al. (Evanston, IL: Northwestern University Press, 2017).

BP Herman Melville, *Battle-Pieces and Aspects of the War*, in Herman Melville, *Published Poems*, ed. Robert C. Ryan et al. (Evanston, IL: Northwestern University Press, 2009).

CM Karl Marx, *Communist Manifesto*, in Karl Marx, *Political Writings*, vol. 1, *The Revolutions of 1848*, ed. David Fernbach, 2 vols. (Harmondsworth: Penguin, 1973), 67–98.

COR Walt Whitman, *The Correspondence*, ed. Edwin Haviland Miller, 6 vols. (New York: New York University Press, 1961–1977).

DN Walt Whitman, *Daybooks and Notebooks*, ed. William White, 3 vols. (New York: New York University Press, 1978).

DTS Walt Whitman, *Drum-Taps and Sequel to Drum-Taps*, reprinted in Ed Folsom and Kenneth M. Price, eds., *The Walt Whitman Archive*, https://whitmanarchive.org.

EPF Walt Whitman, *The Early Poems and Fiction*, ed. Thomas L. Brasher (New York: New York University Press, 1963).

EPM Karl Marx, *Economic and Philosophical Manuscripts* (1844), in Karl Marx, *Early Writings*, ed. Lucio Colletti, trans. Rodney Livingston and Gregor Benton (London: Penguin, 1992), 279–400.

LG 1855 Walt Whitman, *Leaves of Grass: The First (1855) Edition*, ed. Malcolm Cowley (New York: Penguin, 1986).

LG 1856 Walt Whitman, *Leaves of Grass* (Brooklyn, NY: n.p., 1856). Reprinted in *The Walt Whitman Archive*, ed. Ed Folsom and Kenneth M. Price, https://whitmanarchive.org.

LG 1860 Walt Whitman, *Leaves of Grass: Facsimile of the 1860 Text*, ed. Roy Harvey Pearce (Ithaca, NY: Cornell University Press, 1961).

LG 1871 Walt Whitman, *Leaves of Grass* (Washington, DC: n.p., 1871). Reprinted in *The Walt Whitman Archive*, ed. Ed Folsom and Kenneth M. Price, https://whitmanarchive.org.

LGC Walt Whitman, *Leaves of Grass: Comprehensive Reader's Edition*, ed. Harold W. Blodgett and Sculley Bradley (New York: New York University Press, 1965).

LGV Walt Whitman, *Leaves of Grass: A Textual Variorum of the Printed Poems*, ed. Sculley Bradley et al., 3 vols. (New York: New York University Press, 1980).

LOM "Live Oak, with Moss," in *Whitman's Songs of Male Intimacy and Love: "Live Oak, with Moss" and "Calamus,"* ed. Betsy Erkkila (Iowa City: University of Iowa Press, 2011), 1–37.

MC Herman Melville, *Correspondence*, ed. Lynn Horth (Evanston, IL: Northwestern University Press, 1993).

MD Herman Melville, *Moby Dick; or, The Whale*, ed. Harrison Hayford, Hershel Parker, and G. Thomas Tanselle (Evanston, IL: Northwestern University Press, 2001).

MT Herman Melville, *Typee: A Peep at Polynesian Life*, ed. Harrison Hayford, Hershel Parker, and G. Thomas Tanselle (Evanston: Northwestern University Press, 2003).

MWJ Herman Melville, *White-Jacket; or, The World in a Man-of-War*, ed. Harrison Hayford, Hershel Parker, and G. Thomas Tanselle (Evanston: Northwestern University Press, 2000).

NUPM Walt Whitman, *Notebooks and Unpublished Prose Manuscripts*, ed. Edward F. Grier, 6 vols. (New York: New York University Press, 1984).

PTP Herman Melville, *Piazza Tales and Other Prose Pieces 1839–1860* (Evanston, IL: Northwestern University Press, 1987).

PW Walt Whitman, *Prose Works 1892*, ed. Floyd Stovall, 2 vols. (New York: New York University Press, 1963–1964).

SW Karl Marx, *Karl Marx: Selected Writings*, ed. David McLellan (New York: Oxford University Press, 2000).

WJ Walt Whitman, *The Journalism*, ed. Herbert Bergman, 2 vols. (New York: Peter Lang, 1998–2003).

WWC Horace Traubel, *With Walt Whitman in Camden* (Vol. 1, Boston: Small, Maynard, 1906; Vol. 2, New York: D. Appleton, 1908; Vol. 3, New York: Mitchell Kennerley, 1914; Vol. 4, Philadelphia: University of Pennsylvania Press, 1953; Vol. 6: Carbondale: Southern Illinois University Press, 1982).

THE WHITMAN REVOLUTION

INTRODUCTION

The Whitman Revolution

> If man is ever to solve the problem of politics in practice he will have to approach it through the problem of the aesthetic, because it is only through Beauty that man makes his way to Freedom.
>
> —Friedrich Schiller, *On the Aesthetic Education of Man* (1795)

> Walt Whitman, an American, one of the roughs, a kosmos,
> Disorderly fleshy and sensual . . . . eating drinking and breeding,
> No sentimentalist . . . . no stander above men and women or apart from them . . . . no more modest than immodest.
>
> —Walt Whitman, *Leaves of Grass* (1855)

"Unscrew the locks from the doors! / Unscrew the doors themselves from their jambs!" Whitman proclaimed in the 1855 edition of *Leaves of Grass*, in words that powerfully express the new forms of "unlocked" human sexual and social being his poems imagine and command: no more locks, secrets, and silences; no more disgust and shame of the body, sex, and erotic desire; no more doors closed to the splendors of being in contact with the human and natural world. Against the "contemptible dreams" of the past, the poet announces a new way of seeing: "Now I wash the gum from your eyes, / You must habit yourself to the dazzle of the light and of every moment of your life" (*LG* 1855, 48, 81).

Published on or about July 4, 1855, Whitman's first book of poems was as revolutionary in its material form as it was in its language, style, and content. Designed by Whitman and printed at his own expense, the volume was neither quarto sized nor folio sized, but published on large legal forms likely printed by Whitman's friend, Andrew Rome, who owned a small print shop in Brooklyn. The dark green cover is embossed with specimens of lush grass, and the

FIGURE 1. Dark green cover of the 1855 *Leaves of Grass* embossed with specimens of grass and a gold-stamped title that sprouts gonad-shaped roots and leaves. Courtesy of the University of Iowa Special Collections and the Walt Whitman Archive.

gold-stamped title sprouts gonad-shaped roots and leaves as the material sign of the themes of nature, sex, fertility, regeneration, and connectedness announced by the poems and symbolized by the democratic grass (Figure 1): "Sprouting alike in broad zones and narrow zones, / Growing among black folks as among white" (*LG* 1855, 29). The title page bears no author's name, only the title, place, and date of publication: *Leaves of Grass*, Brooklyn, New York: 1855.

Opposite the title page, in an engraved frontispiece drawn from the new art of daguerreotype, the poet embodies himself as a common man dressed in workingman's trousers, a shirt unbuttoned to reveal his undershirt, and a hat

FIGURE 2. Engraved frontispiece of *Leaves of Grass* (1855), by S. Hollyer. Whitman may have enhanced the shading around his crotch to project what he called the "goodshaped and wellhung" democratic men and women he seeks to "breed" through his poems. Courtesy of the Ohio Wesleyan University Bayley Collection and the Walt Whitman Archive.

cocked jauntily on his head (Figure 2). This bearded working-class man, with his gaze trained directly outward to the reader, projects the rebellious proletarian energies of Whitman's first volume of poems: "Washes and razors for foofoos . . . . for me freckles and a bristling beard," the poet declares; "I cock my hat as I please indoors or out" (*LG* 1855, 46, 43). As one critic has argued, Whitman may even have enhanced the shading around his crotch to project what he called the "goodshaped and wellhung" democratic men and women he seeks to "breed" through his poems (Preface, *LG* 1855, 23).[1]

Whitman's title page and picture are followed by a twelve-page, two-column preface in which he declares America's literary independence from the antidemocratic forms and content of the Old World. Against the widely held sentiment that the United States lacked the materials for great art, Whitman asserts: "The United States themselves are essentially the greatest poem. . . . Here are the roughs and beards and space and ruggedness and nonchalance that the soul loves. . . . Here the theme is creative and has vista" (*LG* 1855, 5, 8). Although the preface emphasizes the specifically national dimensions of the American poet, the democratic roots and vista of Whitman's poems are revolutionary and global. "The attitude of great poets is to cheer up slaves and horrify despots," Whitman declares in lines that suggest the origins of his poems in the American and French Revolutions, the working-class and antislavery struggles of the United States and Europe, and the Revolutions of 1848 (*LG* 1855, 15). This international dimension of Whitman's poems needs to be underscored because during the Cold War period—the decade of the 1950s, following the Second World War, when American literature emerged as a distinct field of literary study—it was the primarily democratic individualist and formal dimensions of Walt Whitman that were emphasized while his political and working-class roots, his homoeroticism, and his communal and internationalist vision were suppressed, played down, or forgotten. And yet, as Whitman's major biographer Gay Wilson Allen wrote in an early 1937 essay entitled "Walt Whitman—Nationalist or Proletarian?": "Instead of seeking for an interpretation of Whitman in terms of the American frontier, Jacksonianism, or the American ideology, Whitman should be studied as a configuration of a world-proletarian movement."[2]

The earliest free-verse poem in the 1855 *Leaves of Grass* was not about America at all: it was an impassioned response to the Revolutions of 1848 in France and throughout Europe. Entitled "Resurgemus" (later "Europe, the 72d and 73d Years of These States"), the poem was published on June 21, 1850, in the New York *Daily Tribune*, edited by the socialist and antislavery activist Horace Greeley. The poem, which bears an uncanny resemblance to Karl Marx's 1848 *Communist Manifesto*, responds to the defeat of the Revolutions of 1848 with a triumphant lyric vision of liberty as part of the regenerative law of the universe: "Not a grave of those slaughtered ones, / But is growing its seed of freedom, / In its turn to bear seed, / Which the winds shall carry afar and resow, / And the rain nourish" (*EPF*, 39).

It is these seeds of Revolutionary freedom that Whitman seeks to plant among his readers in the twelve untitled poems of *Leaves of Grass*. At a time when the death-grip of capitalism was tightening its hold over labor, the absolute power of the state was replacing the inalienable rights and sovereignty of the people, and slavery had overwritten freedom as the law of the land with the passage of the 1850 Compromise and the Kansas-Nebraska Act of 1854, Whitman seeks to recall his readers to their Revolutionary birthright.

Whitman's impassioned involvement in the antislavery struggle was fired by his belief that what was happening in America was part of a global democratic advance from enslavement to freedom. "Not only here, on our beloved soil, is this democratic feeling infusing itself, and becoming more and more powerful," he wrote as editor of the Brooklyn *Daily Eagle* in 1846. "The lover of his race—he whose good-will is not bounded by a shore or a division line—looks across the Atlantic, and exults to see on the shores of Europe, a restless dissatisfaction spreading wider and wider every day. Long enough have priestcraft and kingcraft stalked over those lands, clothed in robes of darkness and wielding instruments of subjection. . . . and the Pen shows itself mightier than the Sceptre" (*WJ*, 2: 79).

As I argue in chapter 1, "'The Federal Mother': Whitman as Revolutionary Son," it was not through a reading of Ralph Waldo Emerson or a mystical experience, but amid the passions aroused by the labor and antislavery struggle in America and the Revolutions of 1848 in France and throughout Europe that Whitman broke away from the traditional forms and sentiments of his early poems toward the political inspiration and experimental form of the 1855 edition of *Leaves of Grass*. Whitman projected his radical commitment to the democratic and egalitarian ideals of the American Revolution as a potent female figure whose nurturance, generativity, and power he identified with the law of nature. Her earliest appearance may be as the mysterious "Shape" in Whitman's 1850 poem "Resurgemus," "draped interminably, / Head, front and form, in scarlet folds," who emblematizes the ultimate triumph of "Liberty" as part of the resurrectionary force of nature: "Those corpses of young men . . . / They live in other young men, O, kings, / They live in brothers, again ready to defy you" (*EPF*, 39).

Whitman first used the term *federal mother* in an 1855 self-review of *Leaves of Grass* in the *Democratic Review* as part of his call for a distinctively American literature. "Where in American literature is the first show of America?" the poet asked. "Where is the majesty of the federal mother, seated with more than antique grace, calm, just, indulgent to her brood of children, calling them around her, regarding the little and the large and the younger and the older with perfect impartiality?"[3] Whitman evokes "the federal mother" as an embodiment of the foundational ideals of equality, justice, affection, nurturance, and fraternity he associates with the American Revolution and democracy in America. As my chapter "The Federal Mother" illuminates, this athletic, sexually charged, and at times warlike woman and mother would continue as source, emblem, and muse of Whitman's democratic songs through all editions of *Leaves of Grass*. She also appears as the "divine Mother not only of material but spiritual worlds, in ceaseless succession through time" at the conclusion of Whitman's vision of the future of democracy in *Democratic Vistas* (*PW*, 2: 426).

Although Whitman never directly uses the word *revolution* in the 1855 *Leaves of Grass*, the presence of the American and French Revolutions as the source and inspiration of his democratic songs is evident throughout the poems. Whereas Whitman's 1850 poem on the Revolutions of 1848, which is the earliest free-verse poem in *Leaves of Grass*, evokes the scene of global revolution, his political ballad on the arrest, trial, and return of the fugitive slave Anthony Burns in 1854 (later "A Boston Ballad") focuses on the domestic scene in Boston, where the ghosts of Revolutionary patriots return to haunt and jeer at their countrymen for giving up the hard-won rights of freedom and independence for personal comfort and material wealth.

Scenes from the American Revolution are also evident in several historical vignettes in *Leaves of Grass*, including the heroic representation of John Paul Jones's victory over the British in the opening poem (later "Song of Myself") and the revisionary image of George Washington as a kind of affectionate mother-man in the poem later entitled "The Sleepers." Perhaps most importantly, the Revolution informs Whitman's effort to poeticize and reimagine many of its key terms: *life*, *liberty*, *equality*, *happiness*, *independence*, *inalienable rights*, *social affection*, *sympathy*, *fraternity*, and *the right of revolution*. In Whitman's time, these terms had been passed on to an increasingly alienated and dispossessed working class of small shop owners, craftsmen, artisans, and day laborers as part of the revolutionary legacy of Thomas Paine.[4]

"We have it in our power to begin the world over again," Thomas Paine wrote in his incendiary call for American independence in *Common Sense:* "The birth-day of a new world is at hand," he declared.[5] In the first and longest poem of the 1855 *Leaves of Grass*, Whitman invites his readers to celebrate the birthday of this new person and new world as a celebration of themselves:

I celebrate myself,
And what I assume you shall assume,
For every atom belonging to me as good belongs to you.

I loafe and invite my soul,
I lean and loafe at my ease . . . . observing a spear of summer grass.
(*LG* 1855, 25)

If the first line of the poem—"I celebrate myself"—isolates the first-person singular of the poet as the hero of the poem, the following two conjunctive and parallel lines link the *I* of the poet with the *you* of the reader and the world. These opening lines mark the poles between which the poem swings. The poem begins with the revolutionary potency of the *I*, the self, the individual, and ends with the revolutionary potency of the *you*, the reader, the future:

Failing to fetch me at first keep encouraged,
Missing me one place search another,
I stop some where waiting for you (*LG* 1855, 25, 86)

The lack of a final mark of punctuation in the concluding line, which appears to have dropped off in later reprintings of *Leaves of Grass*, serves nevertheless uncannily to underscore the open-endedness of the process of democratic creation, personal, national, global, and cosmic, toward which the poem moves.

Whitman's rhythmic and fluid free-verse lines not only broke the pentameter; in the words of Ezra Pound, he also broke the "new wood" that would be "carved" and expanded by the poets, writers, and social thinkers who followed him.[6] Presenting himself as an ordinary person, a worker, who speaks as and for rather than apart from the people, Whitman's democratic poet is a breaker of bounds: he is female and male ("I am she who adorned herself and folded her hair expectantly / My truant lover has come and it is dark"), white and black ("I am the hounded slave . . . . I wince at the bite of the dogs"), farmer and factory worker, prostitute and privy washer, citizen of America and citizen of the world: "Of every hue and trade and rank, of every caste and religion, / Not merely of the New World but of Africa Europe or Asia . . . . a wandering savage, / A farmer, mechanic, or artist . . . . a gentleman, sailor, lover or quaker, / A prisoner, fancy-man, rowdy, lawyer, physician or priest." Shuttling between past, present, and future, he is "an acme of things accomplished" and "an encloser of things to be" (*LG* 1855, 107, 62, 40–41, 77).

Whitman's songs are songs not only of workers and occupations but of sex and the body. Celebrating the body as the luxuriant outgrowth of nature and sexual energy as the regenerative law of the universe, Whitman sings of masturbation, the sexual organs, and the sexual act; he was one of the first poets to write openly of the "body electric," female eroticism, homosexual love, and the anguish of repressed desire. By insisting on the relation between democracy and sexual liberation, Whitman was also the first poet to provoke among his unsympathetic readers what was (and still is) the deepest underlying fear of democracy in America: that in its purest form democracy would lead to a blurring of sexual bounds and thus the breakdown of a social and capitalist economy grounded in the management of the body and the polarization of male and female spheres.

More than any other American writer of the nineteenth century, Whitman realized that a truly democratic literature would require a revolution not only in content but in literary *form* and in the traditional definition of *literature* itself: "Of the traits of the brotherhood of writers savans musicians inventors and artists nothing is finer than silent defiance advancing from new free forms. . . . The cleanest expression is that which finds no sphere worthy of itself and makes one" (Preface, *LG* 1855, 13). The elimination of commas as marks of distinction and division in this passage is—like the use of suspension points, the lack of subordination, and the violation of grammatical rule and linear logic throughout the 1855 *Leaves*—a fitting introduction to the formal revolution of the poems.

The twelve untitled poems of the 1855 *Leaves* opened the field of American poetry and world poetry with a new and revolutionary form of free verse. Defying the rules of rhyme, meter, and stanza division and breaking down the generic distinction between poetry and prose, Whitman's verse rolls freely and dithyrambically across the page in what one 1855 reviewer called "a sort of excited prose broken into lines without any attempt at measure or regularity, and, as many readers will perhaps think, without any idea of sense or reason."[7] Despite their unconventional appearance, however, Whitman's poems are neither formless nor lacking in measure and sense. Rather, Whitman returned poetry to a freer and more ancient prosodic practice based on periodic stress, rhythmic recurrence, parallelism, repetition, alliteration, and assonance.

At the base of Whitman's free-verse poetics is the *catalogue*, a sequence of end-stopped lines or thought rhythms linked by parallelism, repetition, and accentual stress. In pursuit of a new measure and a new way of measuring expressive of the modern democratic world, Whitman tried to avoid simile, metaphor, and the highly allusive structure of traditional verse. Like the overall musical ordering of his verse through thematic progression and recurrence, Whitman's catalogues work by juxtaposition, image association, and metonymy to suggest the connectedness of all things: "Every existence has its idiom . . . . every thing has an idiom and tongue," Whitman writes in the poem later entitled "Song of the Answerer." It is the role of the poet as answerer to resolve and connect "every thing": "One part does not counteract another part . . . . He is the joiner . . he sees how they join" (*LG* 1855, 130). By basing his free verse on a single, end-stopped line, Whitman gives to each thought or image a separate breath rhythm; at the same time, each line is fused through various linking devices to the larger structure of the whole as Whitman weaves an overall pattern of unity in diversity.

What some critics regard as formlessness and failure to discriminate is in fact part of Whitman's attempt to invent an egalitarian poetics. His verse form, like the catalogue technique in which it is rooted, is a poetic analogue of democracy, inscribing a pattern of many in one. The following catalogue from "Song of Myself" undoes traditional hierarchies by presenting each person as part of a seemingly indiscriminate mass:

> The bride unrumples her white dress, the minutehand of the clock
> moves slowly,
> The opium eater reclines with rigid head and just-opened lips,
> The prostitute draggles her shawl, her bonnet bobs on her tipsy and
> pimpled neck,
> The crowd laugh at her blackguard oaths, the men jeer and wink to
> each other,
> (Miserable! I do not laugh at your oaths nor jeer you,)
> The President holds a cabinet council, he is surrounded by the great
> secretaries,
> On the piazza walk five friendly matrons with twined arms.

Presented in a sequence of separate end-stopped images, these figures are independent and yet related through the parallel structure of the lines, the patterns of rhythmic stress, and the summary statement of the poet at the end of the catalogue:

> And these one and all tend inward to me, and I tend outward to them,
> And such as it is to be of these more or less I am. (*LG* 1855, 38–39, 40)

The total effect of the passage is to equalize and fuse in one chain brides and opium eaters, prostitutes and presidents, men and women, privileged and dispossessed, by presenting them paratactically on a horizontal plane. In a further display of poetic democracy, the passage turns on the figure of the prostitute by swelling to an eight-stress pattern in the lines that describe her, by presenting her before and next to the president, by dwelling on her for three lines—as opposed to the single line given to the others in the catalogue—and by expressing sympathy for her in a first-person parenthetical aside that changes the rhythm and tone of the sequence.

Whitman achieves a similarly equalizing and unifying effect through his use of anaphora (or beginning repetition), parallelism, and extensive coordinate, conjunctive, and prepositional constructions:

> Through me many long dumb voices,
> Voices of the interminable generations of slaves,
> Voices of prostitutes and of deformed persons,
> Voices of the diseased and despairing, and of thieves and dwarfs,
> Voices of cycles of preparation and accretion,
> And of the threads that connect the stars—and of wombs, and of the
> fatherstuff. (*LG* 1855, 48)

Parallelism and repetition, alliteration and assonance, conjunctions and prepositions are interwoven to connect the "long dumb voices" of the universe on a single spatial and temporal plane. These democratizing strategies are particularly evident in the first edition of *Leaves*, in which Whitman's occasional elimination of commas to separate items in a series has the effect of combining objects in a single mass.

As chapter 2, "Whitman and the Politics of Language," elucidates, for Whitman, as for his revolutionary predecessor in the American epic, Joel Barlow, the question of democratic creation—personal, political, and artistic—came to center on the question of language. "No country can have its poems without it have its own names," Whitman wrote in *The Primer of Words*, a series of notes on language he composed in the 1850s. In the *Primer*, Whitman called upon Americans to "throw off" the rule of standard English in order to create a language commensurate with the "new occasions, new facts, new politics, new combinations" of America (*DN*, 3: 754, 734).

Like the political revolution, the linguistic revolution that Whitman envisioned meant relocating power in the hands of the people and shifting the authority from the rules of dictionaries and grammars to the "real grammar" of the spoken language. "Talk to everybody everywhere," Whitman wrote in a directive to himself. "[K]eep it up—*real* talk—no airs—real questions—no one will be offended." "I love to go away from books, and walk amidst the strong coarse talk of men as they give muscle and bone to every word they speak," he wrote in another note (*DN*, 3: 675, 811). Whitman's notes include long lists of foreign and American words and phrases, a heavily corrected manuscript called "Our Language and Literature," and a homemade volume entitled *Words*, which contains lists of slang, common idioms, and entries on etymology, orthography, philology, and American names.

The notebooks that Whitman kept as he went about talking to "everybody everywhere" served as a kind of laboratory for the linguistic experiments of *Leaves of Grass*. "I sometimes think that the Leaves is only a language experiment," he later told Horace Traubel; "that it is an attempt to give the spirit, the body, the man, new words, new potentialities of speech—an American, a cosmopolitan . . . range of self-expression. The new world, the new times, the new peoples, the new vista, need a tongue according—yes, what is more, will have such a tongue—will not be satisfied until it is evolved" (*DN*, 3: 729n; ellipsis mine).

The range of Whitman's language experiment in the 1855 *Leaves* is evidenced by the fact that of the 34,000 words he used in the poems, many of its most expressive words are used only once. "A characteristic word once used in a poem, speech, or what not, is then exhausted," Whitman wrote in the *Primer* (*DN*, 3: 750). By using strong words only once and by drawing on slang phrases, common idioms, and many foreign terms, especially French (*en masse*, *ensemble*, *rapport*, *résumé*, *nonchalant*, *amies*, *amours*, *élèves*, *accouchement*, *rendezvous*, *cache*, *douceurs*, and *soirée* were among the French terms he used in the 1855 *Leaves*), Whitman sought to revolutionize the possibilities of poetic speech as an instrument of democratic creation. His poems are alive with street talk, with words such as *rowdy*, *swap off*, *top-knot*, *duds*, and the *blab of the pave*; colloquial speech rhythms such as "Washes and razors for foofoos . . . . for me freckles and a bristling beard"; or "You there, impotent, loose in the knees, open your scarfed chops till I blow grit within you"; and nicknames for people of different states and regions that become part of the poet's collective identity: "Kanuck, Tuckahoe, Congressman, Cuff, I give them the same, I receive them the same" (*LG* 1855, 46, 70, 29).[8]

As part of his language experiment in *Leaves of Grass*, Whitman sought to revive the real value of the human and natural world through a pervasive and often comic practice of poetic catachresis, a purposeful misnaming as a means of recomposing by decomposing the nature of things. The 1855 *Leaves of Grass* begins with a catachrestic renaming: "I celebrate myself" wrenches the word *celebrate* from its conventional religious and public ceremonial usage to describe the unleashing—or birthday—of the fullness and plenitude of the person, *myself* and the *self in relation*, that the poet embodies and seeks to call forth. "Divine am I inside and out, and I make holy whatever I touch or am touched from," the poet declares, turning the language of scripture and religious creed to a celebration of the glories of the person and the body: "The scent of these arm-pits is aroma finer than prayer, / This head is more than churches or bibles or creeds." To redeem the body, sex, and nature from their former abjection, Whitman presents a nonsupernatural account of God and soul by redirecting the language of religious worship to the miracle of the spirit in the flesh: "If I worship any particular thing it shall be some of the spread of my own body," he writes in a ritual of nature and body worship that decorously includes, by encoding as nature, the semen and genitals: "You my rich blood, your milky stream pale strippings of my life / . . . / Root of washed sweet-flag, timorous pond-snipe, nest of guarded duplicate eggs, it shall be you" (*LG* 1855, 49).

Through a similar poetics of catachrestic renaming the poet invents a counter-ethics and metaphysics of love that locates God, soul, and spirit within both the individual person and the social being of the person in affectionate and loving relation with the other and the world. The poet finds God not through the institutional medium of Church or clergy, but in his bedroom as comrade and lover: "As God comes a loving bedfellow and sleeps at my side all night and close on the peep of the day, / And leaves for me baskets covered with white towels bulging the house with their plenty" (*LG* 1855, 27). He enacts his relation to nature in the language of a passionate physical love affair that makes it unclear whether he is describing nature or an actual or fantasy lover:

> Prodigal! you have given me love! . . . . therefore I to you give love!
> O unspeakable passionate love!
>
> Thruster holding me tight and that I hold tight!
> We hurt each other as the bridegroom and the bride hurt each other.
> (*LG* 1855, 45)

Here, as in future editions of *Leaves of Grass*, Whitman's revolutionary experiments in the language and style of poetry, his seemingly inappropriate but in fact catachrestic mixture of genres, voices, and tones—of lyric, epic, comedy, and satire, of comrade, mystic, teacher, and rough, of confession, intimacy, hyperbole, and brag—are at the very sources of his poetic practice as a practice of democracy.

"Song of Myself," the title that Whitman gave his major poem in the final 1881 edition of *Leaves of Grass*, is regarded by some as a misnomer because it suggests that the drama of self, nation, and world that the poem enacts has only one character, *I*, when in fact it has at least two: *I* and *you*. But "Song of Myself" also suggests the multiple selves—or *I* and *you*—that "Song of Myself" celebrates and sings. Like the *E pluribus unum* (many in one, one in many) that became the Revolutionary seal of the American republic in 1782, the dialectics of *I* and *you*, self and other, individual and community, is at the center of Whitman's democratic mythos. It is a dialectics that Whitman inscribed in the opening poem of the final edition of *Leaves of Grass*: "ONE'S SELF I sing, a simple separate person, / Yet utter the word Democratic, the word En-Masse" (*LGC*, 1).

The failure to recognize this *you*, this other, this very French "En-Masse" at the democratic heart of Whitman's poems, has led many American and some French critics—including Whitman's French biographer Roger Asselineau—to emphasize the primarily individual dimensions of Whitman's democratic vision: Whitman the individualist, the singer of "Myself," the glorious embodiment of liberal individualism, the possibilities of the self, and American freedom.

It has also led major American philosophers of democracy, such as George Kateb, to dismiss the more collective, affective, and homoerotic dimensions of Whitman's democratic persona. Describing Whitman as "perhaps the greatest philosopher of democracy" and "Song of Myself" as "a work of political theory," Kateb treats "Connectedness" as an ideal of "receptivity and responsiveness" *within* the individual that "is not well illustrated by Whitman's notion of adhesive love, or love of comrades." "Adhesiveness threatens to suffocate the very individual personality that Whitman is trying to promote," Kateb argues, and thus he concludes: "The comradely side of Whitman is not his most attractive because it is not the genuinely democratic one."[9]

Against those critics and philosophers who have sought to comprehend Whitman's democratic poetry and his democratic theory by lopping off the more collective, working-class, and homoerotic dimensions of his work, I want to suggest that the *you* is at least as important as the *I* to Whitman's democratic creation. In fact, this *you* may be Whitman's most revolutionary creation. Conceived in its most literal sense as the *you* of the reader and the future, this *you* enabled Whitman to rewrite the traditionally hierarchical relationship of the poet and reader as a relation of equals: "Stop this day and night with me and *you* shall possess the origin of all poems / . . . / You shall listen to all sides and filter them from yourself" (*LG* 1855, 26; my italics). Whitman also revises the singularity and self-possession of the Emersonian poet by adding sympathy, an other, a *you* to the soul of the poet: "The soul has that measureless pride which consists in never acknowledging any lessons but its own. But it has sympathy as measureless as its pride and the one balances the other and neither can stretch too far while it stretches in company with the other. The inmost secrets of art sleep with the twain. The greatest poet has lain close betwixt both and they are vital in his style and thoughts" (Preface, *LG* 1855, 12).

By figuring the *I* as a relation, a *me* that is also a *you*, and always "stretches in company with the other"—or as Rimbaud would later say, perhaps under the influence of Whitman, "Je est un autre"—Whitman writes *fraternité*, affective community, and the radicalism of the French Revolution into the self-evident truths of liberty, equality, and the pursuit of happiness proclaimed by the Declaration of Independence.[10] The poet enacts this *self in relation* through the erotically charged union of *I* and *you* at the outset of the poem:

> I mind how we lay in June, such a transparent summer morning;
> You settled your head athwart my hips and gently turned over upon
> me,
> And parted the shirt from my bosom-bone, and plunged your tongue
> to my barestript heart,
> And reached till you felt my beard, and reached till you held my feet.
> (*LG* 1855, 28–29)

Who is this *you* who "gently" mounts, penetrates, and makes love to the poet as he lays in the grass? Critics have wondered. Is the poet recounting a kind of romantic descendance of the soul into the body of the poet? Is he having sex with a fantasy lover, a real person, his soul, or himself? Or shall we stop pussyfooting around: Is this a scene of homosexual cocksucking pure and simple, as Charley Shively was one of the first to insist?[11]

One thing is certain. *You* does not decline: it is grammatically indefinite. As the poet tells us: "I dilate you with tremendous breath" (*LG* 1855, 71). *You* is second-person singular and plural, intimate and stranger, "you my soul" and "the other I am," homosexual lover and soul of the universe; and the poet's erotic union with *you* gives birth to the vision and values at the origins of Whitman's democratic voice and song:

> Swiftly arose and spread around me the peace and joy and knowledge
> that pass all the art and argument of the earth,
> And I know that the hand of God is the elderhand of my own,

And I know that the spirit of God is the eldest brother of my own,
And that all men ever born are also my brothers . . . . and the women
my sisters and lovers,
And that a kelson of the creation is love. (*LG* 1855, 29)

At a time when the American government in collaboration with Northern capitalists and Southern slaveholders was seeking to reduce democracy to a laissez-faire pursuit of money and self-interest in the labor and slave marketplace, Whitman seeks to redefine democracy as an affective relation between *I* and *you*—"a kelson"—that links God, woman, man, animals, plants, insects, and weeds in an egalitarian community of comradeship and love.

As later appearances of *you* in "the twenty-ninth bather," "Is this then a touch?" and "The cloth laps a first sweet eating and drinking" sequences suggest, *you* is not only radically fluid but a sex radical who erodes the boundaries between selves, sexes, and persons as the poet—the *I* that is also *you*—licks, sucks, panics, puffs, penetrates, aches, masturbates, ejaculates, breeds, dances, laughs, sings, and swings his way through the poems of *Leaves of Grass* (*LG* 1855, 34, 53, 108).

The full radicalism of Whitman's democratic persona is perhaps most evident in the poet's act of self-naming midway through the opening poem:

Walt Whitman, an American, one of the roughs, a kosmos,
Disorderly fleshy and sensual . . . . eating drinking and breeding,
No sentimentalist . . . . no stander above men and women or apart from
them . . . . no more modest than immodest. (*LG* 1855, 48)

Here again, Whitman's poetic persona moves from the local to the global and the cosmic: he embodies the person ("Walt Whitman"), the nation ("an American"), the working class, or what Whitman called the "ouvrier class" in its more transnational reach ("one of the roughs"), and the universe ("a kosmos").[12] For the first time in the history of American poetry, the poet has a body, sexuality, desires that are not decorously regulated or contained: he eats, drinks, and breeds without self-loathing or shame. By identifying himself as "one of the roughs" and by asserting his disorderly and sensual nature in an unpunctuated sequence that mirrors the unruly flow of the senses, Whitman refuses decorum, hierarchy, and stock sentiment as both lifestyle and literary style.

These revolutionary new forms of bodily, sexual, and social being at the center of Whitman's democratic poetics are the subject of the second part of this book, "In Paths Untrodden," a title drawn from the opening poem of the "Calamus" sequence in the 1860 *Leaves of Grass.* "In Paths Untrodden" features essays on Whitman's sex radicalism as a singer of the politics of the body erotic in "Song of Myself," as a poet who bravely "let flame" in his "Calamus" poems "the burning fires" of erotic passion, love, and affection among and between men (*LG* 1860, 11), and as a radical imaginary whose poems are in fascinating dialogue with that other major poet and sex radical of the nineteenth century, Emily Dickinson.

I was asked to write "'Song of Myself' and the Politics of the Body Erotic" (chapter 3) for a collection of essays on teaching *Leaves of Grass* published by the Modern Language Association in 1990. In teaching "Song of Myself," I begin with the passage in the 1855 preface in which Whitman imagines the ideal poet balanced between the values of "pride" and "sympathy" (*LG* 1855, 12). I use this passage to elicit student reflection on the ways Whitman's vision of a poet stretching within a universe bounded by pride and sympathy had as its political analogue the paradox of an American republic balanced between self and other, liberty and union, the interests of the many and the good of the one.[13] Linking the drama of identity in "Song of Myself" to the political struggles of the United States on the eve of the Civil War, this is one of the first essays to read Whitman's major poem as something other than a primarily personal, mystical, or transcendental poem written under the influence of Emerson.[14]

Chapter 4, "Whitman and the Homosexual Republic," which also appears in the "In Paths Untrodden" part of this book, is one of the most controversial essays on Whitman that I have ever written. As early as 1956 in *Howl and Other Poems*, Allen Ginsberg "outed" Whitman in his visionary encounter with the poet in "A Supermarket in California": "I saw you, Walt Whitman, childless, lonely old grubber, poking among the meats in the refrigerator and eyeing the grocery boys."[15] But the fifties were a time when American literature was still defining itself as a distinctive field of study, and the formalist protocols of T. S. Eliot and the New Critics still reigned in American literary criticism and in the literature classroom. According to F. O. Matthiessen in *American Renaissance: Art and Expression in the Age of Emerson and Whitman*, it was the charge of the literary critic and the teacher to evaluate Whitman's craft as a poet and not private and seemingly irrelevant biographical matters such as his love of men. "The older liberalism was the background from which my writers emerged. But I have concentrated entirely on the foreground, on the writing itself" and "*what* these books were as works of art," he wrote in his canon- and field-defining study of Emerson, Thoreau, Hawthorne, Melville, and Whitman.[16]

This all changed with the publication of Robert K. Martin's major book *The Homosexual Tradition in American Poetry* (1979), which pioneered not only in focusing on Whitman as a homosexual poet but in locating him at the origin of a tradition of homosexual poets that included Hart Crane, Allen Ginsberg, Robert Duncan, and other major contemporary American poets who talked back to Whitman and each other in their shared love of men in their poetry.[17] But even with the precedent of Martin's brave book and his presence at the 1992 Conference at the University of Iowa to honor the hundredth anniversary of Whitman's death, I was not quite prepared for the apparent "scandal" caused by my presentation of a paper entitled "Whitman and the Homosexual Republic."

The essay begins with a letter from Malcolm Cowley to Kenneth Burke dated March 13, 1946: "I'm working on Whitman, the old cocksucker. Very strange amalgam he made between cocksucking and democracy."[18] The comment itself seems "strange" coming from Malcolm Cowley, who in his famous 1959 introduction to the Viking edition of the 1855 *Leaves of Grass* became instrumental in the critical construction of Whitman as neither "cocksucker" nor democrat but as an essentially spiritual poet who was miraculously transformed from party journalist to spiritual poet by a "mystical experience."[19]

Although I did not realize it at the time, the main "scandal" of my talk was the fact that after citing Cowley's letter, I continued to use the vulgar term throughout the talk rather than switching to the more polite and less offensive Latin term *fellatio*. Especially coming from a woman academic, my language appears to have offended and even shocked some of my colleagues. But as I reflect back on this moment, I believe some of the shock came not from my use of the term *cocksucking*, but from my insistence throughout the talk on the public political importance of men loving men to Whitman's theory of democracy and what I call "the Homosexual Republic."

As I note in chapter 5, "Radical Imaginaries: Crossing Over with Whitman and Dickinson," at the time that I wrote this essay I was one of the few scholars who wrote and published work on both Whitman and Dickinson. Oddly, however, I had never put Whitman and Dickinson together in the same essay until 2010, when Éric Athenot, the French translator of *Leaves of Grass*, asked me to give a lecture for a class he was teaching on both poets at the University of Tours in France. This was, I confess, one of the most challenging essays I have ever written.

In her essay "Beginners," Adrienne Rich describes Whitman and Dickinson as "a strange, uncoupled couple" at the origins of the American poetic tradition. "And so they have come down to us," Rich writes: "For Dickinson, the private life, intense, domestic, microcosmic; for Whitman the 'kosmos,' the 'democratic vistas' of the urban panorama, the open road."[20] Rather than finding Whitman and Dickinson to be the archetypal male and female, public and private "couple" at the beginnings of American poetry, however, in writing about them together for the first time, I was surprised to find what sex radicals they *both* were, and how often the sexual, social, and political crises that marked their lives and their poems were in conversation with each other in hitherto unremarked and illuminating ways. By "Crossing Over with Whitman and Dickinson," "Radical Imaginaries" seeks to suggest some of the new social, sexual, political, and aesthetic perspectives that might be opened by moving beyond the "male" and "female," "public" and "private" frames that have structured past approaches to their work.[21]

At the same time that Whitman "split off with the radicals" in 1848 and departed for New Orleans, where his editorials for the *Daily Crescent* resounded with news of the revolutions in France and throughout Europe, Dickinson split with the religious establishment at Mt. Holyoke Seminary in 1848 in order to dedicate herself to writing as a powerful means of talking back to, with, and against her democratic age. In the same year, in February, Karl Marx published the *Communist Manifesto*, which begins with the portentous words "A spectre is haunting Europe—the spectre of Communism" and concludes with a prophetic call for proletarian revolution against the bourgeoisie: "WORKING MEN OF ALL COUNTRIES, UNITE!" (*CM*, 67, 98).

Although we are not used to thinking of Walt Whitman and Karl Marx together, this is because the demonizing rhetorics of the Cold War years have kept us from recognizing the uncanny overlappings of these two major nineteenth-century voices of worker revolution, democracy, and global community in what I call the "Revolutionary Transatlantic." As I argue in chapter 6, "Whitman, Marx, and the American 1848," against the dehumanizing force of capitalism both the poet and the philosopher called for the liberation of man in the fullness of his physical and social being. "[T]he society that is *fully developed* produces man in all the richness of his being, the *rich* man who is *profoundly and abundantly endowed with all the senses*, as its constant reality," Marx wrote in his 1844 *Economic and Philosophical Manuscripts*, in language that anticipates the fully endowed individual and social being whose birthday Whitman celebrates in *Leaves of Grass* (*EPM*, 354). Whereas Marx's early writings define the economic conditions and the revolutionary political struggle out of which *Leaves of Grass* emerged, Whitman's 1855 edition of *Leaves of Grass* embodies and materializes the ideal of human liberation, the "*corporeal*, living, real, sensuous" actualization of both the individual and the species-being, that Marx described in his 1844 *Economic and Philosophical Manuscripts* but rarely elaborated in his later work (*EPM*, 390).

As chapter 7, "Insurrection, the Paris Commune, and *Leaves of Grass*," emphasizes, the scene of revolution in Europe, especially in France, would continue at the center of Whitman's democratic imaginary and future editions of *Leaves of Grass*. In the 1856 *Leaves of Grass*, Whitman highlights the continuity between the American and the European Revolutions by changing the title of "Resurgemus" to "Poem of the Dead Young Men of Europe, the 72d and 73d Years of These States" (later, "Europe, the 72d and 73d Years of These States"). He adds several poems of world address and global revolution, including "Poem of Salutation" ("Salut au Monde!" in the 1860 *Leaves*) and uses the French refrain "*Allons!*" in "Poem of the Road" ("Song of the Open Road" in the 1867 *Leaves*). In the 1860 *Leaves of Grass*, where Whitman began to organize his poems into clusters, two of these clusters bear French titles: "Chants Democratic and Native American" collects Whitman's songs of global and American democracy; and "Enfans d'Adam" celebrates the glories and naturalness of sexual or "amative" love.

During the dark years of scandal and corruption that followed the Civil War, the one bright spot on Whitman's democratic horizon was the insurrections in France. He concludes *Democratic Vistas* (1871) with a "wondrous" news flash from Europe about the defeat of Louis Napoleon III and the popular uprisings in France. These events shaped the 1871 *Leaves of Grass*, which Whitman thought would be the final edition of his *Leaves*. The volume opens with a sequence of "Inscriptions" which reveal the French signature of this and all future editions of *Leaves of Grass*: "ONE'S-SELF I sing—a simple, separate, Person; / Yet utter the word Democratic, the Word *En-Masse*" (*LG* 1871, 7). To keep alive the spirit of revolutionary struggle, Whitman also added a radical grouping entitled "Songs of Insurrection," in which three of the six poems focus on the Revolutions in France in 1792–1793, 1848, and 1870–1871. After the defeat of France in the Franco-Prussian War, 1870–1871, Whitman published his moving elegy "O Star of France. 1870–71," in which he imagines the ultimate triumph of France as the "pale symbol" of his "soul" and its "dearest hopes" for "liberty" and "brotherhood," "reborn, high o'er the European world" (*LGC* 396, 397).

If Whitman aspired to be America's epic poet of democracy in the poems of *Leaves of Grass*, Herman Melville might be seen as Whitman's novelistic counterpart in seeking to write *Moby-Dick; or, The Whale* (1851) as America's prose epic of democracy. But pairing Whitman with Melville, as I was asked to do by Paul Lauter in an essay on the "tribulations of democracy" for the Blackwell *Companion to American Literature and Culture* (2010), seemed at first like a major challenge because Whitman seemed to be so immediately outmatched: Melville was dark, deep, and so profound in his apocalyptic vision of America and the world in *Moby-Dick* that his prophetic novel had to wait until the post–World War I period for audiences to understand it at all. Whitman seemed by comparison, optimistic, hopeful, happy—possibly even a chucklehead! "Do you see O my brothers and sisters?" he assured his readers in *Leaves of Grass*: "It is not chaos or death . . . . it is form and union and plan . . . . it is eternal life . . . . it is happiness" (*LG* 1855, 85).

F. O. Matthiessen put it best in *American Renaissance* when he wrote: "Whitman rode through the years undisturbed by such deep and bitter truths as Melville had found" (179). As I argue in chapter 9, "Whitman, Melville, and the Tribulations of Democracy," this scholarly emphasis on the essential difference between Whitman and Melville has kept us from recognizing the similarly democratic and dystopian impulses out of which both writers emerged. It has also kept us from recognizing the ways their imaginative writings overlap and intersect in their mutual effort to address the political and economic tribulations of democracy before, during, and after the Civil War.

What struck me in writing about Melville and Whitman was at first how alike they were. Both were born in New York City in 1819 at a time of economic depression and political foreboding signified by the Missouri Compromise on the issue of slavery. Neither finished school: one found his "Harvard and Yale" on shipboard as a common sailor, and the other, as a printer's apprentice. In their major writings, both shared a tragic vision of the slave system as a trope for an America propelled not by the revolutionary dream of freedom but by the economics of capitalism. "Who ain't a slave? Tell me that," Ishmael asks at the outset of *Moby-Dick* (*MD* 6). "I am the hounded slave . . . . I wince at the bite of the dogs," Whitman asserts in the opening poem of *Leaves of Grass* (*LG* 1855, 62). At his most radically utopian, in sequences such as "A Squeeze of the Hand" in *Moby-Dick*, Melville sounds remarkably like Whitman in the "Is this then a touch?" masturbatory sequence in *Leaves of Grass* (*LG* 1855, 53).

But Melville's moments of erotic comradeship are always momentary, whereas Whitman's vision of men loving men became the base of his democratic vision. "I say democracy infers such loving comradeship, as its most inevitable twin or counterpart, without which it will be incomplete, in vain, and incapable of perpetuating itself," Whitman wrote in his major post–Civil War reflection on the future of democracy in *Democratic Vistas* (*PW*, 2: 41). While Melville recognizes the power of democratic personality and non-state forms of feeling and love between men in bringing an alternative democratic order and ethos into being, even in his most radical novel, *White-Jacket* (1850), as in his poetic epic *Clarel: A Poem and Pilgrimage in the Holy Land* (1876) and *Billy Budd, Sailor* (published posthumously in 1924), his conservative fear of the anarchic consequences of "unbounded insurrection" lead him to choose imperial figures of law and authority such as Captain Vere against the promise of democratic comradeship and love represented by Billy Budd.

The concluding essay, "Public Love: Whitman and Political Theory," written in 2002, focuses on the centrality of same-sex love between men, not only to Whitman's poetry, but to his democratic politics and his theory of democracy. Whereas in the past Whitman's democratic politics would have been dismissed as irrelevant or even naïve by F. O. Matthiessen and others who emphasized a critical focus on "the writing itself," in recent years there has been an increasing interest in Whitman among political scientists and theorists of democracy such as Samuel Beer and George Kateb, who have pioneered in taking Whitman seriously as a philosopher and theorist of democracy.[22] But they are also characteristic of a tradition in liberal individualist political thought that has failed to acknowledge the centrality of homoerotic love to Whitman's theory of democracy. In reflecting on the relations among sex, tears, politics, poetry, and what I call "public love" that underwrite Whitman's theory of democracy, my essay draws on Jürgen Habermas's theory of a "public sphere" of print, separate from the state or government, in which private persons engage in public discussion about issues of common interest to all.

The essay traces the multiple—and sometimes secret and forbidden—forms of erotic attraction, pleasure, and desire that bring people together in Whitman's writings: from his short story "The Child's Champion" (1841) and early temperance novel *Franklin Evans; or The Inebriate: Tale of the Times* (1842), to the public scenes of George Washington embracing his soldiers in the 1855 *Leaves of Grass*, to Whitman's first use of the phrenological term *adhesiveness* to express the "yearnings" that arouse and draw strangers together in the 1856 *Leaves of Grass*, to his inclusion of an entire sequence of poems on "manly love" entitled "Calamus" in the 1860 edition of *Leaves of Grass*.

Published on the eve of the Civil War, Whitman's attempt to resolve the political crisis of the nation on the level of the body, sex, and homosexual love is evident in the opening poem "Proto-Leaf" (later "Starting from Paumanok"). Introducing a new confessional voice into American poetry, Whitman writes: "I will therefore let flame from me the burning fires that were threatening to consume me / . . . / I will write the evangel-poem of comrades and of love" (*LG* 1860, 11).

This public and liberatory focus on the relation between manly love, political union, and democratic theory is evident throughout the "Calamus" poems. "Affection shall solve every one of the problems of freedom," Whitman affirms, in "Calamus" 5, representing himself as the embodiment of "a new friendship" that will "twist and intertwist" the "States" in bonds of "manly affection" and love:

> The most dauntless and rude shall touch face to face lightly,
> The dependence of Liberty shall be lovers,
> The continuance of Equality shall be comrades.
> These shall tie and band stronger than hoops of iron. (*LG* 1860, 349, 351)

In the history of sexuality and politics, the "Calamus" sequence may be Whitman's most radical sequence of poems. But because Whitman insisted on "manly love" and "adhesiveness" as the foundation of political "Compact" and democratic union in his "Calamus" poems, they have traditionally—and in some sense quite miraculously—been read as an allegory of American democracy.

It was, ironically, Whitman's poems on *amative* love, the phrenological term for physical and sexual love between men and women, which first appeared in the "Enfans d'Adam" cluster (later "Children of Adam") of the 1860 *Leaves of Grass*, that led to his being "the object of two or three pretty serious special official buffetings" (Whitman, *LGC*, 562). Although Whitman does not name his attackers, the first of what he later called "several set-tos with the state" was with Secretary of the Interior James Harlan, who fired Whitman as a clerk in the Bureau of Indian Affairs in June 1865 when he found a marked copy of the 1860 *Leaves of Grass* in Whitman's desk. Harlan described *Leaves of Grass* as "full of indecent passages" and dismissed its author as a "Free Lover" and "a very bad man."[23] But William Douglas O'Connor's ardent defense of Whitman in *The Good Gray Poet: A Vindication* (1866) led to a growth in Whitman's public stature and his literary reputation. At O'Connor's behest, Whitman was also transferred to the attorney general's office, only one day after he was fired by Harlan.

The second and more serious "official buffeting" came on March 1, 1882, when Boston District Attorney Oliver Stevens initiated proceedings to suppress the 1881 edition of *Leaves of Grass*. Perhaps responding to a complaint from the New York anti-obscenity activist Anthony Comstock and the New England Society for the Prevention of Vice, the district attorney informed Whitman's publisher James Osgood and Company that *Leaves of Grass* was "obscene" in accord with the "Public Statutes respecting obscene literature."[24] Whitman at first agreed to remove what Osgood called "the obnoxious features," thinking that the changes involved "about ten lines to be left out, & half a dozen words or phrases" (*COR*, 3: 267). But when he received a full list of the "lines and pages and pieces &c. to be 'expunged,'" which included several passages from "Song of Myself," "Children of Adam," and "The Sleepers," as well as the entire text of "A Woman Waits for Me," "To a Common Prostitute," and "The Dalliance of the Eagles," he demurred: "The list whole & several is rejected by me, & will not be thought of under any circumstances" (*COR*, 3: 267, 270). He withdrew *Leaves of Grass* from Osgood and Company and arranged to have the volume published by Rees Welsh and Company in Philadelphia in 1882.

At a time when women were challenging conventional views of women as essentially wives and mothers and demanding the vote, what Whitman's offending poems had in common was the naming of an active and empowering female body and sexuality that was deemed dangerous to the political body of America. As historian Carroll Smith-Rosenberg observes: "No matter how her mythic representations changed, from the mid-nineteenth century on woman had become the quintessential symbol of social danger and disorder."[25] Not only was *Leaves of Grass* banned in Boston, but those who attempted to publish and circulate Whitman's offending poems were persecuted.

Whitman's third "set-to with the state" occurred with someone he later referred to in conversation with Horace Traubel as "the fool postmaster Tobey" (*WWC*, 1: 18). Whitman alludes to Edward S. Tobey, who was appointed postmaster of Boston by President Grant in 1875 and continued to serve until 1885. These were the very years when the 1873 federal law known as the Comstock Law, which prohibited circulation of "obscene, lewd, or lascivious" material in the US mail, was being challenged by Boston reformers and anarchist free-love advocates and defenders of Whitman's *Leaves of Grass* such as Ezra Heywood, George Chainey, and Benjamin Tucker of Boston. It was Tobey who arrested Ezra Heywood, the president of the New England Free-Love League, for publishing "To a Common Prostitute" and "A Woman Waits for Me" in his magazine *The Word.* The judge finally dismissed charges against both poems as "obscene," and Heywood was acquitted.[26] Although Whitman did not like being associated with the free-love league, the public scandal caused by the attempt to ban *Leaves of Grass* in Boston served only to increase his national fame, the sales of his work, and the substantial royalty check of over one thousand dollars Whitman received in December 1882 when David McKay replaced Rees Welsh and Company as his Philadelphia publisher.

The irony of this public persecution of Whitman's poems on women's bodies and sexuality is that his love songs to and about men loving men, in "Song of Myself," "The Sleepers," "Crossing Brooklyn Ferry," "Song of the Open Road," "Starting from Paumanok," and especially his "Calamus" poems, went virtually unnoticed by the organs of official culture. This seems particularly odd given the fact that Oscar Wilde, who would later serve two years in prison after he was found guilty of homosexual offenses in England in 1895, visited Whitman in Camden in January 1882, only a few months before Oliver Stevens initiated proceedings against *Leaves of Grass* as obscene literature in March 1882. During a return visit in May, Wilde claimed that Whitman confessed his love of men. According to Richard Ellmann, "Wilde would later tell George Ives, a proselytizer for sexual deviation in the Nineties, that Whitman had made no effort to conceal his homosexuality from him, as he would do with John Addington Symonds." "The kiss of Whitman," Wilde said, "is still on my lips."[27]

In his 1966 memoir, *The Circle of Sex*, Gavin Arthur, the grandson and namesake of former US president Chester Arthur, gave an even more vivid account of how the kiss and caress of Whitman was remembered by Edward Carpenter, the English socialist, poet, and advocate for homosexual rights. In 1923, Arthur visited Carpenter's cottage in England, where the seventy-eight-year-old Carpenter stroked, caressed, and made love to the young man in the same manner that Whitman had made love to Carpenter when he visited the poet for several weeks in 1877 and again in 1884. Arthur's tender and loving memory of Carpenter making love to him as Whitman made love to Carpenter literalizes Whitman's "Poets to Come," his love buds as seeds wafted to generations hence, in a real scene of men making love. In the history of Whitman's reception, this erotic remembrance has become part of what Allen Ginsberg has called a "line of transmission"—from Whitman to Carpenter to Arthur to Neal Cassady to Ginsberg himself—that embodies, as Whitman's "Calamus" poems embodied, his vision of erotic love between men as the source of poetic utterance, democratic union, and spiritual communion; or, as Gavin Arthur put it, a "laying on of hands," "in which oneself, as a unit, reunites with the Whole."[28]

The essays in this book cut against the grain of those who have criticized Whitman's sometimes problematic attitudes toward race, especially in the Reconstruction years and beyond, and his arguable embrace of US imperialism. I have done this in *Whitman the Political Poet*, where I raised a number of issues, including Whitman's imperialism and his retrograde views of women, African Americans, and Native Americans, that others have expanded upon in the decades since.[29] *The Whitman Revolution: Sex, Poetry, and Politics* emphasizes a different and more positive vision of Whitman's work and legacy. It is the Whitman who helps the auctioneer in his celebration of the miracle of African American life in the poem later entitled "I Sing the Body Electric": "A slave at auction! / I help the auctioneer . . . . the sloven does not half know his business":

> Gentlemen look on this curious creature,
> Whatever the bids of the bidders they cannot be high enough for him,
> For him the globe lay preparing quintillions of years without one
> animal or plant,
> For him the revolving cycles truly and steadily rolled.
>
> In that head the allbaffling brain,
> In it and below it the making of the attributes of heroes. (*LG* 1855, 121)

Poetry does not matter finally because of what it reveals about the shortcomings of the author. It matters because it enacts a better, more revolutionary future that can still be glimpsed amid our sad and trying present.

For Whitman as for Thomas Paine, the political revolution and the future of democracy were inextricably bound up with the liberation of new forms of sensuous and social being. In a letter to the Frenchman Abbé Raynal, Paine described the American Revolution as the site of a new birth of the person and the world through a revolutionary rebirth of mind and body. "Our style and manner of thinking have undergone a revolution more extraordinary than the political revolution of the country. We see with other eyes; we hear with other ears; and think with other thoughts, than we formerly used."[30]

To give birth to this new democratic person and world, Whitman seeks to revive and extend the revolutionary legacy of Paine's *Common Sense* by emphasizing the fundamental sovereignty, agency, power, equality, and rights of the people against all forms of outside authority and mastery. In "I Sing the Body Electric," Whitman sings the value of the body—every part of the body—and uses the culturally dominant image of the slave auction—to excoriate a national (and global) economy that seeks to objectify the riches of the body—the person—by giving it a cash value in the slave and labor marketplace: "Examine these limbs, red black or white," Whitman writes, "And wonders within there yet. / Within there runs his blood . . . . the same old blood . . the same red running blood; / There swells and jets his heart . . . . There all passions and desires . . all reachings and aspirations" (*LG* 1855, 121).

Whitman's most radical engagement with the underlying impulses of the individual and species-being comes in his dream poem "The Sleepers," in which the poet enters a kind of personal and political dream consciousness that unmasks the ill-assorted sexual and social fantasies, fears, anxieties, and utopian longings that link person, nation, and globe. In this dream landscape Eros seems to wrestle with Thanatos, love with death, for the individual and species-being and the future of democracy worldwide. The poem concludes with an assertion of democratic faith and a radical exercise of the poetic imaginary that restores the losses, sufferings, and wounds of human life in a dream vision of baptismal renewal, democratic affection, and world community:

> The sleepers are very beautiful as they lie unclothed,
> They flow hand in hand over the whole earth from east to west as they
> lie unclothed;
> The Asiatic and African are hand in hand . . the European and
> American are hand in hand;
> Learned and unlearned are hand in hand . . and male and female are
> hand in hand. (*LG* 1855, 114)

This luminous vision of naked bodies flowing hand in hand with other naked bodies "over the whole earth from east to west" powerfully embodies Whitman's revolutionary rethinking of person and world in the poems of *Leaves of Grass*. It also bodies forth the poet's democratic ethos and mythos of a *being in relation* that is grounded in erotic desire and the feelings of sympathy, comradeship, and love.

It is this revolutionary new person and world that Whitman sought to bring into being through the power of song. And it is for this reason that in his later magisterial reflection on both the crisis and possibility of democracy in *Democratic Vistas* (1871), Whitman assigned the major role of bringing a revolutionary new world into being not to law, government, or state but to the poet and the power of the poetic imagination. If you cannot imagine a democratic world, you cannot bring it into being. In Whitman's democratic poetics, the final act of imagining a democratic person and world into being belongs not to the *I* of the poet but to the *you* of the reader and the "En-Masse." "The touch of him tells in action," Whitman wrote of the poet in the 1855 preface to *Leaves of Grass*. His revolutionary aesthetics is an activist aesthetics that incites the reader to the final act of democratic creation of self and poem, nation and world. Or as Whitman wrote in "Poets to Come":

> I myself but write one or two indicative words for the future,
> . . . .
> Leaving it to you to prove and define it,
> Expecting the main things from you. (*LGC*, 14)

As a means of taking Whitman into contemporary history, I want to conclude this introduction with the closing event at the Transatlantic Walt Whitman Association Seminar and Symposium, which met in New York in 2019 to honor the bicentennial of Whitman's birth on Long Island on May 31, 1819. Asked to present a very short version of "The Whitman Revolution" as the concluding address at the "Whitman and New York" Symposium, I was inspired by the luminous vision of Whitman's "Sleepers" flowing "hand in hand over the whole earth from east to west" at the conclusion of my talk to invite the extraordinarily diverse audience of international students, scholars, activists, laborers, and lovers of Whitman from around the world to all join hands. This introduction ends with the same words I spoke during that moment of international handholding at the conclusion of the bicentennial celebration of Whitman's birth: And now as a means of realizing Whitman's democratic vision of new forms of human and social being in the present, I would like us all to join hands in order to embody and affirm the fact that no matter who you are or what country you are from, we can all come together in celebrating the bicentennial of Whitman's birth and realize in the present the democratic dream of global comradeship and love that Whitman imagined in his poems. Right now, we are the Whitman revolution and the answer to the question *why poetry matters*.

PART ONE

REVOLUTIONARY POETICS

CHAPTER ONE

"The Federal Mother"

Whitman as Revolutionary Son

> Perennial with the Earth, with Freedom, Law and Love,
> A grand, sane, towering, seated Mother,
> Chair'd in the adamant of Time.
>
> —Walt Whitman, "America" (1888)

At the close of the Constitutional Convention in 1787, Benjamin Franklin remarked on the radiant sun painted on the back of George Washington's chair: "I have often and often in the course of the Session . . . looked at that sun behind the President without being able to tell whether it was rising or setting. But now at length I have the happiness to know that it is a rising and not a setting sun."[1] In one of his earliest poems, "The Columbian's Song," which was published in the *Long Island Democrat* in 1840, Whitman makes use of the rising-glory rhetoric of the Revolutionary years to express a similar confidence in America's bright future:

O, my soul is drunk with joy,
    And my inmost heart is glad,
To think my country's star will not
    Through endless ages fade.
. . . .
That here at length is found
    A wide extending shore,
Where Freedom's starry gleam,
Shines with unvarying beam. (*EPF*, 12–13)

Echoing the rising-glory rhetoric of such Revolutionary writers as Joel Barlow and Philip Freneau, Whitman goes on to present American union in a series of familial images used during the Revolutionary years to popularize the American cause. Just as American Revolutionary writers, in literature ranging from broadsides and ballads to Jefferson's Declaration of Independence, presented their rebellion against King George in emotionally charged images of sons seeking to save mothers and daughters from the abusive violations of the father, so Whitman presents America as a fraternal band, united by devotion to female liberty and family union:

Nor let our foes presume
        That this heart-prized union band,
Will e'er be severed by the stroke
        Of a fraternal hand.
Though parties sometimes rage,
        And Faction rears its form.
. . . .
Yet should a danger threaten,
        Or enemy draw nigh,
Then scattered to the winds of heaven,
        All civil strife would fly;
And north and south, and east and west,
        Would rally to the cry—
'Brethren arise! to battle come,
For Truth, for Freedom, and for Home,
        And for our Fathers' Memory!' (*EPF*, 13)

In "The Last of the Loyalists," an early fictional tale about the American Revolution, Whitman once again draws on the Revolutionary language of family fracture and patriarchal abuse: "Families were divided; adherents to the crown, and ardent upholders of the rebellion, were often found in the bosom of the same domestic circle." And Vanhome, "the Last Soldier of King George," is associated with stories of cruelty, whippings, starvation, and finally murder inflicted on his orphaned nephew (*EPF*, 102, 104). While the longing for familial harmony and the horror of familial fracture, which are recurrent features of all Whitman's writings, may have personal sources in Whitman's family history, his early writings suggest that these familial images also have ideological roots in the American Revolution.[2]

In a comment on the significance of the American Revolution, Thomas Jefferson said: "May it be to the world, what I believe it will be, (to some parts sooner, to others later, but finally to all,) the signal of arousing men to burst the chains under which monkish ignorance and superstition had persuaded them to bind themselves, and to assume the blessings and security of self-government. . . . All eyes are opened, or opening, to the rights of man."[3] For Whitman, too, the revolt against King George represented not only a revolt against the tyranny of monarchy but a relocation of authority in the individual rather than in the state. It was this relocation of power from the political authority of the state to the inalienable rights of the individual that made the American Revolution not merely a change of regime but the basis for what the founders called a *Novus ordo seclorum* in the Great Seal of the American republic designed in 1782.

Seeking to destroy the king by imagining a new corporate identity for the colonies, Revolutionary writers and artists represented the transformation from an old to a new world order as the replacement of a tyrannical patriarch by a harmonizing and equalizing figure of female power. In the etching *Liberty Triumphs Over Tyranny* (1775), Liberty leans on a pillar with her foot on the neck of a man whose crown and chain, signs of the old oppressive order, lie beside him on the ground. This old order of the patriarch is represented as a barren landscape of war and violence in which a female figure begs release from the male; the new republican order of female liberty is represented as a pastoral landscape of abundance, fertility, and peace in which male and female dance in harmony (Figure 3).

In one of the earliest uses of the term *Columbia* as a figure of the American republic, Freneau presents the reign of Columbia in similar images of harmony and generativity:

> COLUMBIA, hail! immortal be thy reign:
> Without a king, we till the smiling plain;
> Without a king, we trace the unbounded sea,
> And traffic round the globe, through each degree;
> . . . .
> Be ours the task the ambitious to restrain,
> And this great lesson teach – that kings are vain;
> That warring realms to certain ruin haste,
> That kings subsist by war, and wars are waste:

(32)

thoſe who are delegated to *deviſe* and appointed to *execute* public meaſures, be directed to ſuch, as thou in thy ſovereign goodneſs ſhalt be pleaſed to render effectual for the ſalvation of a great empire, and reuniting all its members in one ſacred bond of harmony and public happineſs! Grant this, oh Father, for thy Son Jeſus Chriſt's ſake; to whom, with thee and the holy Spirit, one God, be Glory, Honour and Power now and for ever! A M E N.

FIGURE 3. *Liberty Triumphs Over Tyranny* (1775) by Isaac Taylor. Liberty leans on a pillar with her foot on the neck of a man whose crown and chain signify the old world order of patriarchy. Courtesy of the Library of Congress Rare Book and Special Collections Division.

So shall our nation, form'd on Virtue's plan,
Remain the guardian of the Rights of Man,
A vast Republic, famed through every clime,
Without a king, to see the end of time. ("On Mr. Paine's Rights of Man")[4]

Freneau envisions the female figure of Columbia as a force for freedom, fecundity, and "the Rights of Man" against the tyrannical and destructive power of the king.[5]

Whitman, too, associated the American republic with the potency of a female genius. Already, at age twenty-two, at a Democratic rally in New York, he invoked this female figure in support of the "great principles" of the American Revolution: "The guardian spirit, the good genius who has attended us ever since the days of Jefferson, has not now forsaken us. I can almost fancy myself able to pierce the darkness of the future and behold her looking upon us with those benignant smiles she wore in 1828, '32, and '36. Again will she hover over us, amid the smoke and din of battle."[6] Throughout the 1840s and 1850s, as the issues of slavery, territorial expansion, sectionalism, states rights, and centralized governmental control threatened to split the American union, Whitman continued to appeal to this same female genius of America as a source of personal and political renewal.

It was out of his radical commitment to the ideals of the American Revolution, projected as a potent female muse, that Whitman began to forge his sense of identity and calling as a poet. By identifying his poetic project with the American revolutionary project, he was able to eschew, or at least put off, the sense of orphanage and dispossession that were part of his legacy both as an American and as a Romantic.

This sense of double dispossession frequently experienced by American artists was already evident in the work of Philip Freneau, who celebrated the Revolutionary political break with the king at the same time that as an artist he lamented his dispossession from both the cultural traditions of Europe and the commercial enterprise of America:

> Thrice happy Dryden, who could meet
> Some rival bard in every street!
> When all were bent on writing well
> It was some credit to excel:—
>
> Thrice happy Dryden, who could find
> A *Milbourne* for his sport designed—
> And *Pope*, who saw the harmless rage
> Of *Dennis* bursting o'er his page
> Might justly spurn the *critic's aim*,
> Who only helped to swell his fame.
>
> On these bleak climes by Fortune thrown,
> Where rigid *Reason* reigns alone,
> Where lovely *Fancy* has no sway,
> Nor magic forms about us play—

Nor nature takes her summer hue
Tell me, what has the Muse to do?—

An age employed in edging steel
Can no poetic raptures feel;
No solitude's attracting power,
No leisure of the noon day hour,
No shaded stream, no quiet grove
Can this fantastic century move. ("To an Author," *Poems*, 353)

Whereas Freneau's career as a poet, like Emerson's later, was split between his commitment to American democratic culture and his sense that his poetic muse lay elsewhere in some pastoral realm of the imagination, Whitman fused his role as poet of democracy with the Revolutionary political origins of the American republic.

Amid the passions aroused by the controversy over slavery, and the debates over the 1850 Compromise and the Fugitive Slave Law, Whitman began to break away from the traditional forms and sentiments of his early verse and move toward the political inspiration and experimental form of the 1855 edition of *Leaves of Grass*. His first free-verse poems, "Blood Money," "The House of Friends," and "Resurgemus," emerged out of the political battles over slavery and free soil and the Revolutions of 1848 in Europe. His first recorded lines of free verse in his earliest notebook also arose out of the issue of slavery:

I am the poet of slaves and of the masters of slaves
I am the poet of the body
And I am. (*NUPM*, 1: 67)

Written at a time when Whitman was actively agitating against the extension of slavery in America, these lines anticipate not only the democratic form and content of *Leaves of Grass*, but also Whitman's attempt to unite in his democratic persona the conflicting and paradoxical energies of the nation.

The poet who emerged in the 1855 *Leaves of Grass* as "Walt Whitman, an American, one of the roughs, a kosmos" represents not an escape from politics but a continuation of politics by other means. Whitman invoked as his muse not "Imagination" (a word he rarely used) but "Democracy, ma femme," a potent female figure whose will was inscribed in the natural world—what Whitman called "the politics of nature"—and codified in the Declaration of Independence and the political Constitution of the United States.

"No great literature," Whitman announced in his 1855 preface, "nor any like style of behaviour or oratory or social intercourse or household arrangements or public institutions . . . can long elude the jealous and passionate instinct of American standards." It is the nurturing, equalizing, and unifying functions traditionally associated with women that Whitman proposes as the American standard:

> Will it help breed one goodshaped and wellhung man, and a woman to be his perfect and independent mate? Does it improve manners? Is it for the nursing of the young of the republic? Does it solve readily with the sweet milk of the nipples of the breasts of the mother of many children? Has it too the old ever-fresh forbearance and impartiality? Does it look with the same love on the last born and on those hardening toward stature, and on the errant, and on those who disdain all strength of assault outside of their own? (*LG* 1855, 23)

If in Whitman's poetic iconography the male figure is associated with democratic individualism, the female figure is associated with the federal union: "Where in American literature is the first show of America?" he asked in one of his self-reviews of the 1855 *Leaves of Grass*. "Where is the majesty of the federal mother, seated with more than antique grace, calm, just, indulgent to her brood of children, calling them around her, regarding the little and the large and the younger and the older with perfect impartiality?"[7] Whitman not only invokes the ideals of the American republic, projected as a maternal figure, as the measure of his art. In his attempt to unite within his democratic persona the conflicting energies of the nation—between the one and the many, North and South, urban and agrarian, material and spiritual—his persona also assumes the enfolding, equalizing, harmonizing, and regenerating qualities traditionally associated with women.

The poet's mystical experience at the outset of "Song of Myself" bears the inscription of Whitman's democratic muse:

> Swiftly arose and spread around me the peace and joy and knowledge
> that pass all the art and argument of the earth;
> And I know that the hand of God is the elderhand of my own,
> And I know that the spirit of God is the eldest brother of my own,
> And that all the men ever born are also my brothers . . . . and the
> women my sisters and lovers,
> And that a kelson of the creation is love. (*LG* 1855, 29)

At the end of the poem, in similarly familial images, Whitman sums up his values in language that suggests the Enlightenment ideals of the Declaration of Independence:

> Do you see O my brothers and sisters?
> It is not chaos or death . . . . it is form and union and plan . . . . it is eternal life . . . . it is happiness. (*LG* 1855, 85)

Only occasionally in the 1855 *Leaves of Grass* is this vision of familial harmony fractured by the reality of an economy of masters and slaves, rich and poor; and it is this political reality that continually threatens to fracture not only the United States but the unitary identity of the poet.

These moments of political fracture are frequently presented in visions of an authoritarian male figure menacing liberty and the familial union that is her preserve. In "Europe, the 72d Year of These States," Whitman's poem on the European Revolutions of 1848, brothers unite around the red-robed figure of Liberty to protect her from the "numberless agonies, murders, lusts" perpetuated by "the ferocity of kings" (*LG* 1855, 133). And in "A Boston Ballad," Whitman complains against the increase of government authority—evident in the use of federal commissioners in Boston to enforce the Fugitive Slave Law—portrayed as the corpse of King George returning to rule in America:

> Look! all orderly citizens . . . . look from the windows women.
> The committee open the box and set up the regal ribs and glue those that will not stay,
> And clap the skull on the top of the ribs, and clap a crown on the top of the skull. (*LG* 1855, 136–37)

Like the political orders of "Europe" and "A Boston Ballad," the pastoral order of "There Was a Child Went Forth," which follows the political poems in the 1855 *Leaves*, is menaced by the presence of disruptive male figures. The child's sense of harmony with a blooming female landscape is interrupted by the entrance of an "old drunkard":

> The early lilacs became part of this child,
> And grass, and white and red morningglories, and white and red clover, and the song of the phoebe-bird,
> . . . .

And the field sprouts of April and May became part of him . . . .
wintergrain sprouts, and those of the light-yellow corn, and of the esculent roots of the garden,
And the appletrees covered with blossoms, and the fruit afterward . . . .
and woodberries . . and the commonest weeds by the road;
And the old drunkard staggering home from the outhouse of the tavern whence he had lately risen,
And the schoolmistress that passed on her way to the school . . and the friendly boys that passed . . and the quarrelsome boys . . and the tidy and freshcheeked girls . . and the barefoot negro boy and girl.
(*LG* 1855, 138)

The drunken male figure, who in temperance tracts of the nineteenth century was presented as a primary threat to women, home, and family, is associated with other discordant elements not only in the child's prospect and but in the American landscape. The harmonious image of the "tidy and freshcheeked girls" is sandwiched between the disruptive images of the "quarrelsome boys" and the "barefoot negro boy and girl," images that suggest the disharmonies and inequalities that will ultimately splinter the union in the Civil War.

This dissonance in the garden is paralleled by dissonance in the home of the child:

The mother at home quietly placing the dishes on the suppertable,
The mother with mild words . . . . clean her cap and gown . . . . a wholesome odor falling off her person and clothes as she walks by:
The father, strong, selfsufficient, manly, mean, angered, unjust,
The blow, the quick loud word, the tight bargain, the crafty lure,
The family usages, the language, the company, the furniture . . . . the yearning and swelling heart. (*LG* 1855, 139)

Here again, the prospect of family harmony centered on an idealized maternal figure is threatened by the injustice of a father, who is associated with the celebrated American virtues of strength, self-reliance, and manliness and the aggressively competitive marketplace in which these values thrived. This discordance in the landscape and home of the child is also linked with his sense of uncertainty and doubt about the nature of self and world:

The doubts of daytime and the doubts of nighttime . . . the curious whether and how,

Whether that which appears so is so . . . . Or is it all flashes and specks?
(*LG* 1855, 139)

Associated with a gendered and familial iconography that reflects tensions within the larger body politic of America, the child's doubts suggest some of Whitman's doubts about his own and the nation's identity and future.

Despite these doubts, in the 1856 *Leaves of Grass*, Whitman insisted even more emphatically on the national, and ultimately female, sources of his art. "Poem of Walt Whitman, an American" (later "Song of Myself") was followed in 1856 by "Poem of Women," in which Whitman invokes the woman not only as the source of creative energy but as the generative force of justice and sympathy in the universe:

Unfolded only out of the inimitable poem of the woman can come the poems of man—only thence have my poems come,
Unfolded out of the strong and arrogant woman I love, only thence can appear the strong and arrogant man I love.
. . . .
Unfolded out of the justice of the woman, all justice is unfolded,
Unfolded out of the sympathy of the woman is all sympathy.
(*LG* 1856, 101–2)

Overturning the sentimentalized image of motherhood prevalent in popular literature of the time, Whitman placed at the center of this and subsequent editions of *Leaves of Grass* an athletic, sexually charged mother, who is both source and emblem of the nation.[8]

And yet, if the keynote of the 1856 *Leaves of Grass* is nationalism, there are signs of Whitman's growing uncertainty about his role as the poet of America. Intermixed with the prophetic optimism of several of the poems are darker "patches" in which, as in "Sun-Down Poem" (later "Crossing Brooklyn Ferry"), Whitman for the first time admits his doubts about himself and his work:

It is not upon you alone the dark patches fall,
The dark threw patches down upon me also,
The best I had done seemed to me blank and suspicious,
My great thoughts, as I supposed them, were they not in reality meagre?
Would not people laugh at me? (*LG* 1856, 216)

This dark subtext becomes the main text of "Poem of the Propositions of Nakedness" (later "Respondez"), in which Whitman declares sarcastically:

Let freedom prove no man's inalienable right! Every one who can
  tyrannize, let him tyrannize to his satisfaction!

. . . .

Let there be immense cities—but through any of them, not a single
  poet, saviour, knower, lover!
Let the infidels of These States laugh all faith away! If one man can be
  found who has faith, let the rest set upon him! Let them affright faith!
  Let them destroy the power of breeding faith! (*LG* 1856, 318, 320)

In this vision of poets and lovers being annihilated by a material culture of wealth and infidelity, masters and slaves, Whitman suggests the relation between the political crisis of the nation and his personal crisis of faith as a poet.

The darker, more elegiac tone of the 1860 *Leaves of Grass* expresses a sense of loss and uncertainty brought about not only by the larger political crisis of the nation but by the loss of a real or longed-for love. The relation of Whitman's personal mood to the darkening prospect of the nation is evident in both the material design and the poems of the 1860 *Leaves.* Instead of the vegetation that sprouted out of the title in the dark green cover of the 1855 *Leaves of Grass,* the reddish-brown 1860 *Leaves* bears the image of a globe of the two Americas set on a cloud; on the back cover is the image of a sun on the sea; and on the spine is the image of a butterfly poised on a hand (Figure 4).

Only the image of the butterfly on the hand has a fairly clear positive implication, suggesting both harmony with the natural world and the hope of transformation. The cloud/globe and sun/sea images that enclose the poems are more ambiguous: the globe may be passing out of or being engulfed by a cloud, and the sun may be rising out of or falling into the sea. Just as Franklin's uncertainty about the future of America was reflected in his uncertainty about the sun image on the back of Washington's chair, so Whitman's doubts about American on the eve of the Civil War are reflected in the ambiguous visual iconography which appears on the cover and throughout the 1860 *Leaves.*

"No—it has not yet fully risen," Whitman declares in Poem 20 of the "Leaves of Grass" sequence, linking his poems with the sun emblem in the 1860 *Leaves* and the rising—or falling—glory of America:

Whether I shall complete what is here started,
Whether I shall attain my own height, to justify these, yet unfinished,
Whether I shall make The Poem of the New World, transcending all
  others—depends, rich persons, upon you,

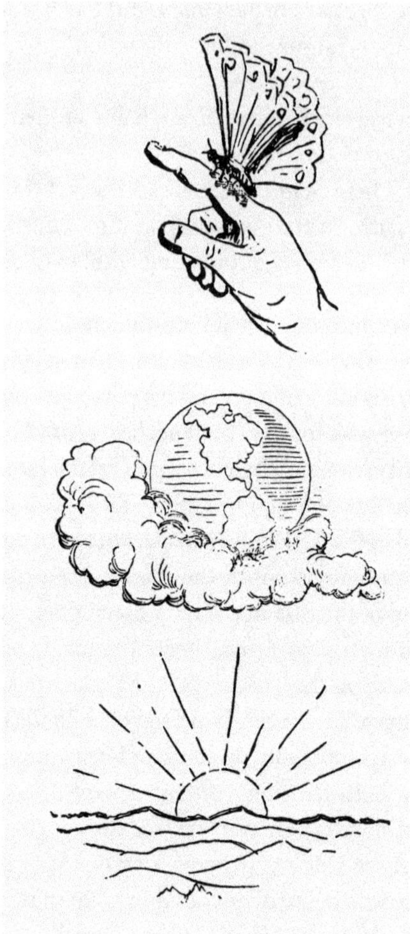

FIGURE 4. Imprints of a butterfly poised on a finger, a globe of the two Americas, and a rising or setting sun that appear on the reddish-brown cover of the 1860 edition of *Leaves of Grass.* These images also appear at the beginning and end of the 1860 *Leaves of Grass* and at the start and conclusion of poems such as "Salut au Monde!," the "Calamus" poems, and "Crossing Brooklyn Ferry." Courtesy of Special Collections, Northwestern University Library.

Depends, whoever you are now filling the current Presidentiad, upon you,
Upon you, Governor, Mayor, Congressman,
And you, contemporary America. (*LG* 1860, 239)

The poet's uncertainty is evident not only in the poems themselves, but in the repetition of the visual icons of globe/cloud, sun/sea, and butterfly/hand throughout the book and the shifting readings that emerge as the icons are placed in relation to one or another of the poems. Thus, the cloud/globe image at the end of "A Boston Ballad" is connected with the betrayal of revolutionary ideals in the battle over slavery, but the same image repeated at the end of "Salut au Monde!" suggests a passage out of the cloud toward national and global union.

The tensions within poet and nation are projected in images of familial fracture, the separation of lovers and brothers, parents and children. In "Poem 1" of "Leaves of Grass" (later "As I Ebb'd with the Ocean of Life"), one of the darker poems of the volume, Whitman's mood of uncertainty is rendered in images of shipwreck and separation from the "fierce old mother," the sea, who "endlessly cries for her castaways":

I, too, but signify, at the utmost, a little washed-up drift,
A few sands and dead leaves to gather,
Gather, and merge myself as part of the sands and drift. (*LG* 1860, 196)

Separated from the unitary power of the mother, Whitman loses his sense of identity and purpose as a poet:

Aware now, that, amid all the blab whose echoes recoil upon me, I have
  not once had the least idea who or what I am,
But that before all my insolent poems the real ME still stands
  untouched, untold, altogether unreached. (*LG* 1860, 197)

The poet seeks to renew his political faith and his poetic utterance by reuniting with both the power of the "fierce old mother" and the heritage of the fathers, which he associates with the fish-shaped island of his birth, his fatherland:

I throw myself upon your breast, my father,
I cling to you so that you cannot unloose me,
I hold you so firm, till you answer me something.

Kiss me, my father,
Touch me with your lips, as I touch those I love,
Breathe to me, while I hold you close, the secret of the wondrous
  murmuring I envy,
For I fear I shall become crazed, if I cannot emulate it, and utter myself
  as well as it.

Sea-raff! Crook-tongued waves!
O, I will yet sing, some day, what you have said to me. (*LG* 1860, 198)

By linking his sense of failure as a poet with a politically resonant image of family fracture—separation from the land of the father and the natural law of the mother—Whitman underscores the connection between his crisis of faith as a poet and his crisis of faith in nation and world.

In "A Word Out of the Sea" (later "Out of the Cradle Endlessly Rocking"), Whitman receives from the sea, again projected as the "fierce old mother," the word and the poetic utterance that fails him in "As I Ebb'd with the Ocean of Life." Writing on the eve of the Civil War, the poet appears to have lost his faith in the vision of "form and union and plan" that characterized the 1855 *Leaves*:

O a word! O what is my destination?
O I fear it is henceforth chaos!
O how joys, dreads, convolutions, human shapes, and all shapes, spring
  as from graves around me!
O phantoms! you cover all the land, and all the sea!
O I cannot see in the dimness whether you smile or frown upon me;
O vapor, a look, a word! O well-beloved! (*LG* 1860, 276)

The word that the poet receives, "Death, Death, Death, Death, Death," might be read as a sign of the regenerative potency of the mother and thus the possibility of transforming the vision of fractured union at the center of the poem into some future union. The poem marks Whitman's transition from being the poet of the revolutionary past to being the poet of the evolutionary future. As the "outsetting bard of love," Whitman rededicates himself to his art as a means of personal and political transformation.

If in "Poem of Women," Whitman celebrated the woman as a creator of athletic individuals, as the political tensions of the nation mounted he laid increasing stress on the mother as a figure of unity, harmonizing and equalizing the separate and potentially divisive energies of her sons and daughters. In a series of notes entitled "Slavery" written in the 1850s, Whitman centered his antislavery appeal on the same images of mother, children, and family fracture that characterized the antipatriarchal rhetoric of the Revolutionary period:

> For this circling Confederacy, standing together with interlinked hands, ample, equal, each one with his grip of love wedged in life or in death to all the rest, we must share and share alike.— Our old mother does not spread the table with a fine dish for one and scraps for another.— She teaches us no such mean and hoggish lesson.— If there be any of good dish, and not enough of it to go completely round, it shall not be brought on at all. If every brother and every sister cannot be supplied, or have an equal chance to be suppled, nobody shall be supplied.— (*NUPM*, 6: 2178–79)

To emphasize this egalitarian vision of America—and the dependence of individual liberty on national unity—in a notebook entry of the late 1850s, Whitman resolved in his poems "to bring in the idea of Mother—the idea of the mother with numerous children—all great and small, old and young, equal in her eyes—as the identity of America."[9] By placing the image of the mother at the center of his political and poetic symbolism, Whitman stresses the organic and federated nature of the American union and the principle of equality on which this union is founded.

In poem 5 of the "Calamus" sequence in the 1860 *Leaves of Grass*, Whitman dedicates himself to the federal mother:

> The old breath of life, ever new,
> Here! I pass it by contact to you, America.
>
> O mother! have you done much for me?
> Behold, there shall from me be much done for you.
> . . . .
> These shall tie and band stronger than hoops of iron,
> I, extatic, O partners! O lands! henceforth with the love of lovers tie
> you.
> . . . .
> For you these, from me, O Democracy, to serve you, ma femme!
> For you! for you, I am trilling these songs. (*LG* 1860, 349, 351)

Overcoming his personal and political crisis by resolving to tie individuals and the nation together "with the love of lovers," Whitman moves away from his earlier emphasis on the poet as a creator of strong individuals to an emphasis on the poet as a creator of national unity. He also shifts in his poems from a primary identification with the male to a primary identification with the traditionally female dimensions of the universe. This new emphasis is reflected in an increased focus on the female as a figure of unitary power.

Ironically, the actual fracture of the union in the Civil War created in Whitman a new sense of his own and the nation's identity and power. His faith in the republican vigor of the nation was strengthened by his vision of the union preparing for war—a vision that, in the first poem of *Drum-Taps* (1865), he projects in the image of Manhattan as an armed mother:

> Forty years had I in my city seen soldiers parading;
> Forty years as a pageant—till unawares, the Lady of this teeming and
>   turbulent city,
> Sleepless, amid her ships, her houses, her incalculable wealth,
> With her million children around her—suddenly,
> At dead of night, at news from the south,
> Incens'd, struck with clench'd hand the pavement. (*DTS*, 5)

Seeking to sustain the republican values of peace and prosperity at the same time that he presses the cause of the union war, Whitman, like the northern political iconographers of the time, presents the union as a female figure who is at once nurturant mother and armed warrior. (Figure 5).

But while Whitman exalts the figure of the union as warrior mother, he also suggests the reality of a divided nation in images of sons being separated from mothers:

> The tearful parting—the mother kisses her son—the son kisses his
>   mother;
> (Loth is the mother to part—yet not a word does she speak to detain
>   him). (*DTS*, 6)

To stress the organic compact of the states, Whitman once again places the family at the center of his war poems. In "Virginia—the West," a poem later included in *Drum-Taps*, Whitman draws on Revolutionary iconography in representing America as a mother violated by the father (Virginia) and protected by her sons (the West):

> The noble sire, fallen on evil days,
> I saw, with hand uplifted, menacing, brandishing,

FIGURE 5. *The Spirit of 61* (1861) by Currier and Ives. Like political iconographers of the time, in *Drum-Taps* (1865), Whitman presents the union preparing for war in the image of an armed woman and warrior. Courtesy of the Library of Congress Prints and Photographs Division.

(Memories of old in abeyance—love and faith in abeyance,)
The insane knife toward the Mother of All.

The noble Son, on sinewy feet advancing,
I saw—out of the land of prairies—land of Ohio's waters, and of
Indiana,
To the rescue, the stalwart giant, hurry his plenteous offspring,
Drest in blue, bearing their trusty rifles on their shoulders.

Then the Mother of All with calm voice speaking,
As to you Rebellious, (I seemed to hear her say,) why strive against me,
and why seek my life?

When you yourself forever provide to defend me?
For you provided me Washington—and now these also. (*LGV*, 3: 648)

In resolving to become the "wound-dresser" of the nation, Whitman as Revolutionary son also became the dresser of the wounded body of the democratic mother. Like a latter-day Son of Liberty, he placed himself in the service of the democratic mother to protect her from the danger that now came from within rather than from outside the republic.

In "After All, Not to Create Only" (later "Song of the Exposition"), which was written in 1871 to commemorate an exhibition at the American Institute in New York, Whitman makes explicit use of the Revolutionary ideology that shapes his relation with his democratic muse. Drawing once again on the rising-glory rhetoric of the American Revolution, Whitman invites the Muse to "migrate from Greece and Ionia," projected as the land of the fathers, to America, where she unites in a familial band with Columbia:

In liberty's name, welcome, immortal! clasp hands,
And ever henceforth sisters dear be both. (*LGV*, 3: 616)

Associating the Old World with kings, caste, war, and the reign of the fathers, Whitman asks the Muse to sing of the New World, which he envisions as a land of workers united in peace and love around the potent figure of the federal mother:

All thine, O sacred Union!
Ships, farms, shops, barns, factories, mines,
City and State—North, South, item and aggregate,
We dedicate, dread Mother, all to thee!

Protectress absolute, thou! Bulwark of all!
For well we know that while thou givest each and all, (generous as God,)
Without thee, neither all nor each, nor land, home,
Nor ship, nor mine—nor any here this day, secure,
Nor aught, nor any day secure. (*LGV*, 3: 623)

Like the vision of America popularized by Currier and Ives prints of the period, Whitman presents the federal mother as both source and sign of American prosperity and progress (Figure 6). He invokes the mother as emblem and protectress of the *Novus ordo seclorum* and *E pluribus unum* that are part of the Revolutionary seal of the American republic, investing her with a political

FIGURE 6. *America* (1870) by Currier and Ives. Like the vision of America popularized by Currier and Ives, Whitman presents the federal mother as a figure of American prosperity and progress. Courtesy of the Library of Congress Prints and Photographs Division.

and spiritual potency—"generous as God"—that is the ultimate source of security for self and world.

If during the Revolutionary period, writers imagined America as a female figure of liberty embattled by the external authority of the king, in the post–Civil War years, the main threat came from within, from a male-powered and increasingly self-interested market economy that repeatedly violated the body of the democratic mother. In opposition to the commercial and material values of the Gilded Age and the aggressively capitalist spirit of the time, Whitman continued to project the future of America in the communal and egalitarian figure of the mother in his 1888 poem "America":

Centre of equal daughters, equal sons,
All, all alike endear'd, grown, ungrown, young or old,
Strong, ample, fair, enduring, capable, rich,
Perennial with the Earth, with Freedom, Law and Love,
A grand, sane, towering, seated Mother,
Chair'd in the adamant of Time. (*LGC*, 511)

Like the sexually charged and spiritually unifying figure of the Virgin that Henry Adams opposed to the divisive and potentially destructive figure of the Dynamo in *The Education of Henry Adams*, Whitman looks to the creative and unifying power of the mother as means of regenerating individual, nation, and world.[10]

The mother Whitman imagines is no mere emblem of the corporate identity of America: "Perennial with the Earth, with Freedom, Law and Love," she bears the traces of a new matriarchal order.[11] "I have sometimes thought," Whitman wrote in *Democratic Vistas* (1871), "that the sole avenue and means of a reconstructed sociology depended, primarily, on a new birth, elevation, expansion, invigoration of woman, affording, for races to come, (as the conditions that antedate birth are indispensable,) a perfect motherhood. Great, great, indeed, far greater than they know, is the sphere of women" (*PW*, 2: 372).

In imagining the *Novus ordo seclorum* as "a new birth" of "woman," Whitman draws once again on the political iconography of America's Revolutionary past. But he also looks forward to the woman-centered quest myths that would shape the work of such Modernist writers as T. S. Eliot, Ezra Pound, Hilda Doolittle, and Ernest Hemingway. Amid the waste and carnage of the post–World War I landscape, these writers looked to feminine figures—the "Hyacinth girl," the "golden, crown, Aphrodite," the Bona Dea, or Maria—as the source of cultural and political transformation.

CHAPTER TWO

Whitman and the Politics of Language

> This subject of language interests me—interests me. I never quite get it out of my mind. I sometimes think the Leaves is only a language experiment—that it is an attempt to give the spirit, the body, the man, new words, new potentialities of speech—an American, a cosmopolitan . . . range of expression. The new world, the new times, the new people, the new vista, need a tongue according.
>
> —Walt Whitman to Horace Traubel,
> *An American Primer* (ellipsis mine)

In *A Backward Glance*, Edith Wharton recalls Henry James's admiration for Walt Whitman: on one occasion, she says, "James, in one of his sudden humorous drops from the heights, flung up his hands and cried out with the old stammer and twinkle: 'Oh, yes, a great genius: undoubtedly a very great genius! Only one cannot help deploring his too-extensive acquaintance with the foreign languages.'"[1] James's ironic comment sums up the critical attitude about Whitman's foreign borrowings: most critics join him in "deploring" Whitman's use of foreign languages.

In *American Renaissance*, F. O. Matthiessen discounts Whitman's use of French words and phrases as "samples of the confused American effort to talk big by using high-sounding terms with only the vaguest notion of their original meaning."[2] In *The Evolution of Walt Whitman*, Roger Asselineau treats Whitman's foreign borrowings as a sign of "the impoverishment of his inspiration" after 1856. In *Literary Democracy*, Larzer Ziff is similarly critical of Whitman's use of foreign terms. Speaking of the "mark of the beery crowd on Whitman," he says: "The mark is also present in the vulgarity of the ill-considered use of foreign terms and the tastelessness of his all-too-easy dismissal of certain British authors."[3]

But Whitman's use of foreign languages is neither merely ignorant nor merely arrogant, as is commonly assumed: his foreign language experiments, like his experiments with literary language more generally, are part of a debate about the relation between language and culture in America that dates back at least as far as Captain John Smith's *Map of Virginia* (1612). Like Smith, who invented several neologisms to describe the unfamiliar flora and fauna of America, Whitman sought to invent a new language to express the unique democratic geography of America. He used foreign terms as a means of expressing the pluralistic, racially diverse, and cosmopolitan nature of American democratic culture.

In using neologisms and foreign terms to assert the special nature of American political experience, Whitman is in the main line of the controversy over national language policy that came to a head during the Revolutionary period. This controversy centered, first, on the question of whether the American republic should have a national language policy and, second, on whether Americans should write and speak in "pure" or American English. In 1781, even before the American Revolution ended, John Witherspoon, the president of Princeton University, expressed alarm at the growing number of Americanisms he found in the speech of his countrymen: "I have heard in this country, in the senate, at the bar, and from the pulpit, and see daily in dissertations from the press, errors in grammar, improprieties and vulgarisms, which hardly any person of the same class in point of rank and literature would have fallen into in Great Britain."[4]

Responding to the same lack of public speech standards, John Adams proposed that America consolidate and extend its political influence by establishing a national language academy. In 1780, he wrote to the Continental Congress, proposing that they establish "the first public institution for refining, correcting, improving, and ascertaining the English language" in order to transmit American ideals of "liberty, prosperity, and glory."[5] Although neither a national language academy nor a national language policy was ever established, Noah Webster's 1828 *American Dictionary of the English Language* became a sort of unofficial standard.

From the first, those favoring an American standard of English insisted on the connection between the American language and the American political system. "It is not to be disputed," Adams averred in his letter to Congress, "that the form of government has an influence upon language, and language in its turn influences not only the form of government, but the temper, the sentiments, and the manners of the people."[6] Perceiving a similar connection between language and politics, Noah Webster wrote what is, in effect, America's declaration of linguistic independence: "As an independent nation," he asserted in *Dissertations on the English Language* (1789), "our honor requires us to have a system of our own, in language as well as government. Great Britain, whose children we are, and whose language we speak, should no longer be *our* standard; for the taste of her writers is already corrupted, and her language on the decline."[7]

Webster's views—while later put into practice by such writers as Joel Barlow in *The Columbiad* (1807)—were by no means universal. The concept of a new American language was vigorously attacked not only in the British press, but also by several prominent Americans, including Benjamin Franklin. The case for the opposition was summed up in 1816 by the distinguished nineteenth-century linguist John Pickering:

> The language of the United States has perhaps changed less than might have been expected, when we consider how many years have elapsed since our ancestors brought it from England; yet it has in so many instances departed from the English standard, that our scholars should lose no time in endeavouring to restore it to its purity, and to prevent future corruption. . . . As a general rule also, we should avoid all those words which are noticed by English authors of reputation, as expressions with which *they are unacquainted*; for although we might produce some English authority for such words, yet the very circumstance of their being thus noticed by well educated *Englishmen*, is proof that they are not in use at this day in England, and, of course, ought not to be used elsewhere by those who speak *correct English*.[8]

Whitman's ideas on language grew out of this national debate about the American language. Like John Adams and Noah Webster, he insisted on the connection between American language and American polity. In a series of notes he wrote during the 1850s in preparation for *Leaves of Grass*, he rejected the British model in language, literature, and government. Finding in British speech and writing a hierarchical system of monarchy and class alien to American democracy, Whitman asserts the need for a new language to express the new American republic. "These States," he wrote in a series of notes on language entitled "The Primer of Words," "are rapidly supplying themselves with new words, called for by new occasions, new facts, new politics, new combinations" (*DN*, 3: 734). Unlike Witherspoon, he declares his love for the rude words he finds in American newspapers, courts, debates, and congressional debates.

In calling for a new American language, Whitman does not attempt to fasten language to any ultimate model: his aim is always to keep language open, flexible, and responsive to the changing contours of the American democratic experience. In this, he is at odds with other poets of his time. Edgar Allan Poe's pursuit of pure poetry engaged him in a perpetual struggle to strip language of its worldliness and referentiality; his experiments in the sound, musicality, and imagery of verse were part of an effort to push language "Out of SPACE—out of TIME."[9] Emerson, too, is fundamentally ahistorical in his view of language. His assertion that "[w]ords are signs of natural facts" expresses a fixed and purist concept of language; in pursuit of some Adamic state in which words are in absolute accord with things, the Emersonian poet must excavate his language—or fossil poetry—out from under the layers of culture in which it is embedded.[10]

Standing flush with the naked universe, Emerson wrote poems that were removed, both physically and linguistically, from the life of his times. For all his belief that "the experience of each new age requires a new confession," he used a language that is—like the language of Bryant, Longfellow, Irving, and Cooper—indistinguishable from the language of his English contemporaries.[11] "Whatever differences there may be," wrote British lexicographer Sir William Craigie, "between the language of Longfellow and Tennyson, of Emerson and Ruskin, they are differences due to style and subject, to a personal choice or command of words, and not to any real divergence in the means of expression."[12] Whitman recognized Emerson's "cold and bloodless" isolation from the life and language of America. "Suppose," he says in an essay on "Emerson's Books,"

> these books becoming absorb'd, the permanent chyle of American general and particular character—what a well-washed and grammatical, but bloodless and helpless, race we should turn out! No, no, dear friend; though the States want scholars, undoubtedly . . . they don't want scholars, or ladies and gentlemen, at the expense of all the rest. They want good farmers, sailors, mechanics, clerks, citizens—perfect business and social relations—perfect fathers and mothers. If we could only have these, or their approximations, plenty of them, fine and large and sane and generous and patriotic, they might make their verbs disagree from

> their nominatives, and laugh like volleys of musketeers, if they should please. (*PW*, 2: 516–17)

If for Emerson the sources of language were in Nature, for Whitman the sources of language were in democratic culture, which included, but was not limited to, natural facts: "Language, be it remember'd," Whitman wrote in "Slang in America," "is not an abstract construction of the learn'd, or of dictionary-makers, but is something arising out of the work, needs, ties, joys, affections, tastes, of long generations of humanity, and has its bases broad and low, close to the ground" (*PW*, 2: 573). For Whitman, language was not removed from, but embedded in historic process. He celebrated the English language, not because he wanted to fit American experience into British speech patterns, but because the multiethnic roots of the English language made it the ideal expressive medium for American democratic culture:

> View'd freely, the English language is the accretion and growth of every dialect, race, and range of time, and is both the free and compacted composition of all. From this point of view, it stands for Language in the largest sense, and is really the greatest of studies. It involves so much; is indeed a sort of universal absorber, combiner, and conqueror. The scope of its etymologies is the scope not only of man and civilization, but the history of Nature in all departments, and of the organic Universe, brought up to date; for all are comprehended in words, and their backgrounds. ("Slang in America," *PW*, 2: 572)

Like John Adams, Whitman equated the evolution of the English language in America with the progress toward realizing the "American ideals" of freedom and happiness.

Whitman's use of foreign languages in his verse was part of his effort to renew and extend the potential of the English language as a democratic medium. Into the so-called purity of New England English, he sought to introduce the ethnic and idiomatic color of American speech. In an essay entitled "The Spanish Element in Our Nationality," he wrote:

> We Americans have yet to really learn our own antecedents, and sort them, to unify them. They will be found ampler than has been supposed, and in widely different and in widely different sources. Thus far, impress'd by New England writers and schoolmasters, we tacitly abandon ourselves to the notion that our United States have been fashion'd from the British Islands only, and essentially for a second England only—

> which is a very great mistake. Many leading traits for our future national personality, and some of the best ones, will certainly prove to have originated from other than British stock. (*PW*, 2: 552–53)

Whitman's desire to keep language and literature open and responsive to the multiethnic sources of American nationality corresponded with his political desire to keep the country open to the immigrants who, after 1850, began coming to America in increasing numbers.

With a similar openness to the "widely different sources" of American nationality, Whitman once speculated that perhaps the sources of a truly native American music might be found not in the transplanted accents of New England English, but in black dialect. This dialect, Whitman says in his "Primer of Words," "furnishes hundreds of outre words, many of them adopted into the common speech of the mass of people." In black speech, Whitman finds "hints of the future theory of the modification of all the words of the English language, for musical purposes, for a native grand opera in America leaving the words just as they are for writing and speaking, but the same words so modified as to answer perfectly for musical purposes, on grand and simple principles" (*DN*, 3: 748). Whitman's words prophesy the development of African American blues and jazz, which are in effect "a native grand opera" and one of America's major contributions to world culture.

With the exception of his brief experiment with black dialect in his post–Civil War poem "Ethiopia Saluting the Colors," Whitman did not draw on the possibilities of black dialect in composing *Leaves of Grass*. But he did introduce several foreign terms—including Spanish, Italian, and French—as part of what he called his "language experiment," his "attempt to give the spirit, the body, the man, new words, new potentialities of speech" in his democratic poems. In this effort to create "an American, a cosmopolitan . . . range of self-expression" commensurate with "the new world, the new times, the new peoples, the new vista," Whitman used French more frequently than any other foreign language.[13] In fact, it is particularly in Whitman's vigorous and extensive use of the French language that we see the political dimensions of his foreign-language experiments.

In a letter to the Princess Royal of England, written in 1797, the British etymologist Sir Herbert Croft reported that during the Revolutionary period Americans considered "revenging themselves on England by rejecting its language and adopting that of France."[14] Although Whitman probably did not know that French had once been considered for adoption as America's national language, his French usage emerged out of similar political sentiments. In championing the language and thought of France, Whitman was not blind to the political implications of his fiercely pro-French position. To be pro-French in early nineteenth-century America could never be a politically or morally neutral position, a mere preference for one country over another. In his book *America and French Culture*, Howard Mumford Jones observes that in America during the early nineteenth century, "the French language was necessarily associated with writers and doctrines held to be atheistic, anarchic, and dangerous."[15]

If, to some, France carried associations with the Enlightenment and rationalism, to many it carried more vivid associations with political revolution, the Reign of Terror, and the reputedly immoral and subversive novels of Eugène Sue and Paul de Kock. Britain, on the other hand, carried associations with monarchy, aristocracy, elitism, and the caste system. Whitman's persistent and sometimes aggressive use of the French language, particularly in his early writings, was a means of flaunting his pro-French sympathies and thus defying the more conservative political and moral attitudes of his countrymen. Just as in the Revolutionary period, American writing participated in the battle between pro-British and pro-French forces—between Federalists and Democrats, conservatives and radicals—so Whitman's poetry, in the tradition of Philip Freneau and Joel Barlow—bears traces of a similar political struggle in the nineteenth century.[16]

Whitman's extensive use of the French language corresponds with the political and social radicalism of his early years. He began to use French while he was editor of the *Aurora* in 1842, at age twenty-three, long before he had any intention of making it part of his politico-literary program. Advertising itself as "the acknowledged journal of the beau monde, the Court Journal of our democratic aristocracy," the *Aurora* filled its columns with borrowings from the French in order to give its articles on New York social life an aristocratic tone.[17] As editor of the *Aurora*, Whitman employed a rather limited store of French words and phrases. These French flourishes were, like his dandyish dress of the time, no more than an affectation, a mannered appeal to the *beau monde*.

After his term as editor of the *Aurora*, Whitman ceased to adorn his journalism with borrowings from the French. Not until his trip to New Orleans in 1848 did Whitman make French words and phrases a recurrent expressive medium in his poetry and prose. Turning away from the affectations of his early journalism, Whitman made a self-consciously literary use of language in the articles he wrote for the New Orleans *Daily Crescent.* In a series entitled "Sketches of the Sidewalks and Levees," for example, his sketches of Dusky Grisette, the *marchande de fleurs*, and Timothy Goujon, the écailler, anticipate the linguistic experiments of literary realism. His street-walking Grisette is an ancestor of Stephen Crane's Maggie. And his transcription of the oyster seller's dialect—"Ah-h-h-h-h-h a bonne marche—so cheap as navair vas—toute frais—var fresh, Ah-h-h come and puy de veritable poisson de la mer—de bonne huitres—Ah-h-h-h-h-h!"—is an early attempt to capture the idioms of American street life.[18]

Writing of "New Orleans in 1848," Whitman observes: "I have an idea that there is much and of importance about the Latin race contributions to American nationality in the South and Southwest that will never be put with sympathetic understanding and tact on record" (*PW,* 2: 606–7). His New Orleans sketches were his first effort to put on record the multiethnic and multilingual nature of America: he used the French language to inject Latin color and accent into the culturally dominant New England strain of American nationality. After his trip to New Orleans, where he came into contact with many "French and Spanish Creole" people, Whitman's French usage became a key element in his struggle for a simultaneously cosmopolitan and native American idiom.

In "America's Mightiest Inheritance," an article on the English language written for *Life Illustrated* in 1856, Whitman remarks: "Great writers penetrate the idioms of their races, and use them with simplicity and power. The masters are they who embody the rude materials of the people and give them the best forms for the place and time." Commenting on the evolution of the English language, he emphasizes the importance of the French contribution: "The Norman Conquest of England brought in profuse buds and branches of the French, which tongue seems always to have supplied a class of words most lacking, and continues its supply to this day."[19]

Not content merely to penetrate and record the idioms of his time, Whitman assumed the role of agent in the evolution of an American language. In an "Appendant for Working-People, Young Men and Women, and for Boys and Girls," he includes, "*A few Foreign Words, mostly French, put down Suggestively.*" Seeking, presumably, the best forms for the "rude materials of the people," Whitman lists the pronunciations and definitions of over one hundred French terms that might be introduced into the spoken language. "Some of these are tip top words," he avers, "much needed in English—all have been more or less used in affected writing, but not more than one or two, if any have yet been admitted to the homes of the common people."[20]

Whitman's list was not as precipitate as it may seem. Of the French words that he put down "suggestively," over half had already appeared in Webster's 1848 *Dictionary*, and of those that did not appear, several could now be found in any standard dictionary. Among the latter are such commonly used French words as *aplomb*, *brochure*, *brusque*, *nonchalant*, *restaurant*, *rôle*, and *repertoire*. Seeking to hasten the process of language growth in America with a few implants of his own, Whitman had in fact anticipated the admission of many French terms into the homes of the common people.

In composing *Leaves of Grass*, Whitman carried on his campaign to enrich the American language with borrowings from the French. Here again, his French usage is not as ill-considered as critics have led us to believe. He incorporated in his verse only about thirty of the French words that he suggested for general usage in 1856. Many of these terms, such as *accoucheur*, *cache*, *douceur*, *ensemble*, *encore*, *façade*, *mélange*, *persiflage*, *rapport*, and *résumé*, were listed in the 1848 *Dictionary* and thus already had some currency in America. He also introduced into his writing several French terms that did not appear in his 1856 list, but most of these can also be found in the 1848 *Dictionary*. In fact, Whitman employed only a few French words—*mon cher*, *ma femme*, *mon enfant*, *en masse*, *trottoir*—that were not already part of American English. By using French terms that were already a part of common parlance, Whitman sought to do for the American language what Chaucer had done for the English.[21]

While French words and phrases are a consistent feature of all his writings, Whitman used a majority of these terms first and most frequently in the more experimental 1855, 1856, and 1860 editions of *Leaves of Grass*. Critics have been quick to remark on Whitman's more unfortunate uses of the French language in passages such as the following:

> I sound triumphal drums for the dead . . . . I fling through my embouchures the loudest and gayest music to them ("Song of Myself," *LG* 1855, 42)

In most cases, however, Whitman's French usage is both precise and effective. When he speaks of "the grandeur and life of the universe" in the 1855 preface, or when he says "The Secretaries act in their bureaus for you" in "A Song for Occupations," his use of French terms seems quite natural (*LG* 1855, 9, 92).

He frequently uses French to suggest sophistication and worldliness, as in "I saw the rich ladies in full dress at the soiree" in "Faces" (*LG* 1855, 127). At other times he uses French for hyperbolic and comic effect: "And the tree-toad is a chef-d'oeuvre for the highest," he exclaims in "Song of Myself" (*LG* 1855, 55). In none of these instances is Whitman's French usage either vulgar or ill-considered.

Although Whitman's French usage was always framed by his political vision, the contexts within which he used the language ranged from the broadly programmatic to the intensely personal. In the 1855 *Leaves of Grass*, for example, he used French as part of his effort to make death less terrifying. In his 1851 address to the Brooklyn Art Union, Whitman called on artists to heighten the beauty and appeal of death: "Nay," he asserts, "May not death itself, through the prevalence of a more artistic feeling among the people, be shorn of many of its frightful and ghastly features."[22] Through the grace and subtlety of the French language, Whitman sought to transfigure the "spectral horror" and "mouldering skull" of death, and thus to create a more poetic feeling about death. In the poem later entitled "Song of Myself," he refers to death as a romantic encounter: "Our rendezvous is fitly appointed . . . . God will be there and wait till we come" (*LG* 1855, 79). The word *rendezvous* suggests death not as a culmination, but as a consummation of a love affair with the great Camerado.

Whitman also refers to death as an *accoucheur* (giver of birth): "To his work without flinching the accoucheur comes," he says in "Song of Myself"; and in "To Think of Time," he writes: "Not a day passes . . not a minute second without an accouchement" (*LG* 1855, 83, 98). His choice of the word *accoucheur*—which Whitman defined in his 1856 list as *Man-midwife*—is particularly effective in suggesting the same hopeful association of birth (*accoucher*), death (*accoucheur*), and sleep (*coucher*) that we find in "The Sleepers." But more importantly, the sexually mixed figure of death as a *Man-midwife* bringing deliverance, and the association of dying (*accouchement*) with labor and childbirth, give unique emphasis to the process of regeneration—personal, political, and spiritual—that is the underlying theme of *Leaves of Grass*.

Associating France with a more open attitude toward sex and the body, Whitman also makes frequent use of the French language in a sexual context. For example, he uses French to heighten the ambiguity of the erotic dream fantasy in the poem later entitled "The Sleepers" in the 1855 *Leaves of Grass*:

I am a dance . . . . Play up there! the fit is whirling me fast.

I am the everlaughing . . . . it is new moon and twilight,
I see the hiding of douceurs . . . . I see nimble ghosts whichever way I look,
Cache and cache again deep in the ground and sea, and where it is neither ground or sea. (*LG* 1855, 106)

Here again, the French words add to the rhythmic and tonal quality of the verse, at the same time that they whisper of hidden delights and the half-formed erotic fantasies of the dream-state. The ambiguity of *douceurs*—suggesting softness, sweetness, honey—and the phrase *cache and cache*—with its suggestion of hole, hidden, treasure—intensify the erotic fantasy of the passage.

On the verso of the only known manuscript page of the first edition of *Leaves of Grass*, Whitman listed three columns of words, presumably a trial vocabulary for the 1856 *Leaves of Grass*. Before each word he wrote *c*, *f*, *g*, or *l*, a code standing for the Celtic, French, Greek, and Latin origins of the word.[23] These words, many of which are used in the 1856 "Broad-Axe Poem," are one further indication of the seriousness with which Whitman sought to create an etymologically diverse language to match the pluralistic culture of America.

Throughout the 1856 *Leaves of Grass*, Whitman used the French language not only to express the democratic pluralism of American culture, but to connect American democracy to the enlightened, republican, and Revolutionary heritage of France. The French language was a consistent feature of Whitman's poems of cosmopolitan vision and international embrace that first appeared in the 1856 *Leaves*. In "Poem of the Road," he uses the French term "*Allons!*"—perhaps an allusion to the first word of the revolutionary French anthem "La Marseillaise"—as an exhortatory refrain to invite the people of all lands to join in the progress toward freedom and regeneration on the open road. He also makes frequent use of French words in such other 1856 poems of universal philosophy as "Poem of Salutation," "Broad-Axe Poem," and "Poem of the Sayers of the Words of the Earth." In fact, through all editions of *Leaves of Grass*, Whitman's favorite borrowings from the French are words of communality, affection, and global embrace: *rapport*, *ensemble*, *en masse*, *rondure*, *mélange*, *résumé*, *mon cher*, *ma femme*, *comrade*, *compagnon*, and *ami*.

The years preceding the Civil War were the period of Whitman's greatest productivity and his most sustained thought about the connection between the American language and democratic culture. Horace Traubel tells us that the notes on language that Whitman collected in "The Primer of Words" were "largely written in the rather exciting five years before the war" (*DN*, 3: 729n). During this same period, Whitman wrote an article on the English language, "America's Mightiest Inheritance." According to C. Carroll Hollis, Whitman also coauthored with William Swinton a book on language entitled *Rambles among Words* in 1859.[24] Here again, in a section attributed to Whitman, language is treated as an outgrowth of national polity: "Over the transformations of a Language the genius of a nation unconsciously presides—the issues of Words represent issues in the national thought." Language, says Whitman, must reflect the multiplicity of habits, heritages and races that make up American nationality: "The immense diversity of race, temperament, character—the copious streams of humanity constantly flowing hither—must reappear in free, rich growth of speech. From no one ethnic source is America sprung: the electric reciprocations of many stocks conspired and conspire. This opulence of race-elements is in the theory of America."[25]

Once again, in naming the diverse roots of American English, Whitman singles out the French contribution: "How much has the French language been to the English! How much has it yet to give! Nation of sublime destinies, noble, naive, rich with humanity, bearers of freedom, upholding on her shoulders the history of Europe for a thousand years!"[26] Here Whitman makes clear the connection between his embrace of the French language and the political role he envisions for France as the enlightened bearer of *liberté*, égalité, *fraternité*—a role that he would later evoke in his 1871 poem "O Star of France. 1870–71."

It is almost as if Whitman saw the proliferation of French terms in English as one more way of strengthening the republican vigor of America. Thus, the period of his most concentrated thinking about language as index and instrument of democratic culture also coincided with his most extensive use of French language in his writings. Whitman introduced more French words into the 1860 *Leaves of Grass*, which was published on the eve of the Civil War, than into any other edition of his poems. He used many French words in the 124 new poems of the 1860 *Leaves*, but he also added several French terms to his earlier poems.

In the 1860 edition, Whitman began organizing his poems into the experimental clusters that anticipate the final structure of *Leaves of Grass*. Two of these clusters—one political, the other sexual, both radical—have French titles. In the political cluster "Chants Democratic"—subtitled "And Native American"—Whitman uses the French term *chants* coupled with the proper

French inversion. The French title may have been prompted by the *chansons* of liberty and internationalism of Pierre-Jean de Béranger, the French national poet and participant in the Revolutions of 1848, with whom Whitman identified in his early years.

The "Chants Democratic" grouping is introduced by a poem with the French title "Apostroph," which begins: "O mater! O fils! / O brood continental!" Here again, Whitman uses the French term *fils* (son) and the French-sounding inversion "brood continental" to express his cosmopolitan theme: his democratic chants are not only songs of native America, but "joyous hymns for the whole earth!" (*LG* 1860, 105, 189). It was also in the 1860 *Leaves* that Whitman changed the title of his most famous poem of international embrace from "Poem of Salutation" in 1856 to the much more effective "Salut au Monde!" It was an auspicious change: The French title would catch the eye of later French writers and advance Whitman's fame and influence in France.[27]

Unlike the "Chants Democratic" cluster, which Whitman broke up and regrouped in later editions, the cluster of poems on sex and the body, to which he initially gave the French title "Enfans d'Adam," became one of the central and most controversial groupings in future editions of *Leaves of Grass*. In this cluster, Whitman carried on his campaign to, as he says in his famous "Letter to Ralph Waldo Emerson" in the 1856 *Leaves*, "celebrate in poems the eternal decency of the amativeness of Nature, the motherhood of all," and to strike out against "the fashionable delusion of the inherent nastiness of sex."[28] In using the French title "Enfans d'Adam" for his group of poems on procreation and amative love, Whitman called attention to their sexual content: the French title would trigger popular notions about the sexual openness and freedom of the French. Looking to the French as an antidote to the deeply rooted Puritan sensibility of New England writers such as Ralph Waldo Emerson, Whitman used "Enfans d'Adam" as another means of championing France's "frankness as opposed to our hypocrisy" in sex directions.[29]

In his "Primer of Words," Whitman observes: "Probably there is this truth to be said about the Anglo-Saxon breed that in real vocal use it has less of the words of various phases of friendship and love than any other race, and more friendship and love" (*DN*, 3: 751). In accord with this observation, Whitman introduced into the 1860 *Leaves of Grass* several French terms of friendship and love, including *amie*, *compagnon*, *mon enfant*, *mon cher*, and *ma femme*. Making use of the phrenological terms *amativeness* and *adhesiveness* to evoke connubial love between men and women and the friendship between men or women, Whitman sought to reaccent these terms with more sexually radical and homoerotic meanings by interweaving several French terms of affectionate address.

However, Whitman's use of these French terms also reveals some of his sexual ambivalence as a man who loved men. Only in his addresses to abstractions does he employ the affectionate term *ma femme*—my woman, my wife. In the opening poem "Proto-Leaf" (later entitled "Starting from Paumanok"), Whitman addresses Democracy as *ma femme*, and he ends "Calamus" 5 with "For you these, from me, O Democracy, to serve you, ma femme! / For you! for you, I am trilling these songs" (*LG* 1860, 351). In "France, the 18th Year of These States," he addresses France as *ma femme*: "I will yet sing a song for you, ma femme" (*LG* 1860, 407). Addressing Democracy and France as *ma femme*, Whitman reveals his depth of affection for both. But he never uses the personal term in his addresses to real women.

Whitman appears to be more interested in finding new French terms of affectionate address to "the young men of the states," who, he says, "never give words to their most ardent friendships" (*DN*, 3: 741). Whereas Whitman employed *ma femme* only in his addresses to abstractions, he frequently used terms such as *amie* [sic], *mon cher*, *mon enfant*, *compagnon*, and *comrade*, which derives from the French word *camarade*, in his intimate addresses to men. In "Proto-Leaf" Whitman asks the young man:

> What do you seek, so pensive and silent?
> What do you need, comrade?
> Mon cher! do you think it is love? (*LG* 1860, 12)

Similarly, in "Poem of the Road," in which Whitman uses the French refrain "*Allons!*" as part of his call to new forms of "adhesiveness" and affection on "the open road," the poet concludes with a kind of intimate proposal of marriage to his companion of the road:

> Mon enfant! I give you my hand!
> I give you my love, more precious than money,
> I give you myself, before preaching and law;
> Will you give me yourself? Will you come travel with me?
> Shall we stick by each other as long as we live? (*LG* 1860, 328)

Associating France with the spirit of *fraternité* and a freer relationship between the sexes—"either sex to either sex," as he once said—Whitman found in the French language words to express some of the ardor of his own love for men.

After 1860, Whitman dropped the use of *mon cher* in "Proto-Leaf" and *mon enfant* in "Poem of the Road." He changed the French *mon cher* to the more paternal *dear son*; and he replaced *mon enfant* with the more political *camerado*. However, he retained the use of *ma femme* to address Democracy and France in all future editions of *Leaves of Grass*. And yet, while some have argued that Whitman toned down the more personal and confessional language in his earlier poems as he moved toward the "good gray" poet of the Civil War and post–Civil War years, just the opposite might be the case. During the Civil War, the bonds of affection among "comrades in arms" and the bonds of affection and love Whitman formed with the hundreds of wounded, sick, and dying soldiers that he visited in the Washington hospitals led to the proliferation of scenes of love and affection between men not only in the poems of "Drum-Taps," but in the more public context of his moving elegy on Lincoln's death, "When Lilacs Last in the Dooryard Bloom'd," in which Whitman expresses his love for the president himself as "comrade lustrous" and lover.[30]

Although Whitman continued to make use of such terms of communality and world embrace as *rapport*, *résumé*, *en masse*, and *rondure*, he used French more sparingly in his poems written after the Civil War. He relied on such terms as *debris*, *promenade*, *grandeur*, and *rendezvous*, which had been thoroughly assimilated into American English. When he introduced new French words into his 1867 Civil War poems, they were such commonly used military terms as *bivouac*, *accoutrements*, *manoeuvre*, and *reveille*. And yet, when Whitman returned to cosmopolitan and international themes in such poems of the 1870s as "Song of the Exposition," "Proud Music of the Storm," "Thou Mother with Thy Equal Brood," and "Passage to India," he continued to use the French language as vigorously as in his early years.

In fact, the ongoing importance of France and the French language to Whitman's democratic vision is suggested by the fact that the 1867 *Leaves of Grass* opens with an "Inscription" in which Whitman pairs his "*Chant*" of "ONE'S SELF" with "the word of the Modern, the word EN-MASSE," a French term used to describe the collectivity or the body of the people together. In the 1871 *Leaves of Grass*, this invocation of what Whitman called "a simple, separate Person" and "the word Democratic, the word *En-masse*" would continue in "One's Self I Sing," the opening "Inscription" and French signature of all future editions of Whitman's democratic epic.[31]

In a 1976 address to the Bicentennial Conference on Early American Literature, Robert Spiller commented on his exclusion of Jewish and African American people from his analysis of American national literature and character:

> Only immigrations from European countries other than Great Britain followed a course close enough to our model to suggest inclusion here, even though the remarkable achievements of the Jews and blacks in contemporary American literature suggest that—given a slightly different model—their contributions to our culture would lend themselves to similar analyses.[32]

Despite some of the failures of Whitman's foreign-language experiments (and there were not as many howlers as critics have led us to believe), he should be credited with proposing a "slightly different model" of American national character than the New England–centered model on which Spiller, F. O. Matthiessen, Perry Miller, and others founded American literature as a distinct field of study during the Cold War years. Rather than being grounded in what Matthiessen called the mid-nineteenth-century American literary "Renaissance," Whitman's model was grounded in the American Revolution.[33] It was a model that set itself against those who sought to define American language and literature in accord with British or New England standards of judgment and taste. But it was also a model that participates in ongoing debates about the multilingual, sexually and racially diverse, and native and transnational origins of American-language literature.

If American language and literature are merely a continuation of British English and its literary tradition in America, then perhaps Whitman erred in his attempt to incorporate a range of foreign and especially French terms into his democratic epic. Perhaps, in fact, he should have heeded the early warnings of John Witherspoon and John Pickering and used no word in public speech and writing that did not accord with British standards of "correct English." But if American language and literature are to express not only the *New England* mind but the entire mind and character of the American people, then perhaps Whitman was ahead of his time. His foreign-language experiments anticipate modernist and later efforts to expand the expressive power and range of English, from Ezra Pound to Jay Z, at the same time that they participate in current attempts to reconstruct American literature in accord with less racially, sexually, and nationally limited definitions of American language and culture.

PART TWO

"IN PATHS UNTRODDEN"

CHAPTER THREE

"Song of Myself" and the Politics of the Body Erotic

I CELEBRATE myself,
And what I assume you shall assume,
For every atom belonging to me as good belongs to you.

—Walt Whitman, *Leaves of Grass* (1855)

In teaching "Song of Myself," I begin with a passage from the 1855 preface to *Leaves of Grass* in which Whitman imagines the ideal poet balanced between the values of pride and sympathy:

> The soul has that measureless pride which consists in never acknowledging any lessons but its own. But it has sympathy as measureless as its pride and the one balances the other and neither can stretch too far while it stretches in company with the other. The inmost secrets of art sleep with the twain. The greatest poet has lain close betwixt both and they are vital in his style and thoughts. (*LG* 1855, 12)

This vision of a poet stretching within a universe bounded by pride and sympathy had as its political analogue the paradox of an American republic poised between self-interest and public virtue, liberty and union, the interests of the many and the good of the one. The secret not only of Whitman's art but of the American Union, the paradox of many in one, would eventually become the opening inscription and balancing frame of *Leaves of Grass* (1881):

> One's-Self I sing, a simple separate person,
> Yet utter the word Democratic, the word En-Masse. (*LGC*, 1)

Balanced between the separate person and the people en masse, the politics of *Leaves of Grass* is neither liberal nor bourgeois in the classical sense of the terms; rather, the poems inscribe the republican ideals of early nineteenth-century artisan radicalism, emphasizing the interlinked values of independence and communality, of personal wealth and commonwealth.

Whitman's concern with the problem of individual power, balance, and social union was in part a response to the political turmoil of the 1840s and 1850s—a time when traditional republican values were being eroded as America was transformed from an agrarian to an industrial economy and the political union was itself dissolving under the pressure of the contradiction of slavery in the American republic. This essay reads "Song of Myself" as a poem that grows out of, and responds to, revolutionary ideology and the specific political struggles of America on the eve of the Civil War.

Just as the American Revolution had led to a relocation of authority inside rather than outside the individual, so Whitman's myth of origins focused not on the exploits of a historic or mythic figure of the past but on the heroism of a self who was, like the nation, in the process of creation. Whitman mythologized what he called the "entire faith and acceptance" of the American republic in a poetic persona who is at once a model of democratic character and a figure of democratic union (*PW*, 2: 729). Speaking of the analogy between the individual and the body politic, he observed: "What is any Nation—after all—and what is a human being—but a struggle between conflicting, paradoxical, opposing elements—and they themselves and their most violent contests, important parts of the One Identity, and of its development?"[1]

The drama of identity in "Song of Myself" is rooted in the political drama of a nation in crisis—a nation, as Lincoln observed at the time, living in the midst of alarms and anxiety in which "we expect some new disaster with each newspaper we read."[2] Through the invention of an organic self who is like the Union, many in one, Whitman seeks to balance and reconcile major conflicts in the American body politic: the conflicts between "separate person" and "en-masse," individualism and equality, liberty and union, the South and the North, the farm and the city, labor and capital, black and white, female and male, religion and science. These conflicts are played out in individual sections of the poem as the poet moves toward two particularly intense moments of crisis: one in section 28 and the other in section 30. The specific nature of the crisis is unclear, but both involve a momentary loss of balance.

"Swing Open the Doors!" Whitman had declared in one of his Brooklyn *Daily Eagle* editorials in 1846. "We must be constantly pressing onward—every year throwing the doors wider and wider—and carrying our experiment of democratic freedom to the very verge of the limit" (*WJ*, 1: 481). Like the American republic, "Song of Myself" is an experiment in self-government that both tests and illustrates the capacity of a muscular and self-possessed individual for regulation from within. The poem might be read as a democratic performance in which the poet approaches the limit of sexual excess and hellish despair but is eventually restored to an inward economy of equity and balance.

In his famous moment of self-naming in section 24, Whitman stresses his sexually turbulent nature:

> Walt Whitman, an America, one of the roughs, a kosmos,
> Disorderly fleshy and sensual . . . . eating drinking and breeding,
> No sentimentalist . . . . no stander above men and women or apart from
> them . . . . no more modest than immodest.
>
> Unscrew the locks from the doors!
> Unscrew the doors themselves from their jambs! (*LG* 1855, 48)

Here as throughout the poem Whitman celebrates and indeed flaunts his representative status as a poet who absorbs into the "kosmos" of his body and his poem what he called in his journalism the "turbulence and destructiveness" and "freaks and excesses" of American democracy.

It is on the sexual level, through a release of libidinous energies, that Whitman's democratic poet undergoes his first major trial of self-mastery. The main challenge comes from the onslaught of touch in section 28. The poet records a moment of crisis in which his hitherto balanced persona, stimulated by a masturbatory fantasy, is taken over by the sense of touch:

> Is this then a touch? . . . . quivering me to a new identity,
> Flames and ether making a rush for my veins,
> Treacherous tip of me reaching and crowding to help them,
> My flesh and blood playing out lightning, to strike what is hardly
> different from myself,
> On all sides prurient provokers stiffening my limbs,
> Straining the udder of my heart for its withheld drip. (*LG* 1855, 53)

Stimulated and stiffened by the "treacherous" fingertips of himself, the poet loses his bodily balance. Carried away by a solitary act of onanism, he also loses the balance between self and other, body and soul, that is part of the democratic design of poet and poem. Here we might ask why a masturbation fantasy occurs at the very center of a poem about democracy. Why is the main battle in this epic of American democracy fought not on the battlefield but within the self, on the level of the body and the senses? And why is masturbation represented in the language of political insurrection? What exactly is the relation between the fear of democracy and the fear of the unruly body in Whitman's poem and in mid-nineteenth-century America?

Presented in the language of a violent mass insurrection in which touch, as the "red marauder," usurps the governance of the body, the entire sequence has a fairly marked political nuance:

> No consideration, no regard for my draining strength or my anger,
> Fetching the rest of the herd around to enjoy them awhile,
> Then all uniting to stand on a headland and worry me.
>
> The sentries desert every other part of me,
> They have left me helpless to a red marauder,
> They all come to the headland to witness and assist against me.
>
> I am given up by traitors;
> I talk wildly . . . . I have lost my wits . . . . I and nobody else am the greatest traitor,
> I went myself first to the headland . . . . my own hands carried me there. (*LG* 1855, 53–54)

The poet's "worry" in this passage is at once personal and political. The vision of insurrection and violence within the democratic body of the poet relates not only to the impending crisis of the Civil War but also to the very theory of America itself. If the individual is not capable of self-mastery, if balance is not the natural law of the universe, if the storms of (homo)sexual passion can usurp the constitution of body and body politic, then the theory of America would be cankered at its source. Just as the insurrection within the body of the poet comes from his own hand, so in the political sphere the main threat to democracy appeared to come from within the body of the republic. The entire sequence links the danger of democracy with the danger of a sexually unruly body. And it is on the level of sex and the body that the poem tests the democratic theory of America.

Whitman resolves the bodily crisis of his protagonist symbolically by linking the onslaught of touch—as a sign of unruliness in body and body politic—with the regenerative energies of the universe:

> You villain touch! what are you doing? . . . . my breath is tight in its throat;
> Unclench your floodgates! you are too much for me.

Blind loving wrestling touch! Sheathed hooded sharptoothed touch!
Did it make you ache so leaving me?

Parting tracked by arriving . . . . perpetual payment of the perpetual
loan,
Rich showering rain, and recompense richer afterward.

Sprouts take and accumulate . . . . stand by the curb prolific and vital,
Landscapes projected masculine full-sized and golden. (*LG* 1855, 54)

The moment of sexual release is followed by a restoration of balance as the ejaculatory flow merges with, and is naturalized as, the regenerative flow of the universe. The parallel lines, alliteration, and consonance formally mark the restoration of balance at the same time that they inscribe the process of parting and arriving, efflux and influx, that is the generative rhythm of the universe and the main pattern of the poem as the poet advances and retreats, absorbs and bestows.

Read closely, the sequence also provides a useful corrective to the popular image of Whitman as the poet of sexual excess. Whitman does not celebrate masturbation in "Song of Myself." On the contrary, his attitude is closer to the antimasturbation tracts published by Fowler and Wells, the distributors of the first edition of *Leaves of Grass*.[3] Whitman presents masturbation as an instance of bodily disturbance—a muted sign perhaps of the unruliness of his own sexual passion for men—and a trope for disorder in the political sphere. As a figure of democratic unruliness in body and body politic, masturbation becomes the sexual ground on which Whitman tests the democratic theory of America. By demonstrating the restoration of bodily balance after taking democracy to the very limit in masturbation and orgasm, Whitman both tests and enacts poetically the principle of self-regulation in individual and cosmos that is the base of his democratic faith.

"Is this then a touch? . . . . quivering me to a new identity," the poet asks at the beginning of his masturbatory sequence (*LG* 1855, 53). Within the gloriously regenerative economy of "Song of Myself," (homo)erotic touching is safe and natural, quivering the poet not to a new and marginal identity as a homosexual in heterosexual America but toward the experience of cosmic unity evoked in the lengthy catalogue of section 33. But while Whitman successfully manages the onslaught of touch within the symbolic order of his poem, the unruly body—both his own and the bodies of others—would remain a source of anxiety and perturbation in his dream of democracy.

If section 28 enacts a loss of bodily balance in masturbation, section 38 enacts a loss of self in empathetic identification with others. This crisis appears to be connected to the end of section 33, where the poet begins identifying with scenes of suffering, carnage, and death: "I am the man . . . . I suffered . . . . I was there," he says (*LG* 1855, 62). Some of these scenes are linked with the nation's history: the "condemned" witch and "hounded slave" in section 33, the Texas war in section 34, and the American Revolution in section 35. While the poet's descent into the American past is presumably intended as a heroic record of personal and national creation, the weight of human suffering and tragedy in the battles he describes registers anxiety about the impending dissolution of the Union and the blood "falling" not only over the past but over the future of America.

The structures of human misery that entrap the human life threaten to overwhelm the poet in sections 37 and sections 38. As he assumes the identities of a prisoner, a mutineer, and a criminal, he becomes static, impotent, caged:

> Askers embody themselves in me, and I am embodied in them,
> I project my hat and sit shamefaced and beg. (*LG* 1855, 68)

No longer "afoot" with his vision, the poet has fallen from the state of democratic grace. His shamefaced beggar is the very antithesis of the proud, self-confident person who straddled continents and cocked his hat as he pleased indoors or out at the outset of the poem.

Having lost his democratic balance between self and other, pride and sympathy, the one and the many, the poet undergoes his second crisis of self-mastery in section 38:

> Somehow I have been stunned. Stand back!
> Give me a little time beyond my cuffed head and slumbers and dreams
> and gaping,
> I discover myself on the verge of the usual mistake. (*LG* 1855, 68)

The poet appears to be on the verge of losing faith in the divine potency of the individual and the regenerative power of the universe. He resolves the crisis by remembering the divinity of Christ—the "overstaid fraction"—as a living power that resides within rather than outside every individual.

Whitman's concern throughout "Song of Myself" with the problem of self-mastery is related to his anxiety about the increasing centralization of institutional authority, whether in the areas of finance, capital, and trade or in response to the issues of slavery, territorial expansion, and the state of the Union. "You cannot legislate men into morality," he had declared as early as 1842 in an article on popular sovereignty in the New York *Aurora* (*WJ*, 2: 132), and later, in a Brooklyn *Daily Eagle* editorial on government, he asserted: "*Men* must be 'masters unto themselves,' and not look to presidents and legislative bodies for aid" (*WJ*, 2: 301). He later elaborated his position in *Democratic Vistas* (1871):

> That which really balances and conserves the social and political world is not so much legislation, police, treaties, and dread of punishment, as the latent eternal intuitional sense, in humanity, of fairness, manliness, decorum, &c. Indeed, this perennial regulation, control, and oversight, by self-suppliance, is *sine qua non* to democracy; and a highest widest aim of democratic literature may well be to bring forth, cultivate, brace, and strengthen this sense, in individuals and society. (*PW*, 2: 421)

By imaginatively embodying the individual's capacity for balance—between self and other, body and soul, material and spiritual—and by inspiring his readers to their own acts of self-creation, Whitman sought in his poems to cultivate and strengthen "this perennial regulation, control, and oversight, by self-suppliance" as the "*sine qua non* to democracy" in individuals and society.

This concept of balance not only as a principle of self-regulation in humanity but as a principle of unity in the cosmos is the culminating lesson of "Song of Myself." In section 50, the poet finds the "word unsaid" of the universe in the regenerative order of creation:

> Do you see O my brothers and sisters?
> It is not chaos or death . . . . it is form and union and plan . . . . it is
> eternal life . . . . it is happiness. (*LG* 1855, 85)

Like the self-evident truths of "life, liberty, and the pursuit of happiness" enunciated in the Declaration of Independence, Whitman's declaration of faith is rooted in an Enlightenment Revolutionary vision of "form and union and plan" as the natural law of the universe.

Having communicated his lesson of equity and balance, Whitman takes leave of his readers. Moving toward dusk, death, and the future, he enacts his message of faith by joyously dissolving into the elements of earth, air, fire, and water:

> I depart as air . . . . I shake my white locks at the runaway sun,
> I effuse my flesh in eddies and drift it in lacy jags.
>
> I bequeath myself to the dirt to grow from the grass I love,
> If you want me again look for me under your bootsoles. (*LG* 1855, 86)

The death of the poet and the completion of the poem correspond, like the fifty-two weeks of the year and the fifty-two sections of his poem, with the completion of the regenerative cycle of the earth. The poet's departure enacts the promise of eternal life not through personal immortality or spiritual transcendence but by merging with the regenerative processes of universal creation. Existing under, rather than above, the "soles" of his readers, the poet becomes the "uniform hieroglyphic" and "sign of democracy" he began by contemplating as he loafed in the grass.

While the poem, like the final edition of *Leaves of Grass* (1881), inscribes an arc of development from life to death, body to spirit, summer to autumn, dawn to dusk, self to other, and poet to reader, it has no beginning, middle, or end in the traditional sense. The poem moves not by narrative line but by association and recurrence, in the form of a circle. The concluding lines of "Song of Myself" return cyclically to the beginning, with this difference: as the poet had predicted, the reader has now assumed the active and creative role of the poet contemplating the meaning of the grass:

You will hardly know who I am or what I mean,
But I shall be good health to you nevertheless,
And filter and fiber your blood.

Failing to fetch me at first keep encouraged,
Missing me one place search another,
I stop some where waiting for you (*LG* 1855, 86)

Through the use of present tense and present participles in the final lines, the poet becomes, like the grass, perennially present, waiting in perpetuity not in the past but somewhere down the road in the future where the reader may encounter him. The image of an open-ended process appears to be underscored by the lack of a period at the end of the poem in some versions of the 1855 *Leaves of Grass*. But as it turns out, some editions of the 1855 *Leaves of Grass* have a period at the end of the poem, and thus the period appears to have dropped off while the book was being printed.

"A great poem is no finish to a man or woman but rather a beginning," Whitman asserted in the 1855 preface to *Leaves of Grass*. "Has any one fancied he could sit at last under some due authority and rest satisfied with explanations and realize and be content and full? To no such terminus does the greatest poet bring . . . he brings neither cessation or sheltered fatness and ease. The touch of him tells in action" (*LG* 1855, 22). In the final lines of "Song of Myself," Whitman refuses the traditional authority and closure of art. His democratic poetics is an activist poetics that incites the reader to the final act of creation—of self and poem, nation and world.

CHAPTER FOUR

Whitman and the Homosexual Republic

The dependence of Liberty shall be lovers,
The continuance of Equality shall be comrades.

These shall tie and band stronger than hoops of iron.

—Walt Whitman, "Calamus" 5 (*Leaves of Grass*, 1860)

In a letter dated March 13, 1946, Malcolm Cowley wrote to Kenneth Burke: "I'm working on Whitman, the old cocksucker. Very strange amalgam he made between cocksucking and democracy."[1] The letter itself seems strange coming from Malcolm Cowley, who in his famous 1959 introduction to the Viking edition of the 1855 *Leaves of Grass* became instrumental in the critical construction of Whitman as neither "cocksucker" nor democratic poet but as an essentially spiritual poet who had been miraculously transformed from hack journalist to prophetic poet by a "mystical experience."[2] But Cowley's private and public comments are characteristic of a critical tradition that has insisted on silencing, spiritualizing, heterosexualizing, or marginalizing Whitman's sexual feeling for men.[3] Recent works on Whitman by gay critics and others have sought to name the sexual love of men that earlier critics insisted on silencing. But while these approaches have emphasized the centrality of Whitman's sexuality and homosexuality to his work, they have also tended to maintain a distinction between Whitman the private poet and Whitman the public poet, Whitman the homosexual poet and Whitman the poet of democracy, that unduly privatizes and totalizes Whitman's sexual feeling for men.[4] It is this distinction between private and public, homosexuality and democracy, that I would like to question and problematize in this chapter by exploring what Cowley very aptly called the "very strange amalgam" of "cocksucking and democracy" in Whitman's work.

I would like to begin by describing a brief public service announcement produced by the Philadelphia Lesbian and Gay Task Force as a means of reflecting on the uses to which Whitman may and may not be put in contemporary American culture. A young man stands at the Delaware River's edge, with the Walt Whitman Bridge in the background, and says:

> Hey, I just found out Walt Whitman was gay . . . you know the guy they named the bridge after. I wish I had known that when I was in high school. Back then, I got hassled all the time by the other kids, 'cause I'm gay—and the teachers—they didn't say anything. Why didn't they tell me Walt Whitman was gay?

All six television stations in the Philadelphia market refused to air this public service announcement, arguing that it was too "controversial" and that it "advocated a particular lifestyle." When two of the stations called the Walt Whitman Poetry Center, the director said that to tell the world that Whitman was gay "would really be detrimental to the Center. A lot of our programming is geared to teens. Kids don't need a lot to scare them off."[5]

At issue in this controversy was not the question of whether Whitman was gay; there seemed to be widespread if covert agreement that he was. At issue was the idea that Whitman's gayness must not be aired publicly because such public airing would be detrimental to the American public and "scare" young kids. What the controversy suggests, finally, is the extent to which Whitman, as the poet of the people, the poet of democracy, and the American poet, has also become an American public property whose image is bound up with the maintenance of American public health and American national policy. It is not only the academic and critical establishment but those in positions of social and cultural power, and, I would add, the national government itself, that are heavily invested in keeping Whitman's sexuality, and specifically his sexual love of men, out of any discussion of his role as the poet of democracy, and the American poet.[6] In other words, if we can control Whitman's sexuality, we can also control the sexuality of the nation.

Against those who insist on separating Whitman's work into an either/or proposition—either Whitman the private poet or Whitman the public poet, Whitman the poet of gay men or Whitman the democratic poet, Whitman the homosexual or Whitman the poet of the American republic—I would like to argue that we take Whitman seriously when, in the preface to the 1876 centennial edition of *Leaves of Grass*, he says of the "ever new-interchange of adhesiveness, so fitly emblematic of America" that "the special meaning of the 'Calamus' cluster of 'Leaves of Grass' (and *more or less running through the book*, and cropping out in 'Drum-Taps,') mainly resides in its *political significance.*" "It is," Whitman goes on to say, "by a fervent, accepted development of comradeship, the beautiful and sane affection of man for man, latent in all of the young fellows, north and south, east and west—it is by this, I say, and by what goes directly and indirectly along with this, that the United States of the future, (I cannot too often repeat,) are to be most effectually welded together, intercalated, anneal'd into a living union" (*PW*, 2: 471; my italics).

In arguing for the political significance of adhesiveness as a fervent passion among and between men in the "Calamus" poems, *Drum-Taps*, and throughout *Leaves of Grass*, I do not mean to return to older interpretations of Whitman's love poems to men as allegories of American democracy. Rather, I mean to argue the centrality of Whitman's sexual love of men to the democratic vision and experimental poetics of *Leaves of Grass* and to Whitman's hopes for welding the American republic into a "living union," especially in the post–Civil War period. In making this argument, I shall explore the ways the discourse of democracy intersects with material transformations in labor, industry, and social relations in the nineteenth century in the United States to construct homosexuality as a type of pathology.[7] But in exploring the emergence of homosexuality as a modern type and sensibility in nineteenth-century America and in Whitman's work in particular, I want to try to avoid the tendency among critics, despite their distinction between what Jeffrey Weeks calls "homosexual behavior, which is universal, and a homosexual identity, which is specific," to construct both homosexual behavior and homosexual identity as transhistorical and monolithic categories.[8]

This essay insists on the fact that the word and the category *homosexual* did not exist when Whitman began writing. As he himself put it in "The Primer of Words": "The lack of any words . . . is as historical as the existence of words. As for me, I feel a hundred realities, clearly determined in me, that words are not yet formed to represent" (*DN*, 3: 745–46; ellipsis mine). The words Whitman did use to articulate and name his erotic feeling for men were the words of democracy—of comradeship, brotherhood, equality, social union, the glories of the laborer and the common people. But Whitman also used other languages. And thus, against those who tend to treat homosexuality as an a priori or monolithic given in Whitman's work, I want to argue the fluidity of Whitman's articulation of same-sex love among men as the language of democracy intersects with other languages, including the languages of temperance, sexual reform, artisan republicanism, labor radicalism, phrenology, heterosexual love, familial and especially father-son relationships, and spirituality in Whitman's attempt, as he says, to express "a hundred realities, clearly determined in me, that words are not yet formed to represent."

In past approaches to Whitman's work, there has been a tendency to discuss the arc of Whitman's poetic development as if he emerged miraculously as a "homosexual poet" in the 1860 *Leaves of Grass* and then disappeared or was sublimated just as miraculously during the Civil War and in the post–Civil War period. As Charley Shively and Michael Moon have pointed out, however, Whitman's desire to name his erotic attraction to men is already evident in his early story "The Child's Champion" (1841, later entitled "The Child and the Profligate") and in his temperance novel *Franklin Evans; or The Inebriate* (1842), both published in the *New World*, a popular and widely circulated workingman's magazine. But while these stories name a kind of sexual cruising among men in the city, to which youths newly arrived from the country were particularly prone, they also locate physical relations among men under the sign of intemperance, thus rendering them potentially dangerous to the healthy and virtuous personal relationships and republican body the stories advocate. Although the profligate is transformed into a provider by his erotic attraction to the child, and he sleeps that night with the young boy folded in his arms, the narrator makes it clear that this is not a totally "unsullied affection": "Fair were those two creatures in their unconscious beauty—glorious, but yet how differently glorious! One of them was innocent and sinless of all wrong: the other—O to that other, what evil had not been present, either in action or to his desires!" (*EPF*, 76).

Similarly, while *Franklin Evans* seems driven by a narrative urge to kill off women and heterosexual marriage in order to affirm the primacy of social and erotic bonding among men, these relationships are associated with intemperance as a sign of drinking, carousing, and other forms of bodily excess and therefore at odds with the temperance and virtue necessary for a healthy republican body politic. When Franklin Evans is transformed from inebriate into temperance advocate, the transformation is figured in the political language of republican regeneration and manifest destiny: "Now man is free! He walks upon the earth, worthy the name of one whose prototype is God! We hear the mighty chorus sounding loud and long, Regenerated! Regenerated! . . . Victory! victory! The Last Slave of Appetite is free, and the people are regenerated!" (*EPF*, 221, 223; ellipsis mine).

Sometime in the 1840s this apparent antithesis between unhealthy sexuality among men and a healthy republican body politic begins to shift in Whitman's work, as he moves toward articulating a position different from but often expressed in the same language as such popular male purity and antimasturbation tracts as Sylvester Graham's *A Lecture to Young Men, on Chastity* (1834) and Orson Fowler's *Amativeness: Or, Evils and Remedies of Excessive and Perverted Sexuality* (1844), in which masturbation and sexual play among men are presented as destructive to the physical and moral health of a productive, reproductive, and ultimately heterosexual American republic.[9] In Whitman's 1854 notebooks, in which he begins working toward the experimental language and form of *Leaves of Grass*, he insists on locating the soul and vision in the body and matter. And in an early version of the famous touch sequence in "Song of Myself," he represents masturbation (which also doubled in the nineteenth century as a code word for sex among and between men) as a source at once of sexual ecstasy, mystical vision, and poetic utterance:

> I do not wonder that one feeling now, does so much for me,
> He is free of all the rest,—and swiftly begets offspring of them, better than the dams.
> A touch now reads me a library of knowledge in an instant,
> It smells for me the fragrance of wine and lemon-blows,
> It tastes for me ripe strawberries and melons.—
> It talks for me with a tongue of its own,
> It finds an ear wherever it rests or taps. (*NUPM*, 1: 75–76)

Just as in "Song of Myself," in which the pleasures of touching, either oneself or "what is hardly different from myself," and the orgasmic spilling of male seed give rise to a regenerative vision of "Landscapes projected masculine full-sized and golden" (*LG* 1855, 53, 54), so in his notebook entry Whitman reverses the nonreproductive figuration of masturbation and same-sex touching in the male purity tracts, associating the sexual pleasure of "He" who "is free of all the rest" and "better than the dams" with the "offspring" of vision, voice, poetic utterance, and a gloriously reproductive image of nature and world.

This figuration of the body, sexuality, and same-sex love among men as the site of ecstasy, vision, and poetic utterance becomes even more emphatic in the first edition of *Leaves of Grass*. In his long opening poem, later entitled "Song of Myself," the poet describes the "sexual experience" that is at the origins of his democratic voice and vision:

> I believe in you my soul . . . . the other I am must not abase itself to you,
> And you must not be abased to the other.

Loafe with me on the grass . . . . loose the stop from your throat,
Not words, not music or rhyme I want . . . . not custom or lecture, not even the best,
Only the lull I like, the hum of your valved voice.

I mind how we lay in June, such a transparent summer morning;
You settled your head athwart my hips and gently turned over upon me,
And parted the shirt from my bosom-bone, and plunged your tongue to my barestript heart,
And reached till you felt my beard, and reached till you held my feet.
(*LG* 1855, 28–29)

"Isn't this cocksucking plain and simple?" Charley Shively asks, arguing that in this passage, "Whitman demonstrates part of his Americanness by placing cocksucking at the center of *Leaves of Grass*."[10] But before we completely literalize this passage as a direct representation of cocksucking among men, it is important to recognize that the "I" and "you" are unspecified and ungendered in the passage and that the passage has also been read as a representation of what James E. Miller calls an "inverted mystical experience."[11]

Rather than posing cocksucking and mysticism as antithetical readings, however, or arguing that Whitman seeks consciously to disguise his homosexuality through the language of the soul, I would like to suggest that this passage is paradigmatic of the ways the languages of sexuality and spirituality, same-sex love and love between men and women, private and public, intersect and flow into each other in Whitman's work. It is unclear finally whether Whitman is describing sexuality in the language of spiritual ecstasy or a mystical experience in the language of sexual ecstasy, for he seems to be doing both at once.

What is clear is that the democratic knowledge that the poet receives of an entire universe bathed in an erotic force that links men, women, God, and the natural world in a vision of mystic unity is associated with sexual and bodily ecstasy, an ecstasy that includes but is not limited to the pleasures of cocksucking between men. In other words, what we have here is precisely what Malcolm Cowley called the strange amalgam "between cocksucking and democracy" in Whitman's work. Giving tongue is associated at once with sexuality, including sexuality between men, democracy, spiritual vision, and poetic utterance.

This amalgam between men loving men and democracy would become even more emphatic in Whitman's work as the actual political union—on which Whitman staked his identity as a democratic poet—began to dissolve. In traditional readings of Whitman's life and work, it is argued that at some time in the late 1850s Whitman had a love affair that caused him to turn away from his public role as the poet of democracy toward the privacy of love. To disguise the real "homosexual" content of his "Calamus" poems in the 1860 *Leaves of Grass*, it is argued, Whitman interspersed more public poems of democracy, such as "Calamus" 5 (later "For You O Democracy"), with more private and personal poems of homosexual love. Joseph Cady argues that Whitman's attempt to invent a "new order based on his private experience as a homosexual" was only partially successful because in the "least satisfying" strain of "Calamus," Whitman does not sustain his separation and conflict but seeks to "translate" his experience into the language of the common culture.[12]

But this notion of a neat division between the more revolutionary impulses of the private poet of homosexual love and the more conventional impulses of the public poet of democracy is not born out by a close reading of the "Live Oak, with Moss" sequence, the original manuscript of twelve poems of "manly love" out of which the "Calamus" poems emerged. In this sequence, it is precisely in and through rather than against the more conventional language of democratic comradeship, phrenological adhesiveness, and brotherly love that the poet articulates his sexual feelings for men. "I dreamed in a dream of a city where all men were like brothers," Whitman wrote in the poem that would become "Calamus" 34 (later "I Dream'd in a Dream"):

> O I saw them tenderly love each other—I often saw them, in numbers,
> walking hand in hand;
> I dreamed that was the city of robust friends—Nothing was greater
> there than manly love—it led the rest,
> It was seen every hour in the actions of the men of that city, and in all
> their looks and words.— ("Live Oak, with Moss" IX, *LOM*, 31)

What this poem suggests is that, in its most visionary realization, the dream of democracy will give rise to a city—and ultimately an American republic—in which men loving men can live and love and touch openly—a dream city, I might add, that we are still very far from achieving despite the fact that the first lines of "Calamus" 34 ("I dreamed in a dream, I saw a city invincible") are now inscribed on the Camden city hall (*LG* 1860, 373).

Although the "Live Oak, with Moss" sequence and the "Calamus" sequence bear the traces of a rather appealing crisis of representation in which

Whitman realizes that he may not speak for everybody, there is no distinct separation between the poet of democracy and the poet of "manly love." Like other poems in the "Live Oak" sequence and the "Calamus" sequence, "I Dreamed in a Dream" marks not so much a conflict between Whitman the democratic poet and Whitman the lover of men but a shift in Whitman's conceptualization of his role as a democratic poet that locates his personal and sexual love for men at the center of his vision, role, and faith as the poet of democracy. Thus, in the opening poem of "Calamus," later "In Paths Untrodden," the poet avows his desire "To tell the secret of my nights and days, / To celebrate the need of comrades" (*LG* 1860, 342). While these lines might be read as a sign of the separation and conflict between private and public poet, they might also be read paratactically as an example of the ways the poet's "secret" love of men is articulated together with, in the same language as and as the very condition of, his celebration of comrades in the "Calamus" poems.

"Lover and perfect equal!" Whitman exclaims in "Calamus" 41 (later "Among the Multitude"), suggesting the ways the proliferation of the eighteenth-century natural law philosophies of equality and natural rights came to underwrite and in some sense produce homosexuality simultaneously with the emergence and spread of democracy in the United States. It is no coincidence that the proliferation of the rhetoric (if not the reality) of democratic equality during the Age of Jackson corresponded with the emergence of the temperance movement, the male purity crusade, and an increasing cultural anxiety about drinking, masturbation, same-sex sexuality, and other forms of bodily excess and indulgence among and between men. In other words, democracy, particularly in its more egalitarian and fraternal forms, might be said to have simultaneously produced, affirmed, and demonized the modern homosexual as a distinct identity and role.

In *Whitman the Political Poet*, I argued that the "Calamus" poems were Whitman's most radical sequence of poems both personally and politically.[13] But in this essay, I would like to revise that reading to suggest that the "Children of Adam" poems (originally entitled "Enfans d'Adam") may indeed be the more sexually radical sequence that Emerson and the censors who banned *Leaves of Grass* in Boston in 1882 always believed it to be. In accounts of Whitman's poetic development, "Children of Adam" has been treated as an afterthought, a sequence of poems that Whitman added to the 1860 *Leaves of Grass* in order to provide a legitimizing heterosexual context for the actually more radical love poems to men in the "Calamus" sequence. A notebook entry suggests that Whitman initially conceptualized "Children of Adam" as a companion piece to his "Calamus" poems: "A string of Poems, (short, etc.) embodying the amative love of woman—the same as *Live Oak Leaves* do the passion of friendship for man" (*NUPM*, 1: 412). But whatever Whitman's initial intentions, the "Children of Adam" poems do not read as a neatly heterosexual counterpart to his poems of passion for men in the "Calamus" sequence. (And here it is perhaps important to remember that the term *heterosexual* actually came later than the term *homosexual* in the construction of modern sexuality.) While the "Children of Adam" poem "A Woman Waits for Me" consistently provoked nineteenth-century censorship for its representation of an athletic, sexually charged, and desiring female body, the poem is in fact atypical in its emphasis on the amative, and ultimately procreative and eugenically productive, love between men and women.

"Singing the phallus" and the "bedfellow's song," many of the "Children of Adam" poems are not about women or procreation or progeny at all but about amativeness as a burning, aching, "resistless," emphatically physical yearning for young men (see "From Pent-Up Aching Rivers"). Whereas in the "Calamus" poems physical love among men is limited to touching and kissing, in the "Children of Adam" poems Whitman, in the figure of a "lusty," "tremulous," and insistently "phallic" Adam, names and bathes his songs in an active, orgiastic, and physical sexuality among men. "Give me now libidinous joys only!" the poet exclaims in "Enfans d'Adam" 8 ("Native Moments"), evoking scenes of nonreproductive sexual play and pleasure among men:

> I am for those who believe in loose delights — I share the midnight
> orgies of young men,
> I dance with the dancers, and drink with the drinkers,
> The echoes ring with our indecent calls,
> I take for my love some prostitute — I pick out some low person for
> my dearest friend,
> He shall be lawless, rude, illiterate — he shall be one condemned by
> others for deeds done;
> I will play a part no longer — Why should I exile myself from my
> companions? (*LG* 1860, 311)

Even the poem later entitled "A Woman Waits for Me" is as much a celebration of a deliciously phallic male sexuality as it is a celebration of reproductive love between men and women. Associating the "woman" of the title with traditionally masculine activities, the language of the poem slips ambiguously between a celebration of same-sex and opposite-sex love. Moreover, in later revisions of the "Enfans d'Adam" poems, Whitman actually edited out several more explicit "heterosexual" references while retaining the emphasis on an insistently phallic and physical male sexuality. Thus, after Whitman's later deletion of the phrase "I take for my love some prostitute" the passage ends up underscoring the "libidinous joys" and "loose delights" of his "Native Moments" with men.

Whereas in the 1860 *Leaves of Grass* the "Enfans d'Adam" poems are immediately followed by "Poem of the Road" ("Song of the Open Road"), "To the Sayers of Words" ("A Song of the Rolling Earth"), "A Boston Ballad," and then the "Calamus" sequence, in the final edition of *Leaves of Grass* the "Calamus" poems immediately follow the "Children of Adam" poems, which immediately follow "Song of Myself." Rather than suggesting a neatly "heterosexual" and "homosexual" pairing, however, this final arrangement further underscores the fluid relationship between the "lusty," "phallic," and ultimately nonreproductive and nonmonogamous sexual play and pleasure among men in the "Children of Adam" poems and the less insistently phallic but nonetheless explicitly physical lover and democrat of the "Calamus" poems. "Touch me, touch the palm of your hand to my body as I pass, / Be not afraid of my body," says the naked Adamic speaker in the final poem of the "Children of Adam" sequence, as he steps quite imperceptibly into the "paths untrodden" and more emphatically (but not exclusively) homoerotic contexts of the "Calamus" poems (*LGC*, 111).

Against popular associations of masturbation and excessive adhesiveness among men with solitude, impotence, and emasculation, it was Whitman's invention not only to extend the meaning of *adhesiveness*, the phrenological term for friendship between men or women, to same-sex love between men as a virile and socially productive force for urban, national, and international community, but also to extend *amativeness*, the phrenological term for procreative love between men and women, to include physical and procreative love among men. Implicit in the sexual and social vision of "Children of Adam" is a new world garden and a new American republic ordered not by the marital, procreative, familial, and monogamous bonds between men and women but by the sexually and socially productive and nonmonogamous relations among men. While the term "Children of Adam" appears to refer to *all* the children produced presumably by Adam and Eve, as the exclusive reference to Adam in the title suggests, these children are also the male children produced and "prepared for" by the "act divine" and "stalwart loins" of a phallic and virile Adam, whose sexual union with men bears both the creative and procreative seeds of his poetry and the ultimate realization of the American republic and the democratic future.

In his important article "'Here is Adhesiveness': From Friendship to Homosexuality," Michael Lynch argues that when in the 1856 edition of *Leaves of Grass* Whitman wrote, "Here is adhesiveness, it is not previously fashioned—it is apropos," in reference to exclusively same-sex relationships among men, his words marked a major shift toward a definition of the homosexual and heterosexual as distinct types: "Whitman's restriction of Adhesiveness to male-male relationships opened the way for an understanding of same-sex expression of a sexual instinct that was polar to an opposite-sex expression of it." Rather than representing the emergence of what Lynch calls a "distinct 'homosexual identity' and 'homosexual role,'" I would argue that Whitman's "Calamus" and "Children of Adam" poems suggest just the opposite.[14] By conceptualizing and articulating his love for men in the language of democratic comradeship and celebrating physical pleasure among men in the context of male and female amativeness and procreation, Whitman in fact suggests the extent to which the bounds between private and public, male and female, heterosexual and homosexual, are still indistinct, permeable, and fluid in his work.

In most critical discussions of Whitman's life and work, it has become almost axiomatic to argue that Whitman's "homosexual" crisis of the late 1850s was sublimated in the figure of the "wound-dresser" during the Civil War and ultimately silenced and suppressed in the "good gray" politics and poetics of the post–Civil War period. Here, again, however, a close reading of Whitman's Civil War writings suggests just the opposite may be the case: that in fact the discourses of desire among men and the occasions and contexts for their expression in Whitman's work actually proliferated during the Civil War.[15] "How I love them! how I could hug them, with their brown faces, and their clothes and knapsacks cover'd with dust!" Whitman exclaims in the opening poem of *Drum-Taps*, later "First O Songs for a Prelude," as the fire of his passion for men bursts forth along with and in the same language as the "torrents of men" and "the pent fire" of the Civil War in "Rise O Days from Your Fathomless Deeps" (*DTS*, 6, 36, 37).

Rather than sublimating his feelings for men, the historical role Whitman played in visiting thousands of soldiers in the Washington hospitals and the poetic role he played as the "wound-dresser" actually enabled a range of socially prohibited physical contacts and emotional exchanges among men. Soothing, touching, hugging, and kissing the sick and dying soldiers, the private poet merges with the public, female with male, "wound-dresser" with soldier, lover with democratic patriot, in Whitman's poems of the Civil War. "Many a soldier's loving arms about this neck have cross'd and rested, / Many a soldier's kiss dwells on these bearded lips" ("The Dresser," *DTS*, 34).

The intensity of Whitman's passion for men, released and allowed by the "manly" context of war, is particularly evident in "Vigil Strange I Kept on the Field One Night," which along with "When I Heard at the Close of the Day" is perhaps Whitman's most powerful and lyrically moving expression of same-sex love. But it is also important to recognize the ways the languages of manly love, paternal affection, military comradeship, and maternal care intersect and mingle in the poem.

> VIGIL strange I kept on the field one night,
> When you, my son and my comrade, dropt at my side that day,
> One look I but gave, which your dear eyes return'd, with a look I shall never forget;
> One touch of your hand to mine, O boy, reach'd up as you lay on the ground;
> Then onward I sped in the battle, the even-contested battle;
> Till late in the night reliev'd, to the place at last again I made my way;
> Found you in death so cold, dear comrade—found your body, son of responding kisses, (never again on earth responding;). (*DTS*, 42)[16]

As the poet carefully envelopes his "dearest comrade," his "son" and "soldier," and his "boy of responding kisses" in a blanket and buries him "where he fell," he, in effect, prepares the ground which, as in "A March in the Ranks Hard-Prest, and the Road Unknown," "A Sight in Camp in the Day-Break Grey and Dim," and "As I Toilsome Wander'd Virginia's Woods," will enable him to carry on amid what he called the "malignancy," butchery, and surrounding darkness of the war.

The centrality of the Civil War in testing and affirming not only the American union but a range of physical and emotional bonds of affection and intimacy among men as the future of the American republic is most explicitly expressed in "Over the Carnage Rose Prophetic a Voice," which, with the exception of the opening and closing lines, was transferred from the 1860 "Calamus" sequence into *Drum-Taps* (1865):

> OVER the carnage rose prophetic a voice,
> Be not dishearten'd—Affection shall solve the problems of Freedom yet;

> Those who love each other shall become invincible—they shall yet
> make Columbia victorious. (*DTS*, 49)

As in "I Dream'd in a Dream," the poet affirms the relation between "manly affection," physical touch among men across class and state bounds, and the dreams of democracy:

> It shall be customary in the houses and streets to see manly affection;
> The most dauntless and rude shall touch face to face lightly;
> The dependence of Liberty shall be lovers,
> The continuance of Equality shall be comrades.
>
> These shall tie you and band you stronger than hoops of iron;
> I, extatic, O partners! O lands! with the love of lovers tie you. (*DTS*, 50)

Rather than representing a retreat from the privacy of same-sex love, in Whitman's writings of the post–Civil War period this love actually proliferates, even in the most public context of Whitman's famous wartime elegy for Abraham Lincoln, "When Lilacs Last in the Dooryard Bloom'd," where the poet mourns the death of Lincoln as "comrade lustrous" and lover.

The Civil War not only affirmed "manly affection" as the ground of a new democratic order; it also gave Whitman a more militant and combative language in which to express his commitment to the ongoing struggle for this order in the post–Civil War period. "I know my words are weapons, full of danger, full of death," the poet declares in "As I Lay with My Head in Your Lap, Camerado," urging his readers to join him in the democratic struggle:

> For I confront peace, security, and all the settled laws, to unsettle
> them;
> I am more resolute because all have denied me, than I could ever have
> been had all accepted me;
> I heed not, and have never heeded, either experience, cautions,
> majorities, nor ridicule;
> And the threat of what is call'd hell is little or nothing to me;
> And the lure of what is call'd heaven is little or nothing to me;
> . . . Dear camerado! I confess I have urged you onward with me, and
> still urge you, without the least idea what is our destination,
> Or whether we shall be victorious, or utterly quell'd and defeated.
> (*DTS*, 19)

Ironically, it was in the fields and hospitals of the Civil War that Whitman came closest to realizing his democratic and homosexual dream of a "new City of Friends." Included among the poems of demobilization, "As I Lay with My Head in Your Lap, Camerado" registers uneasiness as the poet moves away from the democratic promise of wartime comradeship toward the potentially oppressive structures of a peacetime—and heterosexual—economy. Addressing a "you" who is, as in "Calamus," both personal lover and democratic comrade, the poet expresses a renewed dedication to a boundless democratic "destination" that will include and indeed be grounded in same-sex love among men.[17]

It is ironic that the iconography of the good gray poet came to dominate Whitman's public image and later critical treatments of his life and work during the very years when we have the most specific historical documentation in Whitman's notebooks and in his affectionate correspondence with Peter Doyle (Figure 7) and Harry Stafford (Figure 8) of his emotional and loving attachments to young working-class men.[18] "What did I get?" Whitman said of his service in the Washington hospitals during the Civil War: "Well—I got the boys, for one thing: the boys: thousands of them: they were, they are, they will be mine. . . . I got the boys: then I got Leaves of Grass: but for this I would never have had Leaves of Grass—the consummated book (the last confirming word): I got that: the boys, the Leaves: I got them" (*WWC*, 3: 582; ellipsis mine).

In addition to the extensive correspondence that Whitman carried on with the young men he met during the Civil War, Whitman's notebooks and his correspondence with Peter Doyle and Harry Stafford provide a particularly moving record of his emotional and loving attachments to young working-class men. "Dear Boy," Whitman wrote in 1868 to Peter Doyle, a streetcar driver and ex-Confederate soldier whom he met in Washington in 1865: "I think of you very often, dearest comrade, & with more calmness than when I was there—I find it first rate to think of you, Pete, & to know you are there, all right, & that I shall return, & we will be together again. I don't know what I should do if I had't you to think of & look forward to." "My darling," he wrote in 1869, "if you are not well when I come back I will get a good room or two in some quiet place . . . and we will live together, & devote ourselves altogether to the job of curing you." "Good night, my darling son," he wrote in 1870, "here is a kiss for you, dear boy—on the paper here—a good long one. . . . I will imagine you with your arm around my neck saying Good night, Walt—& me—Good night, Pete—" (*COR*, 2: 47, 84, 104; ellipses mine).

In a notebook entry that appears to refer to the "*enormous* PERTURBATION" of his "FEVERISH, FLUCTUATING" emotional attachment to Peter Doyle, Whitman wrote:

FIGURE 7. Whitman and Peter Doyle, ca. 1869. Photograph by M. P. Rice, Washington, DC. "Dear Boy," Whitman wrote to Doyle from New York in 1868, "I think of you very often, dearest comrade, & with more calmness than when I was there" (*COR*, 2: 47). Courtesy of the Ohio Wesleyan University Bayley Collection and the Walt Whitman Archive.

> Depress the adhesive nature
> It is in excess—making life a torment
> Ah this diseased, feverish disproportionate adhesiveness.
> Remember Fred Vaughan. (*NUPM*, 2: 889–90)[19]

In Whitman criticism, this entry is usually cited as an instance of the poet's attempt to suppress his sexual desire for men in order to transform himself into the safer and more publicly acceptable image of the good gray poet. But

FIGURE 8. Whitman and Harry Stafford, who wears a ring that Whitman gave him on the little finger of his right hand. Photograph by Augustus Morand around October 1878. "Dear Hank," Whitman wrote Stafford in 1881: "I realize plainly that *if I had not known you . . . I should not be a living man to-day . . . you, my darling boy, are the central figure of them all—*" (*COR*, 3: 215). Courtesy of the Sheffield England Library Edward Carpenter Collection and the Walt Whitman Archive.

at no place in his notebooks does Whitman suggest that "adhesiveness" is itself "diseased." Rather, like the male purity tracts, what Whitman suggests is that it is "adhesiveness" in excess that makes "life a torment" and must be brought under control. "PURSUE HER NO MORE," Whitman wrote, coyly changing the object of his passion from him to her (*NUPM*, 2: 887). But the change once again suggests the fluidity and convertibility of male and female identities and desires in Whitman's work. What is perhaps most telling here is that the poet's perception of "adhesiveness" as "diseased" and "disproportionate" and in excess does not change even if the object of his excessive attachment is a woman.

Although the intimacy between Whitman and Doyle appears to have subsided in the years following Whitman's paralytic stroke in 1873 and his move to Camden, New Jersey, to live with his brother George, by the mid-1870s he had entered into a passionate love relationship with Harry Stafford, a young man of eighteen to whom Whitman gave a ring as a sign of his deep affection. "My nephew & I when traveling always share the same room together & the same bed," Whitman wrote in 1876 to arrange for a room (and a bed) with Stafford on one of his trips to New York (*COR*, 3: 68). Their ardent and turbulent relationship lasted several years and had a major impact on Whitman's life. "Dear Hank," Whitman wrote Stafford in 1881, "I realize plainly that *if I had not known you . . . I should not be a living man to-day*—I think & remember deeply these things & they comfort me—*& you, my darling boy, are the central figure of them all*—" (*COR*, 3: 215; ellipsis mine).

In addition to leaving a written legacy of images of male-male desire that been central to the constitution of modern homosexual identities and communities, Whitman also left a visual legacy of portraits, a small cache of "chum" photographs taken with his boyfriends: Peter Doyle in the 1860s (Figure 7), Harry Stafford in the 1870s (Figure 8), Bill Duckett in the 1880s (Figure 9), and Warren (Warrie) Fritzinger in the 1890s (Figure 10). Although these photographs were not "published" until after Whitman's death in 1892 (and they are still little known or remarked upon by Whitman scholars), they were circulated among Whitman's friends and critics during his lifetime and used in the decade after his death to canonize Whitman as the good gray poet, as in Richard Maurice Bucke's edition of Whitman's letters to Doyle in *Calamus* (1897); and, as in John Addington Symonds's *Walt Whitman: A Study* (1893) and Eduard Bertz's *Walt Whitman: Ein Charakterbild* (1905), to circulate Whitman's visual image as part of the cultural capital of a newly emerging international homosexual community.

As Ed Folsom powerfully argues in his essay "Whitman's Calamus Photographs," these revisionary portraits stage new identities and new versions of the family, marriage, and social relationships that blur the traditional roles of mother, father, husband, wife, brother, lover, and friend.[20] Through their stunning visual enactments of the ways Whitman might be said to speak not so much *for* woman, bride, wife, and mother but *as* woman, bride, wife, and

FIGURE 9. Whitman and Bill Duckett, ca. 1886. Photograph attributed to Lorenzo S. Fisler. Sometime between 1886 and 1892, Duckett, who was Whitman's housemate in 1886 and companion in the late 1880s, posed as one of Thomas Eakins's nude models. Courtesy of the Ohio Wesleyan University Bayley Collection and the Walt Whitman Archive.

mother, these "family" and "marital" photographs further suggest the mixture and fluidity of gender identity and performance in Whitman's work. In fact, the photographs are all the more striking because they were taken during the last twenty-five years of Whitman's life, the very years when he is said to have sublimated his sexual passion for men in the more conventional roles of "wound-dresser," the "good-gray poet," and the patriotic nationalist. They were also taken at a time when greater public restraints were being placed on the popular and primarily working-class genre of "chum" photographs.[21]

FIGURE 10. Whitman on the Camden wharf with Warren Fritzinger, who was his nurse and companion during the last three years of his life. Photograph by John Johnson, 1890. "I like [Warrie's] touch and he is strong, a font of bodily power," Whitman told Horace Traubel in 1889: "he has that wonderful indescribable combination—rarely found, precious when found—which, with great manly strength, unites sweet delicacy, soft as a woman's" (*WWC*, 6: 83). Courtesy of Charles E. Feinberg and the Walt Whitman Archive.

In support of the idea of the increasing split between the private and public in Whitman's works in the postwar years, as Whitman the lover of men gives way to the iconography of "the good gray poet," critics have emphasized the changes that Whitman made in his "Calamus" poems after he was fired from his job at the Department of the Interior for moral turpitude in 1865.[22] But here again, a close study of the changes that Whitman made in future editions of *Leaves of Grass* reveals no clear pattern of suppressing or even toning down his love poems to men. In fact, Whitman's decision to delete three poems from "Calamus"—"Who Is Now Reading This?," "I Thought That Knowledge Alone Would Suffice," and "Hours Continuing Long"—suggests that he sought not to tone down or suppress his expression of "manly love" but to suppress the more anguished dimensions of his love for men and to blur the distinction between public and private love he expressed in "I Thought That Knowledge Alone Would Suffice." Moreover, in "The Base of All Metaphysics," the one poem that Whitman added to the "Calamus" sequence in 1871, he represents "The dear love of man for his comrade, the attraction of friend to friend" as the "base and finalè too for all metaphysics," underlying the philosophies of Plato, Socrates, and Christ and the systems of German philosophy represented by Kant, Fichte, Schelling, and Hegel (*LGC*, 121).

This representation of same-sex love between men as the base of a new social order underlies the visionary democracy of *Democratic Vistas* (1871). In this major attempt to come to terms with the problems of democracy in America, Whitman concludes that "intense and loving comradeship, the personal and passionate attachment of man to man" represents "the most substantial hope and safety of the future of these States." "It is to the development, identification, and general prevalence of that fervid comradeship, (the adhesive love, at least rivaling amative love hitherto possessing imaginative literature, if not going beyond it)," Whitman explains in a footnote, "that I look for the counterbalance and offset of our materialistic and vulgar American democracy, and for the spiritualization thereof." Amid what he called the aggressive selfism, vulgar materialism, and widespread corruption of the Gilded Age, Whitman looked not to marriage or to the traditional family but to "the personal and passionate attachment of man to man" as the social base and future hope of the American republic. "I say democracy infers such loving comradeship, as its most inevitable twin or counterpart, without which it will be incomplete, in vain, and incapable of perpetuating itself" (*PW*, 2: 414–15).

So, if what I have been arguing is correct, why did Whitman not just out with it in his famous exchange with Victorian literary critic John Addington Symonds in 1890, when Symonds asked him outright if his "conception of Comradeship" included the possibility of "semi-sexual emotions & actions" between men? Whitman could have said, "Yes, John, *Leaves of Grass* is, indeed, about cocksucking and democracy. You found me out." Instead, he disavowed Symonds's "morbid inferences" about the "Calamus" poems as "undream'd," "unreck'd," and "damnable" and cautioned him about the necessity of construing "all parts & pages" of *Leaves of Grass* "by their own ensemble, spirit & atmosphere" (*COR*, 5: 72, 73).

Although Whitman's response is coy, it also seems right to me for all the reasons I have been trying to suggest. Whitman and Symonds were speaking two different, though not entirely separable languages. Whereas Havelock Ellis and John Addington Symonds were central figures in the process of medicalizing and singling out homosexuality—or what they called "sexual inversion"—as abnormal and pathological, Whitman was talking about physical and emotional love between men as the basis for a new social and religious order.[23] Given his representation of male sexual love as the source of spiritual and poetic vision and the ground for a new democratic social order, and given Ellis's and Symonds's medicalization of physical love between men as "sexual inversion" and "abnormal instinct," it makes sense that Whitman would disavow Symonds's attempt to medicalize and sexually categorize the "Calamus" poems as "morbid inferences" contrary to the "ensemble, spirit & atmosphere" of *Leaves of Grass* (*COR*, 5: 72, 73).

Whitman's famous assertion, in this same letter to Symonds, that he had fathered six children is, to say the least, disingenuous. But it is not wholly at odds with the amative, reproductive, and familial languages and contexts in which he expressed the loving relationships among and between men. In fact, given the languages of paternal, maternal, and familial affection in which Whitman carried on his relationships and correspondence with Fred Vaughan, Peter Doyle, Harry Stafford, and some of the soldiers he met during the war, including Tom Sawyer and Lewis Brown, one might argue that Whitman was thinking of some of the "illegitimate sons" he adopted, fathered, and mothered over the course of his life.

In his attempt to give Whitman's conception of comradeship and his "Calamus" poems only one reading, Symonds in some sense anticipates the tendency among recent critics to treat Whitman's homosexuality as a single, transhistorical presence. Against those who see in Whitman's work an instance of what Symonds called "sexual inversion" or what Michael Lynch has called "a distinct 'homosexual identity'" or "'homosexual role,'" I have been arguing that we read Whitman's expression of sexual, emotional, and social intimacy among men not as a singular homosexual presence but as the complex, multiply located, and historically embedded sexual, social, and discursive phenomenon it was.[24]

To those who insist on dividing Whitman the private poet and Whitman the public poet, Whitman the lover of men and Whitman the poet of democracy, or in Malcolm Cowley's apt phrase, "cocksucking and democracy," I have been trying to suggest that when they are read within what Whitman called the "ensemble, spirit & atmosphere" of his work, the homosexual poet and the American republic refuse any neat division; they intersect, flow into each other, and continually break bounds. "Who need be afraid of the merge?" Whitman asked in "Song of Myself." The answer to that question is still, in the new millennium, we all are.

CHAPTER FIVE

Radical Imaginaries

Crossing Over with Whitman and Dickinson

ONE'S-SELF I sing—a simple, separate Person;
Yet utter the word Democratic, the word *En-Masse.*

—Walt Whitman, *Leaves of Grass* (1871)

The Soul selects her own Society –
Then – shuts the Door –
To her divine Majority –
Present no more –

—Emily Dickinson (1862)

A decade ago, among American scholars, those who worked on Walt Whitman and those who worked on Emily Dickinson tended to divide into two distinct groups. Those who worked on Whitman, almost exclusively men, rarely ventured into Dickinson studies, which was dominated mostly by women, and those who worked on Dickinson had little to say about Whitman, except to negate his spread-eagle poetics and politics in comparison with the serious experimental art of Emily Dickinson. In recent years, this appears to have changed. But as someone who began my career by crossing over, focusing in my classes and scholarship on both Whitman and Dickinson, I would like to begin by imagining what a social and poetic encounter between the bard of Manhattan and the belle of Amherst might have looked like.[1]

Whitman might solicit intercourse with Dickinson as a woman waiting to breed a hardy race of poets and democratic children as he does in "A Woman Waits for Me":

A woman waits for me, she contains all, nothing is lacking,
Yet all were lacking if sex were lacking, or if the moisture of the right
man were lacking.

. . . .
Without shame the man I like knows and avows the deliciousness of
his sex,
Without shame the woman I like knows and avows hers.
(*LGC*, 101, 102)

Dickinson would likely flee, as she does the "Silver Heel" of the erotically overbearing "Sea" "Man" she encounters in "I started Early – Took my Dog –."[2] But Whitman would persist:

It is I, you women, I make my way,
I am stern, acrid, large, undissuadable, but I love you,
I do not hurt you any more than is necessary for you,
I pour the stuff to start sons and daughters fit for these States, I press
with slow rude muscle,
I brace myself effectually, I listen to no entreaties,
I dare not withdraw till I deposit what has so long accumulated within
me. (*LGC*, 102–3)

Dickinson would be put off by the collectivity and impersonality of Whitman's love call. Driven by a "suppressed and ungratified desire for distinction," according to her childhood friend Emily Fowler Ford, Dickinson would find Whitman vulgar "like a Frog," low class, and more interested in sex and breeding than "women," love, or her in particular.[3] She had nothing against sex; she too dreamt of "Wild nights – Wild nights!" but it was more dreamy, romantic, and personal. She liked the tease and the foreplay, especially with her sister-in-law Sue, who inspired many of her poems. "Wild nights – Wild nights! / Were I with thee," Dickinson writes:

Rowing in Eden –
Ah – the Sea!
Might I but moor – tonight –
In thee! (*Poems*, 269)

Unlike the sexually and rhetorically prone woman, or women, of Whitman's "A Woman Waits for Me," Dickinson's woman lover is active, athletic even, as she joyously rows in a "Sea" of orgasmic feeling and fantasizes entering and mooring herself within—rather than being penetrated by—her lover. Dickinson was more likely a top than a bottom, and in her poems she occasionally speaks as a man rather than a woman. Although Whitman's "A Woman Waits for Me" celebrates a healthy, athletic, and sexually charged female being who had been unnamed by his culture, the speaker of his poem is insistently, and even embarrassingly, phallic and nationalistic. In other poems, such as "Song of Myself," "The Sleepers," and especially the "Calamus" poems, Whitman fluidly assumes both male and female roles, often revealing his preference—contre Dickinson—as bottom rather than top.

What I want to suggest by this opening sexual and poetic encounter between Whitman and Dickinson is that while they have been treated as diametrical opposites of each other by literary critics, she an essentially private poet raised in a genteel upper-class household in rural Massachusetts, and he an essentially public political poet raised in a working-class household in Brooklyn and the bustling city of New York,[4] both were not only sex radicals but radical imaginaries in the nineteenth-century United States. As different as they may seem, their lives and works and the various "myths" and critical contests that have attended their reception are often surprisingly parallel, in conversation with each other, and mutually illuminating in relation to the major political, social, sexual, racial, and cultural struggles that marked their time and ours. In this essay, I want to sketch out several instances of personal and poetic intercourse between Whitman and Dickinson as a provocation to a renewed understanding of the many crossings between them.

Politics

While it is certainly true to say that Dickinson was not an overtly political poet in the same sense that Whitman was, it is simply not true to say that she had no politics and no ideological investment in a particular order of power. Dickinson was, in fact, born into a more publicly active and politically engaged family than Whitman. Whereas Whitman's father was a house builder, a party Democrat, and a Thomas Paine radical, Dickinson's father, Edward Dickinson, was a conservative Whig who served as a state representative, senator, and member of the Massachusetts Governor's Council in the 1840s. Between 1853 and 1855, at a time of intensified struggle over the issue of slavery, he served as a representative to Congress from the Tenth District of Massachusetts. Edward Dickinson was a possible candidate for governor of Massachusetts in 1859 and a nominee for lieutenant governor in 1860 and 1861. Later, in 1873, only a year before his death, he was elected again to serve in the Massachusetts General Court.[5]

Like Whitman, who was raised among brothers named George Washington, Thomas Jefferson, and Andrew Jackson Whitman, Dickinson lived in a political house (Figure 11). Although she did not share her father's public political commitment, as I have argued in "Emily Dickinson and Class," she

FIGURE 11. Emily Dickinson's home in Amherst, Massachusetts. "It is so much easier to do wrong than right – so much pleasanter to be evil than good," Dickinson wrote in a revolutionary manifesto to her friend Jane Humphrey from her room on the second floor in 1850. "I dont wonder that good angels weep – and bad ones sing songs" (*Letters*, 1: 82). Courtesy of the Todd-Bingham Picture Collection, Yale University Library.

shared many of his class values and social fears in response to Jacksonian democracy, the masses, foreigners, the Irish, Negroes, labor, social reform, and westward expansion at a time when the aristocratic class-based values of the past were being eroded under the pressure of an increasingly democratic and industrial capitalist society of new money and new men.[6]

Dickinson's political values and fears are evident in a letter she wrote to her brother Austin from Mt. Holyoke College in 1847, in which she mocks the state of political non-knowledge and removal in which girl students are kept as she queries Austin for information about the political happenings of the time:

> Wont you please tell me when you answer my letter who the candidate for President is? I have been trying to find out ever since I came here & have not yet succeeded. I dont know anything more about affairs in the world, than if I was in a trance. . . . Has the Mexican war terminated yet & how? Are we beat? Do you know of any nation about to besiege South Hadley?[7]

FIGURE 12. Daguerreotype of Emily Dickinson taken at Mt. Holyoke in December 1847 or early 1848. "Wont you please tell me when you answer my letter who the candidate for President is?" Dickinson wrote her brother Austin from Mt. Holyoke College in 1847. "I dont know anything more about affairs in the world, than if I was in a trance" (*Letters*, 1: 49). Courtesy of the Amherst College Library.

Dickinson's intense engagement with "affairs in the world," especially the Mexican War (1846–1848), which many New Englanders saw as an imperialist land grab aimed at extending slavery and the "Slave Power," and the presidential campaign, which would result in the election of Zachary Taylor and a major Whig victory in 1848, suggests that one of the reasons she left Mt. Holyoke after only one year is that she felt isolated and removed from a whole world of political "affairs" and dialogue to which she had grown accustomed in the Dickinson house (Figure 12). Written at a time when the Massachusetts legislature had resolved that the Mexican War was "unconstitutionally commenced by order of the President,"[8] Dickinson's letter mocks the politics of manifest destiny and President Polk's expansionist ambition to annex Mexico;

it also registers a more local Whig fear that New England was itself under siege, not by the republic of Mexico, but by the nationalist, imperialist, and proslavery forces of Polk and the Democrats.

Whereas Dickinson was a student at Mt. Holyoke College, one of the first colleges for women in the United States, Whitman was a printer's apprentice, journalist, and later editor of the Brooklyn *Daily Eagle* (1846–1848), where he wrote articles in support of the laboring masses, social reform, and the expansionist policies of President Polk, including the Mexican War. By 1848, however, Whitman was fired by the *Eagle* owner, when he "split off with the radicals" in opposing the expansion of slavery into the western territories. At about the same time, Dickinson "split" with the religious establishment at Mt. Holyoke Female Seminary, where she was found "without hope" of religious salvation.[9] She returned home in 1848, after only one year.

Revolution and Poetry

The Compromise of 1850, which extended slavery into the territories and strengthened the Fugitive Slave Law by requiring that fugitive slaves be returned to their Southern masters, sent Whitman literally raging into verse. Under the pressure of political events, his savage attack on congressmen who supported slavery rather than freedom and his celebration of the Revolutions of 1848, in four poems published in 1850, broke the pentameter and began to move toward the free-verse line of *Leaves of Grass*. "God, 'twas delicious! / That brief, tight, glorious grip / Upon the throats of kings," Whitman declared in "Resurgemus," the earliest of his poems to be included in the 1855 *Leaves of Grass* (*EPF*, 38).

At the same time that Whitman was celebrating the revolutionary struggle for liberty as part of the natural law of the universe, Dickinson inaugurated her own revolution against the orthodox sexual ideologies of her time. She resisted marriage, rebelled against domestic ideology, and saw housework as a plebeian interference with her writing. Mocking the politics of housework—"mind the house – and the food – *sweep* if the spirits were low"—and the true womanly ideals of "meekness – and patience – and submission –," Dickinson issued her own revolutionary manifesto in a letter to her friend Jane Humphrey in January 1850:

> Somehow or other I incline to other things – and Satan covers them up with flowers, and I reach out to pick them. The path of duty looks very

> ugly indeed – and the place where *I* want to go more amiable – a great deal – it is so much easier to do wrong than right – so much pleasanter to be evil than good, I dont wonder that good angels weep – and bad ones sing songs. (*Letters*, 1: 82)

As Dickinson's identification of her desire to write with Satan suggests, at a time when the Calvinist orthodoxy of the fathers was breaking down, she retained the language, imagery, and conscience of New England Puritanism without the faith. "Christ is calling everyone here," she wrote to Humphrey again in 1850, "and I am standing alone in rebellion" (*Letters*, 1: 94). While her friends and family converted to the Congregational religion during the many revivals that passed through Amherst and the surrounding community in the 1840s and 1850s, Dickinson refused to give herself up and become a Christian.

Living at a time of major political, social, religious, and epistemological breakdown perhaps best signified by the political collapse, blood violence, and ongoing social questions raised by the Civil War, Dickinson, who was eleven years younger than Whitman, dedicated herself to writing at about the same time that Whitman did, not as a retreat into privacy but as a radical act of the imagination, a higher order of culture, and a powerful means of talking back to, with, and against her democratic age.

Radical Imaginaries

On or about July 4, 1855, Whitman published the first edition of *Leaves of Grass*. Designed by Whitman and printed at his own expense, everything about the book was revolutionary: the volume was oversized with clusters of leaves embossed on its dark green cover; its title, which was printed in gold, sprouted lush sperm-shaped roots and leaves, suggesting the motifs of the body, sex, fertility, and regeneration that figure throughout the poems (Figure 1). The title page bears no author's name, only an engraved frontispiece of himself as a day laborer, a common man who speaks as and for rather than apart from the people (Figure 2). "The attitude of great poets is to cheer up slaves and horrify despots," Whitman announced in a twelve-page preface that sounds the cry of revolt implicit in the design of the 1855 *Leaves* (*LG* 1855, 15).

The twelve "untitled" poems that follow the preface make good Whitman's declaration of literary independence. Defying the rules of rhyme, meter, and stanza division and breaking down the distinction between poetry and prose,

Whitman's verse rolls freely and rhythmically across the page. The long opening poem, later entitled "Song of Myself," and the five poems that follow are all entitled "Leaves of Grass," while the last four poems, separated only by two horizontal bars, are untitled. All of the poems appear to flow together as part of a single florid growth entitled *Leaves of Grass*. The poet's epic subject is not Virgil's arms and the man, but the self that is at the center of the American myth of origins. "I celebrate myself," Whitman begins:

> And what I assume you shall assume,
> For every atom belonging to me as good belongs to you. (*LG* 1855, 25)

The opening *I* and the closing *you* are the bounds of an agonistic arena in which the poet commands, questions, challenges, wrestles, fondles, and makes love to the reader, finally sending the reader into the world bearing the seeds of democratic creation.

Whitman had inky fingers: he presided over every aspect of the material and poetic production of the 1855 *Leaves of Grass*, including the reviews, among them three rave reviews he wrote of himself. "An American bard at last!" he exuded in the *United States and Democratic Review*: "One of the roughs, large, proud, affectionate, eating, drinking, and breeding, his costume manly and free."[10]

Whitman played the market and failed to gain an audience for his radical poems. Dickinson refused to go to market. "Publication – is the Auction / Of the Mind of Man –," she wrote, in a poem that associates print publication with blackness, wage slavery, and the degradations of both the slave auction and the capitalist marketplace:

> Poverty – be justifying
> For so foul a thing
>
> Possibly – but We – would rather
> From Our Garret go
> White – unto the White Creator –
> Than invest – Our Snow – (*Poems*, 788)

Making use of the language of both antislavery and artisan republican protest against wage labor as a new form of slavery to constitute herself and her writing as part of an elect community of whiteness, Dickinson resists the "foul" values of the commercial marketplace: "reduce no Human Spirit / To

Disgrace of Price –" (*Poems*, 788). Her refusal to publish was not so much a private act as it was an act of social and class resistance to the commercial, democratic, and increasingly amalgamated and mass values of the national marketplace.

If Whitman looked upon his poems as material seeds of present and future artistic and democratic creation, Dickinson described her poetry as another form of letter writing and "News" addressed to her "countrymen":

This is my letter to the World
That never wrote to Me –
The simple News that Nature told –
With tender Majesty

Her Message is committed
To Hands I cannot see –
For love of Her – Sweet – countrymen –
Judge tenderly – of Me (*Poems*, 519)

Here, as elsewhere in her writing, Dickinson presents her poetry not as a "private" production but as a form of "public" address—a "letter to the World"—whether imaginary or real. Like Whitman, Dickinson was also engaged in her own form of material production and "publication." Between 1858 and 1864, she gathered over 800 of her poems into 40 hand-sewn booklets. Binding four to five folded sheets of paper together in groupings of eighteen to twenty poems, Dickinson, in effect, converted traditional female thread-and-needle work into a different kind of housework and her own form of productive industry. She appears to have been engaged in a kind of home or cottage industry, a precapitalist mode of manuscript production and circulation that avoided the commodity and use values of the commercial marketplace.[11]

Along with the manuscripts that she produced and bound with string and thread herself, Dickinson also engaged in a more aristocratic form of "publication" by circulating her poems in letters to her friends. While only ten of her poems were "printed" during her lifetime, including seven in the *Springfield Republican*, beginning in the early 1850s Dickinson, like Whitman, broke down the distinction between poetry and prose by circulating hundreds of her poems in letters to a select republic of "countrymen" that engaged her in dialogue with some of the most powerful cultural and social figures of her time.[12] Her network of known correspondents included Samuel Bowles, the editor of the *Springfield Republican*, one of the most influential newspapers in the country, and an outspoken supporter of antislavery, women's suffrage, the Republican Party, and Abraham Lincoln; Josiah Gilbert Holland, the literary editor of the *Springfield Republican*, a founding editor of *Scribner's Monthly* in 1870, and the popular author of numerous novels and books, including a *Life of Abraham Lincoln* (1865); Thomas Wentworth Higginson, a well-known writer, Unitarian minister, liberal republican advocate of abolition and women's rights, and colonel who led one of the first regiments of black troops during the Civil War; Thomas Niles, the editor of Roberts Brothers, a major publishing house in Boston; Judge Otis P. Lord, a leading figure in Massachusetts politics and law; and Helen Hunt Jackson, one of the most highly acclaimed women writers of her time.

Homoerotic Poetics

The heteronormatizing mythologies that have attended the critical reception and criticism of Whitman and Dickinson have obscured the extent to which homoerotic love was at the very origins of their poetic voice and vision. Whitman supposedly fell in love with an octoroon on his trip to New Orleans in 1848, and as suggested in his poem "Once I Passed Through a Populous City," this New Orleans romance inspired his poems. Dickinson supposedly fell in love with a married minister, Charles Wadsworth, on a visit to Philadelphia in 1855, and it was her lifelong love of him that inspired her to withdraw from society, wear white, and devote herself to poetry. Both of these "myths" fly in the face of the reality of same-sex love in their lives, letters, and poems. Whitman's "Once I Passed Through a Populous City" was originally addressed to a man rather than a woman, so romances with other women have been proposed; and there is no evidence that Dickinson even met Wadsworth, let alone fell in love with him in 1855, so other men have been proposed.

And yet, as early as his temperance novel *Franklin Evans; or The Inebriate* (1842), Whitman evoked the urban subculture of sexual cruising and man love to which he would seek to give voice in *Leaves of Grass*: "Through me forbidden voices, / Voices of sexes and lusts . . . . voices veiled, and I remove the veil" (*LG* 1855, 48). At the outset of his long opening poem, later "Song of Myself," Whitman insists on the body, sexuality, and love between men as the site of ecstasy, vision, and poetic utterance:

> I mind how we lay in June, such a transparent summer morning;
> You settled your head athwart my hips and gently turned over upon me,

And parted the shirt from my bosom-bone, and plunged your tongue to my barestript heart,
And reached till you felt my beard, and reached till you held my feet.
(*LG* 1855, 28–29)

Rather than posing sex between men and mysticism as antithetical readings, as past critics have done, this passage is representative of the ways the languages of sexuality and spirituality, same-sex love and love between men and women, private and public, intermix and flow into each other in Whitman's work.[13]

In the early 1850s, Dickinson and her friend and later sister-in-law, Susan Gilbert, began writing poems together. Despite the later efforts of Dickinson's brother Austin literally to cut out and mutilate the traces of his sister's lifelong love relationship with Sue, it is clear from Dickinson's extant letters and poems that it was Dickinson's explosive and transgressive love for Sue that called forth and validated the volcanic persona who would emerge in her poems as "Loaded Gun" and "Vesuvius at Home."[14] In her multiple incarnations as "absent lover" and a "real beautiful hero," "Imagination" and an "Avalanche of Sun," an "Emblem of Heaven" and the "garden *unseen*," Gilbert served finally as a bewitching muse-like presence who poeticized Dickinson's world and inspired her own art of song. "You sketch my pictures for me," Dickinson wrote Sue in 1853, "and 'tis at their sweet colorings, rather than this dim real, that I am used, so you see when you go away, the world looks staringly, and I find I need more vail" (*Letters*, 1: 229).

In "One Sister have I in the house –," one of Dickinson's earliest extant poems, she represents Sue as a bird whose "different" tune becomes a source of sustenance in the journey from adolescence to adulthood. In stanzas 3 and 4, she wrote:

She did not sing as we did –
It was a different tune –
Herself to her a music
As Bumble bee of June.

Today is far from childhood,
But up and down the hills,
I held her hand the tighter –
Which shortened all the miles –

Even in this sisterly song of praise, however, there are ambiguous references to a "hum" that "Deceives" and eyes that "lie," references that suggest that

Sue's "different tune" was also a source of tension and struggle between them (*Poems*, 5).[15]

Love Crisis

Sometime around 1858 both Whitman and Dickinson appear to have suffered a personal love crisis during the very years when the political union was moving inexorably toward the fracture and blood carnage of civil war. The primary evidence for Whitman's crisis is a small sheaf of twelve poems of male intimacy and love entitled "Live Oak, with Moss" that the poet copied into a notebook in spring 1859. Although the work was first published by Fredson Bowers in 1953 and hailed as a "gay manifesto" by Herschel Parker and others over the past few decades, the exact nature of this love affair remains a mystery. Whitman may be alluding to a break with Fred Vaughan, who lived with or near him at the time they were written, or possibly with another man, or even several men over a span of time.[16] What is clear is that these poems represent a revolutionary break with the past and a radical new departure in literary, sexual, and social history in their moving evocation and affirmation of the hitherto unnamed and unnamable bonds of erotic passion, love, and affection among and between men. The poems also record a crisis of poetic vocation in "Live Oak" V, in which the poet renounces his earlier desire "to strike up the songs of the New World" in order to pursue his relationship with his lover. "I can be your singer of songs no longer—," the poet writes: "I have found him who loves me, as I him, in perfect love, / With the rest I dispense—" (*LOM*, 17).

The primary evidence for Dickinson's love crisis is a sequence of three "Master" letters, written between 1858 and 1861 with no evidence they were ever posted, in which she presents herself in the figure of "Daisy," a "Bird" hit by a "bullet" and someone with "a Tomahawk in my side," to a mysterious unknown "Master." Although much critical ink has been spent seeking to identify which man broke Dickinson's heart, these letters read more like a metaphysical complaint against the nature of things, perhaps addressed to God or some other patriarchal master of the universe.

The real source of Dickinson's wound may be her loss of Sue to religion, marriage, and family, a story she movingly retells in "Ourselves were wed one summer – dear –":

Ourselves were wed one summer – dear –
Your Vision – Was in June –

And when Your little Lifetime failed,
I wearied – too – of mine – (*Poems*, 596)

Although Dickinson used the term in other poems of the time, the syntactical oddness of "Ourselves" in this wedding poem to another woman suggests the "difference" of their female marriage—the autoerotic awakening to an enriched consciousness of self that a woman may feel in loving someone who is like rather than different from herself. Dickinson's poetic construction might be paraphrased to read: we married ourselves when we married each other, a phrasing that recalls the auto- or homoerotic mirroring of self that Whitman evokes in the opening poem of *Leaves of Grass* when he asks: "Is this then a touch? . . . . quivering me to a new identity / . . . / My flesh and blood playing out lightning, to strike what is hardly different from myself" (*LG* 1855, 53). While Whitman's free-verse line is very different from Dickinson's, the ellipses that he used in the 1855 *Leaves of Grass* are similar to Dickinson's dashes in rhythmically marking—and expressing—pause, break, and sometimes fracture.

Sue's vision in "June" appears to telescope two events: her profession of faith in August 1850 and her marriage to Dickinson's brother, Austin, in July 1856. Associating their relationship with the creative bloom of summer, Dickinson experiences her loss of Sue to religion and marriage, as a kind of social death in which Sue is "yielded up" to the masculine and heteronormative orders of husband and God (*Letters*, 1: 210). The speaker overcomes her own experience of death and waste by yielding "her" self—not to man or God—but to the "light" and call of her poetic muse:

And overtaken in the Dark –
Where You had put me down –
By Some one carrying a Light –
I – too – received the Sign – (*Poems*, 596)

Having received the "Sign" of her poetic vocation as another kind of religious and marital vow, Dickinson describes the difference of her own election in lines that suggest the heroism of her rededication and the anguish of her loss:

'Tis true – Our Futures different lay –
Your Cottage – faced the sun –
While Oceans – and the North must be –
On every side of mine

'Tis true, Your Garden led the Bloom,
For mine – in Frosts – was sown –

And yet, one Summer, we were Queens –
But You – were crowned in June – (*Poems*, 596)

Whereas Sue's life is contained within the daily round of cottage and sun, Dickinson lives sterile and witchlike, on the margins, facing the open spaces of "Oceans" and "the North."

Once again Sue is associated with the creativity and bloom of a garden, but it is a garden circumscribed by the round of the male order signified by sun/son. The reference to Sue's "Bloom" may refer to the birth of her son, Edward, on June 19, 1861. Like Whitman sowing the seeds of his poems, Dickinson sows her own garden—her poems—in "Frosts" that suggest the cold and desolation of her separation from Sue, her existence on the margins of the social order, and a barrenness that gives birth to poems rather than children. In their separation, Dickinson suggests that both have lost some of the potency of their primal bond together when they were "Queens" under another law. And thus, the "crown" of power Sue receives as the Bride of Christ and man is also a crown of limits, suffering, and thorns.

The story is not unlike the story Whitman tells in his 1859 elegy "A Word Out of the Sea" (later "Out of the Cradle Endlessly Rocking") with its dark undertone of the "fierce old mother" the sea whispering "Death, Death, Death, Death, Death" in response to the former joy of the he-bird and the she-bird nesting their "four light-green eggs." Identifying with the he-bird's loss of his mate, Whitman bids farewell to male/female love, marriage, and family, and rededicates himself to his poems as the expression of unsatisfied love:

O you demon, singing by yourself—projecting me,
O solitary me listening—never more shall I cease imitating,
perpetuating you,
. . . .
Never more the cries of unsatisfied love be absent from me.
(*LG* 1860, 276)

On the eve of the Civil War, both Whitman and Dickinson appear to intersect in practicing a compensatory poetics in response to the "real reality" of human loss, misery, and "Death" ("Calamus" 2, *LG* 1860, 344).

Representing herself as the "Empress of Calvary," in an 1861 poem, Dickinson evokes her dedication to her art as an alternative form of marriage and religion:

Title divine, is mine.
The Wife without the Sign –
Acute Degree conferred on me –
Empress of Calvary –
Royal, all but the Crown –
Betrothed, without the Swoon
God gives us Women – (*Poems*, 194)

Whereas for Whitman, death is "strong and delicious," associated with the "angry moans" of "the fierce old mother" the sea, as the generative source of a "thousand responsive songs" and "My own songs, awaked from that hour" (*LG* 1860, 277), for Dickinson, death is an exigent male figure, a signifier of the all-powerful "He," the "Blond Assassin" and sadistic bringer of loss, pain, change and the finality of death, against whom and in competition with whom she writes her poems.

"I had a terror – since September – I could tell to none – ," Dickinson wrote in April 1862, "and so I sing as the Boy does by the Burying Ground – because I am afraid – " (*Letters*, 2: 404). Whatever the sources of Dickinson's "terror"—a personal love crisis, a failure of religious belief, the advent of the Civil War, the collapse of an older New England social order, the horrifying prospect of everlasting "Death," metaphysical angst, or all these together—her poems powerfully register the disintegrative emotional and psychic effects of social transformation and political crisis that marked Dickinson's years of greatest productivity during and after the Civil War.

In the 1860 *Leaves of Grass*, Whitman registered a similar terror of America as graveyard rather than garden. "O give me some clue!" he asked "the savage old mother," the sea, in "A Word Out of the Sea":

O a word! O what is my destination?
O I fear it is henceforth chaos!
O how joys, dreads, convolutions, human shapes, and all shapes, spring
  as from graves around me!
O phantoms! you cover all the land, and all the sea!
O I cannot see in the dimness whether you smile or frown upon me.
  (*LG* 1860, 276)

Although Whitman would later delete this passage from "Out of the Cradle Endlessly Rocking" on the occasion of the American centennial in 1876, on the eve of the Civil War, Whitman's prospect and the "terror" of annihilation that gives rise to song were much closer to Emily Dickinson.[17]

The Civil War

The blood carnage and horrific loss of human life during the Civil War tested Whitman's democratic faith and deepened Dickinson's searing critique of American providential history. Whitman visited the sick, wounded, and dying soldiers in Washington hospitals, suffered the amputation and violence of the war physically and psychically, and, by 1863, rededicated himself to what he called "the work of my life . . . making poems . . . I *must* be continually bringing out poems" (*COR*, 1: 185; ellipses mine).

Although critics have traditionally emphasized Dickinson's isolation from the war and history and the merely personal sources of the crisis she suffered in the years immediately preceding and following the start of the war, as Shira Wolosky and others have argued, in poems such as "'Tis so appalling – it exhilarates –" and "Revolution is the Pod," the war crisis appears to have set "Fright at Liberty," inspiring Dickinson to a "Bloom" of creative power in the very midst of the "over Horror," "rattle" of "Systems," and "Death" signified by the Civil War (*Poems*, 337, 1044).[18] Of the 1,789 poems in Franklin's variorum edition of *The Poems of Emily Dickinson*, over half were written during the years of the Civil War between 1861 and 1865, and of these, almost 300 were written in 1863, a year of crisis and turning point in the war, when even Union victories such as Gettysburg had become scenes of horrific bloodletting and mass death on both sides.

"I, myself, in my smaller way, sang off charnel steps," Dickinson wrote during the war (*Letters*, 2: 436). For Dickinson, the Civil War became the larger historic ground against and through which she enacted her own "charge within the bosom" against "The Cavalry of Wo –" ("To fight aloud, is very brave –"; *Poems*, 138). The massive carnage, suffering, and death of the Civil War propelled Dickinson into further doubts about republican destiny, divine providence, and the nature of things, a fuller withdrawal from society, and a renewed dedication to art as a higher order of culture. Against the self-sacrificial patriotism of local "soldier-hearts" like Frazar Stearns, an Amherst boy who died in the war—"His big heart shot away by a 'minie ball'" (*Letters*, 2: 397)—and against Lincoln's public rhetoric of blood sacrifice for the cause of Union or the sin of slavery, several of the poems Dickinson wrote during and after the war express doubt about the larger meaning and value of war, suffering, and sacrificial death.

In "It feels a shame to be Alive – / When Men so brave – are dead –," the speaker wonders if sacrifice of human lives "In Pawn for Liberty –" or for the United States ("for Us") is worth the price:

> The price is great – Sublimely paid –
> Do we deserve – a Thing –
> That lives – like Dollars – must be piled
> Before we may obtain?
>
> Are we that wait – sufficient worth –
> That such Enormous Pearl
> As life – dissolved be – for Us –
> In Battle's – horrid Bowl? (*Poems*, 524)

Similarly in "My Portion is Defeat – today –," Dickinson presents a starkly realistic evocation of the "Bone and stain" of the battlefield—of "Moan" and "Prayer" and "Chips of Blank – in Boyish Eyes"—but the scene has no meaning beyond "Death's surprise, / Stamped visible – in stone –" (*Poems*, 704). Dickinson resists Lincoln's redemptive reading of the Civil War in the Gettysburg Address (1863) and the Second Inaugural Address (1865) as a blood sacrifice for "a new birth of freedom" or a "mighty scourge" sent by a "true and just God" to rid the nation of "American Slavery."[19]

When Whitman returned to book publication with the printing of *Drum-Taps* (1865) and *Sequel to Drum-Taps* (1865–1866), he sought like Lincoln to locate the butchery and unreason of the Civil War within a redemptive narrative of democratic sacrifice and rebirth. But in poems such as "A March in the Ranks Hard-Prest, and the Road Unknown," his dark and unmeaning prospect is closer to Dickinson. The army of soldiers marching in darkness along an unknown road come upon a "large old church" made into "an impromptu hospital," where pews become beds for soldiers, the gleams of light amid "shadows of deepest, deepest black," and the hellish cast of flame and smoke all reflect an ambivalent response to the war as a site of redemption and a descent into hell. The soldier stops momentarily to minister to the wounds of a fellow soldier:

> At my feet more distinctly, a soldier, a mere lad, in danger of bleeding
> to death, (he is shot in the abdomen;)
> I staunch the blood temporarily, (the youngster's face is white as a lily;)
> (*DTS*, 45)

Unrelieved by any larger teleology that would give meaning and significance to the "bloody forms" of war, the soldier is swept back into the ranks marching in darkness along an unknown road:

But first I bend to the dying lad—his eyes open—a half-smile gives
he me;
Then the eyes close, calmly close, and I speed forth to the darkness.
(*DTS*, 45)

The "half-smile" of "the dying lad" represents a sustaining gesture of comradeship, love, and human affirmation—possibly redemptive—shooting its light into the surrounding darkness as the soldier falls back into line and speeds forth "in darkness marching, on in the ranks / The unknown road still marching" (*DTS*, 45).

Here as in his elegy for the death of President Lincoln, "When Lilacs Last in the Dooryard Bloom'd," Whitman resists any larger religious vision. He insists on a fully secular account of the war in which the passions of manly love and comradeship and the everyday heroism of ordinary men and boys—the common and unknown soldiers who fought the war, North, South, and West—become the only hope for the future of democracy in America.

Immortality

For both Dickinson and Whitman, the Civil War represented a trial, a crucible, a darkness from which neither fully returned in the post–Civil War period. If "Boston had solved the universe," as Adams wrote in *The Education of Henry Adams*, Emily Dickinson had not.[20] In a poem written toward the close of her life, she expresses the pain of living in an era of unbelief using the same figure of amputation that Whitman had used to evoke both the war's carnage and the dismembered union:

Those – dying then,
Knew where they went –
They went to God's Right Hand –
That Hand is amputated now
And God cannot be found –

The abdication of Belief
Makes the Behavior small –
Better an ignis fatuus
Than no illume at all – (*Poems*, 1581)

Unlike Dickinson, Whitman did not mourn the death of God, but he did lament the apparent loss of faith in democracy amid the aggressive selfism, greed, and economic and political scandal of the Gilded Age and beyond.

Both poets became critics of a decline, a loss, in post–Civil War America, she from a conservative country point of view, he from the point of view of ordinary laborers and the democratic radicalism of his antebellum years. Although Dickinson sees "New Englandly" and Whitman sees from the point of view of the increasingly disenfranchised urban workers, both make use of similar figures—artisans, laborers, craftsmen, art—to emblematize a set of individual and communal values that has been lost. At a time when the local Amherst economy was being pressed into production of cash crops for the national market, Dickinson's "The Products of my Farm are these" links poetic creation—"With Us, 'tis Harvest all the Year"—with the self-sufficiency and barter of an older agricultural economy (*Poems*, 1036). In "Sparkles from the Wheel," Whitman identifies with the "works" and "copious golden jets" unleashed by "a knife-grinder" at "his wheel," displaying a craftsmanship rapidly being replaced by wage labor and the assembly line values of speed, profit, and efficiency (*LGC*, 389–90).

In the post–Civil War years, Whitman and Dickinson may have had much more to say to each other. And it wouldn't have been about sex. After his paralytic stroke in 1872, Whitman moved to Camden, New Jersey, where he still had his "boys" and his art; and Dickinson withdrew into the Dickinson Homestead, but she still had her art and her community of friends. "Some – Work for Immortality – / The Chiefer part, for Time –," Dickinson wrote in 1863, setting the new commercial economy of money, exchange, and free-flowing cash—"The Bullion of Today"—against the "Slow Gold," "the Currency / Of Immortality –" that she associates with the transcendent work of art. "One's – Money – One's – the Mine –," she writes, invoking contemporary political debates about the gold standard as opposed to the free circulation of greenback notes (*Poems*, 536). While Dickinson's "Work for Immortality" and the forms in which she circulated it look backward toward a set of Federalist and country values embodied in the figure of George Washington, her work also looks forward to the increasing valorization of art as an aesthetic object separate from the messiness of politics and history that came to be the dominant mythos of literary modernism and that still shapes the ways Dickinson's work is interpreted today.[21]

Whitman worked for "Immortality," too, but as he suggests in "Poets to Come" (1867), the immortality he sought would be achieved somewhere down the road, in poets, "orators, singers, musicians" and others who would carry on the work of democratic creation: "I myself but write one or two indicative words for the future, / I but advance a moment only to wheel and hurry back in the darkness" (*LGC*, 14). But even here, in this seemingly public poem,

Whitman evokes a persona, a poet, who is as coy, elusive, and dark as Emily Dickinson.

By reading Whitman and Dickinson in private and public, as poets whose unsettled and unsettling *interiors* existed *inside* rather than *outside* the political and social struggles of their times, I have tried to move beyond the "public" and "private" frames that have too often structured past approaches to their work. I have tried to suggest some of the new social and aesthetic perspectives that might be opened by reading—or more properly rereading—the relation between Whitman and Dickinson *within* the social and political histories that they lived, suffered, wrote about, and resisted.

PART THREE

THE REVOLUTIONARY TRANSATLANTIC

CHAPTER SIX

Whitman, Marx, and the American 1848

An increase in wages arouses in the worker the same desire to get rich as in the capitalist, but he can only satisfy this desire by sacrificing his mind and his body.

—Karl Marx, *Economic and Philosophical Manuscripts* (1844)

Here and there with dimes on the eyes walking,
To feed the greed of the belly the brains liberally spooning,
Tickets buying or taking or selling, but in to the feast never once going;
Many sweating and ploughing and thrashing, and then the chaff for
  payment receiving,
A few idly owning, and they the wheat continually claiming.

—Walt Whitman, *Leaves of Grass* (1855)

"Man *lives* from nature . . . nature is his *body*, and he must maintain a continuing dialogue with it if he is not to die." "How it deadens one's sympathies, this living in a city!" "The same unholy wish for great riches enters into every transaction of society, and more or less taints its moral soundness." "It is our task to drag the old world into the full light of day and give positive shape to the new one." Is this Walt Whitman or Karl Marx? Karl Marx or Walt Whitman?[1] I begin with this confusion of voices because it is so common to view Whitman and Marx as antitheses of each other that we have forgotten the uncanny overlappings of these two major nineteenth-century voices of revolution, democracy, and global community. The Whitman we inherited from the Cold War came to us curiously clipped of his political and working-class roots, his homoeroticism, and his communal vision: Whitman the individualist, the singer of "Myself," the glorious embodiment of liberal individualism, the possibilities of the self, and American Freedom.[2] The Marx we inherited from the Cold War, and who endures in American criticism and the American national fantasy today, comes to us clipped of his humanist and millenarian roots not only in German philosophy, but in the Enlightenment and revolutionary traditions of France and America: Marx the Communist, the antagonist of the individual, of privacy, and property, who celebrated the subjection of individual freedom to the totalitarian state.

On the hundredth anniversary of *Leaves of Grass* in 1955—in the very midst of McCarthyism, anticommunism, and the Cold War—there could be no conversation between the major democratic poet and the major political philosopher of the nineteenth century because they worked dialectically as negations of each other. But even a half century later, at a time when we have articles and books on Whitman and on just about everything, I could still not find a single article on Whitman and Marx. Why not? Whitman and Marx continue to be kept apart not only by a disciplinary logic that organizes and segregates fields—literature, philosophy, political theory, economics, poetry—but also by a Cold War manichean ideology of good versus evil, democracy versus communism, native versus foreign—that continues to haunt and, indeed, to saturate the way we do both American studies and American foreign policy.[3]

Having marked the 150th anniversary of the publication of *Leaves of Grass*, I want to open the transatlantic conversation between Whitman and Marx as a means of challenging the disciplinary, national, and field boundaries and the demonizing rhetorics of the Cold War that have kept Whitman and Marx, the poet and the philosopher, America and Europe, democracy and communism apart. Writing in 1837 to his father of his attempt as a student to bring philosophy, law, poetry, and history together, Marx observed: "[I]t is the juxtaposition of these different things that gives it different relationships and truths."[4] Reading Whitman through the lens of Marx, and Marx through the lens of Whitman, embodies and poeticizes Marx by giving his key terms—human, liberty, labor, community, species-being—a local habitation and a name; it also politicizes and theorizes Whitman's democratic poetry by situating it within larger debates about labor, slavery, capital, and class.

The subject Whitman/Marx is fascinating in what it tells us about nineteenth-century political and cultural exchange across the boundaries of the nation-state. It locates Whitman's revolutionary poetics in relation to a more global democratic struggle for human liberation and popular cultural expression. It links Whitman with an international network that includes, at the very least, England, France, Germany, and the United States. And it highlights the ways global vision—so important to Whitman's reception and circulation throughout the world and already evident in his political poems of 1850—shaped the first edition of *Leaves of Grass*. In the context of the global crisis of capital which Marx predicted and the possibility of global union which Whitman envisioned, the subject of Whitman/Marx also has a pressing relevance and urgency to the ongoing struggles over capitalist dominance, democratic freedom, world union—and peace—today.

This fascinating subject of Whitman and Marx warrants a longer comparative study of their multiple convergences, from their birth within one year of each other, Marx in 1818 in Trier, Rhineland, and Whitman in 1819 in Long Island, New York; to their mutual engagements in journalism, political radicalism, the labor movement, democratic struggle, and the revolutions of 1848; the centrality of France to their political vision; their common view of the importance of the discovery of America to what Marx called the rise of the bourgeoisie and Whitman called the advance of democracy; their respective political calls to workers to unite against the growing power of capital and the state, Marx in the *Communist Manifesto* and Whitman in his early journalism and "The Eighteenth Presidency!"; their response to the Civil War and their mutual admiration for Lincoln; their shared glee at the uprisings of the Paris Commune in 1871; and their virtually simultaneous effort to come to terms with the national and increasingly global conflict between capitalism and democracy, Marx in the first and only published volume of *Capital* in 1867 and Whitman in *Democratic Vistas*, which first appeared as essays on "Democracy" and "Personalism" in 1867 and 1868 and then as a political pamphlet in 1871.

In this essay, I focus on the dialectics of the young Whitman and the young Marx in the years leading up to revolutions of 1848, the *Communist Manifesto* (1848), and the publication of the first edition of *Leaves of Grass* (1855).

Roots

Whitman's family origins and upbringing were more radical than Marx's. Whereas Whitman came from a freethinking, working-class family, and his father was one of the increasingly disenfranchised artisan laborers of the competitive capitalist marketplace that Marx would write about in his 1844 Paris manuscripts, or *Economic and Philosophical Manuscripts*, and later in *Capital* (1867), Marx was raised in a bourgeois Jewish German family; his attorney father converted to Lutheranism in order to gain respectability in the primarily Catholic city of Trier in the Prussian Rhineland. Whitman briefly attended a

Brooklyn poverty school, but he received his main education during the 1830s in the print trade, journalism, and Democratic party politics, whereas Marx studied law and then philosophy at the University of Berlin.

Whitman was raised on the radical political and religious philosophies of Thomas Paine, Constantin Volney, and the revolutionary Enlightenment.[5] His father subscribed to and Whitman "often read" the *Free Enquirer*, a socialist magazine edited by Robert Dale Owen and Frances Wright, which sought through the rhetoric of a "war of class" to unite the grievances of New York City workers in an anticapitalist and anticlerical platform.[6] Whereas Whitman early identified with the working class in its protest against the betrayal of the American Revolution through the increasing dominance of government, big business, and the monied classes in American life, Marx still lived in an Old World aristocratic order of state censorship and autocratic rule, in which a bourgeois revolution had not yet occurred and industrial transformation had just begun. Nevertheless, the Rhineland province, where Marx was born, had been annexed to France during the Napoleonic wars (1798 to 1815). Here as elsewhere in Germany, the Enlightenment and French revolutionary traditions of individual rights, freedom, and popular sovereignty would remain alive, as instanced by the insurrections in Germany inspired by the revolutions in France in 1830 and 1848. For Whitman and for Marx, a commitment to individual freedom (not free trade but freedom of the person), popular sovereignty, and the example of France—especially the French Revolution and the Revolutions of 1848—would become a shaping presence in their life and work. Despite outsetting differences, their lives began to converge.

Under the influence of the materialist and natural law philosophies of Paine's *The Age of Reason* (1794), Wright's *A Few Days in Athens* (1822), and especially Volney's *The Ruins, or Meditation on the Revolutions of Empires* (1791), which was first translated into English in 1802 by Joel Barlow and Thomas Jefferson, Whitman, at age twenty-one, dreamed of writing a "wonderful" philosophical book focused on an "enlightened" critique of money and property that sounds remarkably like Marx's life's work: "Therein should be treated on, the nature and peculiarities of men, the diversity of their characters, the means of improving their state, and the proper mode of governing nations."[7] As a student of law at the University of Berlin, Marx in his turn struggled against the traditions of German idealism by writing what he called an "unhappy opus" that sought "to elaborate a philosophy that would cover the whole field of law" (*SW*, 10).

During these same years, both wrote lyric poetry: Marx wrote several volumes of "purely idealistic" poems, which he later burned (*SW*, 10, 13), and Whitman published several early poems of "flashing hope, and gloomy fear" in the *Long Island Democrat*.[8] For both, poetry became a means of escaping the gloom of history and the real, or what Marx called the "opposition of 'is' and 'ought' which is the hallmark of idealism" (*SW*, 10). "The whole scope of a longing that sees no limits," he wrote, "is expressed in many forms and broadens poetry out" (*SW*, 10). For early Marx and early Whitman, poetry became one form through which each expressed a utopian social desire, "a longing that sees no limits," as each sought an appropriate form—philosophy, poetry, journalism, fiction, public speaking, political activism—through which to engage with and change the world.

In his effort to reconcile the real and the ideal, "what is and what ought to be" (*SW*, 10), Marx came under the early and powerful influence of the Young Hegelians at the University of Berlin, where Hegel had been a professor of philosophy until his death in 1831. Writing to his father of the dramatic philosophical transformation brought by his reading of Hegel, Marx sounds more like Whitman than Whitman at this time: "I left behind the idealism which, by the way, I had nourished with that of Kant and Fichte, and came to seek *the idea in the real itself. If the gods had before dwelt above the earth, they had now become its centre*" (*SW*, 12; my italics). Whereas Whitman moved away from the more materialist, sensuous, and body-centered poetics of the 1855 *Leaves of Grass*, in which the soul as eros inseminates and has no existence apart from the body, toward the Hegelian idealism of *Democratic Vistas*, "Passage to India," and other post–Civil War writings, Marx moved in the opposite direction: from Romantic idealism, to Hegel as a means of reconciling the ideal with science and history, to the historical materialist method which he and Frederick Engels set forth in the *German Ideology* (written in 1846) and which became the base of Marx's later work in the *Grundrisse* (1857–1858) and *Capital*.

But, while Whitman and Marx appear to move in opposite directions, in their early years and at critical moments throughout their writings, their works and voices also converge.[9] In their early work, for example, both shared a common interest in the philosopher Epicurus, a figure who played a central role in the philosophy of Marx and the poetic vision of Whitman. In 1841 Marx completed a doctoral dissertation—"The Difference between Democritus' and Epicurus' Philosophy of Nature"—in which he argued in support of Epicurus's materialist view of human freedom and the ability to act in nature against the deterministic vision of Democritus. Similarly drawn to Epicurus as a figure who triumphs over fate through an ethics of simplicity, virtue, and pleasure in the natural and the human world, Whitman incorporated a scene from Frances Wright's *A Few Days in Athens*—one in which Epicurus expounds on his "philosophy of the Garden"—into an early poetic sketch for *Leaves of Grass* entitled "Pictures":

> He shows to what a glorious height the man may ascend,
> He shows how independent one may be of fortune—how triumphant over fate.[10]

Both found in Epicurus a figure of human agency, of human self-making, that would become important to their vision of labor and history as forms of human self-creation.

By the time Whitman came of age in 1840, he had acquired a reputation as a "well-known locofoco of the town" and "champion of the Democracy."[11] Identified with the radical wing of the New York Democratic party, Whitman was during these years more advanced in his knowledge of both practical politics and labor conditions under capitalism than Marx, whose attacks on church and state were still being launched on the abstract level of theory and Hegelian logic. Marx planned to pursue a career as a professor of philosophy, but he was stopped short by the reactionary power of the Prussian state when in 1842 his friend Bruno Bauer and other progressives at the University of Bonn were fired for unorthodox religious and political views. Like Whitman in the 1840s, Marx turned to journalism and the power of the print public sphere to give voice to social criticism and promote political change. "The philosophers have only interpreted the world in various ways; the point is to change it," Marx wrote in "Theses on Feuerbach" (*SW*, 173).

In 1842, Whitman became editor of the *Aurora*, a daily newspaper in New York City, and Marx began to write for and then edit the *Rheinische Zeitung* (Rhenish Gazette), a newspaper published in Cologne and supported by liberal industrial interests. Whereas Marx's early political journalism makes use of liberal and Enlightenment rhetorics of freedom and rationality to defend freedom of the press and convince his primarily bourgeois readers that religious and political repression is a logical contradiction in the administration of the Prussian state, Whitman's editorials for the penny press seek to educate his primarily working-class readers in the democratic ideals of independence, freedom, and citizenship by imbuing them "with a feeling of respect for, and confidence in, themselves" (*WJ*, 1: 124).

Unlike Marx's articles for the *Zeitung*, which are aimed at bringing about a bourgeois revolution in a country that did not yet have a political constitution, Whitman's editorials already register the glaring contradiction between the revolutionary ideal of American democracy and the actual conditions of American capitalism. "If we were asked the particular trait of national character from which might be apprehended the greatest evil to the land," Whitman wrote in 1842, "we should unhesitatingly point to the *strife for gain* which of late years has marked, and now marks, the American people" (*WJ*, 1: 97; my italics). The triumph of capital over republican virtue was dramatically symbolized for Whitman in the public willingness to desecrate the graves of the revolutionary founders in the name of accumulating "ill won heaps of gold." "Even the battle spots where our old soldiers fought and died, are not beyond the reach of this pollution. The very hill made sacred by the blood of freedom's earliest martyrs, is sold and trafficked for" (*WJ*, 1: 98).

In another editorial, Whitman reflects, through the story of "Lively Frank," on the wretched conditions of laborers throughout New York City: "If some potent magician could lift the veil which shrouds, in alleys, dark streets, garrets, and a thousand other habitations of want, the miseries that are every day going on among us—how would the spectacle distress and terrify the beholder!" In his vision of "delicate women . . . working themselves even to illness . . . young boys forced by the circumstances wherein they are bred, to be familiar with vice and all iniquity; [and] girls, whom absolute starvation drives at length to ruin, worse than starvation" (*WJ*, 1: 63, 64; ellipses mine), Whitman had already begun to mount his own attack on American capitalism from the viewpoint of the laboring class in language that anticipates Marx's first engagement with the struggle between labor and capital a few years later in his 1844 Paris manuscripts.[12]

Capitalism and Democracy

Marx first addressed "economic questions" in articles written for the *Zeitung* on the right of peasants to gather wood from landed estates and the "conditions" of the Moselle wine-growers.[13] But it was not until 1843, when the *Zeitung* was banned by the Prussian state and Marx was forced into self-exile in France, that he had his first direct contact with working-class revolutionaries and began to make the acquaintance of French democrats and socialists, including Pierre-Joseph Proudhon, Pierre Leroux, and Louis Blanc. It was here, too, that Marx reconnected with Engels, whom he first met in 1842, and the two began a friendship and an intellectual collaboration that would last for the rest of their lives.

"[I]t is our task," Marx wrote shortly before he left for Paris in 1843, "to drag the old world into the full light of day and to give positive shape to the new one."[14] By joining the cause of labor radicalism to his desire to "give positive shape" to a new world, Marx caught up with Whitman, who had in effect already gone to France in his political imagination. In Marx's 1844 Paris manuscripts, the voices of Marx and Whitman begin to converge in their common response to the struggle between labor and capital throughout the Atlantic world from Cologne, Brussels, London, and Paris to New York City.

Marx's Paris manuscripts draw on German idealism (especially Hegel and Ludwig Feuerbach), French politics (especially socialism), and English economic theory (especially Adam Smith and David Ricardo) to analyze the death grip of capital on human and social life. As I argue elsewhere in this volume, Whitman's journalism and stories of the 1840s draw on Revolutionary ideology, Jeffersonian republicanism, and labor and other forms of social radicalism to critique the increasing dominance of capital in American life.[15] Marx and Whitman begin with the same economic fact: "The devaluation of the human world grows in direct proportion to the increase in value of the world of things" (*EPM*, 323–24). Both respond to the same social conditions: Whitman criticized capitalist accumulation, monopoly, the oppression of workers and women, the corruption of businessmen and lawyers, religious institutions, child labor, economic depression, and the worker as slave; Marx focused on "Rag-and-bone-men," "enslavement to capital," the bureaucratic state, and many of the same social conditions (*EPM*, 292, 285). "An increase in wages arouses in the worker the same desire to get rich as in the capitalist, but he can only satisfy this desire by sacrificing his mind and his body," Marx wrote of the grip of "dead capital" on "real individual activity" (*EPM*, 286, 284); "For [money] we work and toil, and sweat away our youth and manhood, giving up the improvement of our minds and the cultivation of our physical nature," Whitman wrote, "weakly thinking that a heap of money, when we are old, can make up to us for these sacrifices" (*WJ*, 2: 104).

The dominance of capital and the corresponding growth of corporate monopolies and "immense monied institutions" represented, in Whitman's view, a threat to the life of the individual, the American republic, and the possibilities of democracy worldwide: "Reckless and unprincipled—controlled by persons who make them complete engines of selfishness—at war with everything that favors our true interests—unrepublican, unfair, untrue, unworthy—these bubbles are kept afloat solely and wholly by the fever for gaining wealth. . . . The same unholy wish for great riches enters into every transaction of society, and more or less taints its moral soundness" (*WJ*, 2: 103). Under capitalism, Marx wrote, persons and objects are emptied of their "real content" and replaced by capital: "[T]he same capital stays the same in the most varied natural and social circumstances"; "money, which appears to be a means, is the true power and the sole end" (*EPM*, 336, 365).

Whereas Whitman speaks as an I and We, as a working-class man to other working-class men and women, Marx speaks from an objective point of view, of the worker as they, as object of his analysis rather than subject to whom he speaks. What Whitman describes in the language of artisan republicanism and labor radicalism, Marx analyzed as the commodification of the laborer, the objectification of labor, and the consequent alienation of the worker from his work, the products of his labor, and the natural world. Against the dehumanizing force of capitalism, Marx and Whitman called for the liberation of man in the fullness of his physical and social being. "[T]he society that is fully developed produces man in all the richness of his being, the rich man who is profoundly and abundantly endowed with all the senses, as its constant reality" (*EPM*, 354), Marx wrote in language that anticipates the fully endowed individual and social being, the laborer poet who steps forth in the 1855 *Leaves of Grass* and sings:

> I believe in the flesh and the appetites,
> Seeing hearing and feeling are miracles, and each part and tag of me is
> a miracle. (*LG* 1855, 49)

But, while Whitman and Marx converge in their millennial vision of human and democratic possibility, their political paths diverge. Their solutions to the social contradictions of their time are quite different: Marx advocates the end of private property in communism: "*Communism* is the *positive* supersession of *private property* as *human self-estrangement*, and hence the true *appropriation* of the *human essence* through and for man; it is the complete restoration of man to himself as a *social*, i.e. human, being" (*EPM*, 348). Whitman advocates a more radical commitment to democracy. "Swing Open the Doors!" he proclaimed in an 1846 editorial for the Brooklyn *Daily Eagle*, striking a pose that projects his political views on free trade, open banking, open immigration, free soil, free men, and free women: "We must be constantly pressing onward—every year throwing the doors wider and wider—and carrying our experiment of democratic freedom to the very verge of the limit" (*WJ*, 1: 481). Whereas Marx's contradictions are philosophical—between man and nature, man and man, existence and being, objectification and self-affirmation, freedom and necessity, individual and species—and his resolution utopian, Whitman's contradictions are political—between freedom and slavery, labor and capital, individual and state, state and union—and his resolution is on the way to becoming a democratic poetics. His phrases roll with the participial rhythms of the 1855 *Leaves*, and his open-door image anticipates the democratic challenge he hurls at his readers in the opening poem: "Unscrew the locks from the doors! / Unscrew the doors themselves from their jambs!" (*LG* 1855, 48).

Although Whitman never questioned the relations of private property and free enterprise at the foundation of the American system, his political and labor journalism of the forties reveals the signs of dispossession, dehumanization, and degeneration in American life and the growing inequality between rich and poor, capital and labor, that were the true legacy of Jacksonian democracy.[16] Like Marx, Whitman recognized that the economics of capitalism "enters every transaction of society" and "taints its soundness," but, by focusing on the corruption of American government by Northern capital and Southern slaveholders, he avoided the potential contradiction between the free-enterprise society in which he lived and the harmonious and egalitarian society of his dreams. Envisioning the commercial spirit as an essentially benign, civilizing, and unifying force, Whitman never carried his critique of capitalism to an attack on the concept of free enterprise itself.

The American 1848

"Where is, at this moment, the great medium or exponent of power, through which the civilized world is governed?" Whitman asked in an 1846 editorial for the Brooklyn *Daily Eagle*. "The pen is that medium of power," he responded, which could "sway the energy and will of congregated masses of men" and hurl "destruction on every side!" At this very moment "unknown and unnoticed, a man may be toiling on to the completion of a book destined" to convulse "the social and political world" and "gain acclamations . . . from admiring America and astonished Europe!" (*WJ*, 2: 62; ellipsis mine). Whitman appears to prophesy the revolutionary poet of the 1855 *Leaves of Grass*, but he might also be prophesying the revolutionary pamphlet published by Marx and Engels in 1848 under the title *The Manifesto of the Communist*

Party. The political crisis of 1848 in Europe and the Americas would provide the historical occasion for the poet and the philosopher, the democrat and the communist, to rock the world.

In the years leading up to the Revolutions of 1848, Whitman and Marx moved toward increasingly radical positions that located them outside the political mainstream of their respective countries and led both of them to begin thinking about forms of human freedom and community that might be realized outside the institutionalized forms of government and the state.[17]

In 1845 Marx was expelled from France for his political journalism. He went to Brussels, where he carried on his political collaboration with Engels and became part of a diasporic community of radical German émigré laborers and intellectuals who worked across national borders to bring about revolutionary change throughout Europe, and especially in Germany. After Marx left France, he applied to emigrate to the United States, where he might have become part of the radical German émigré community in New York City. He might even have met Walt Whitman at one of the German beer halls such as Pfaff's, where artists and revolutionaries gathered. But, after spending several years traveling from Belgium, to England, to France, to Germany and back again, he finally settled in London in 1848 and resided there for the remainder of his life (Figure 13).

In London Marx joined a workingmen's movement called the League of the Just and later the Communist League, which Engels described as "the first international workers' movement of all time."[18] It was for this group of primarily German émigré workers that Marx and Engels composed the *Communist Manifesto*, which was published in German in January 1848 just one month before the revolutions broke out in Paris on February 21. During this same time, Whitman was dismissed as editor of the Brooklyn *Daily Eagle* when he refused to support the proslavery position of the *Eagle*'s owner and the Democratic Party. He joined the Free Soil Party and in August 1848 was elected a delegate to the Free-Soil convention in Buffalo, where the party nominated Martin Van Buren for the presidency on a platform of "Free-soil, free speech, free labor, and free men." To support what he called the "genial and enlightened doctrines of the Free Soil [Party]," Whitman founded the Brooklyn *Weekly Freeman*, which would, he announced in the first issue of September 9, 1848, "oppose, under all circumstances, the addition to the Union, in the future, of a single inch of slave land, whether in the form of state or territory."[19] In 1850, as talk of southern secession mounted, the Congress approved a series of compromise measures, including the admission of

FIGURE 13. Karl Marx, 1861. Photograph by Richard Beard. As "the complete restoration of man to himself as a *social*, i.e. human, being" (*EPM*, 348), Marx's vision of communism as a state of sensuous, corporeal, human being is finally closer to the state of being *in relation* that Whitman embodies in *Leaves of Grass* than it is to the Soviet Stalinist state that came to define Communism during the Cold War years and beyond. Courtesy of Art Resource and Wikimedia Commons.

California as a free state, a stricter Fugitive Slave Law, and the extension of slavery in the territory acquired in the war against Mexico.

The scene of political crisis both national and transnational that culminated in the American crisis over labor, freedom, and slavery and the Revolutions of 1848 catalyzed a new direction in the work of both Marx and Whitman. In 1848 Marx and Engels published *The Manifesto of the Communist Party*, the most important political pamphlet ever written. Whitman published four political poems that anticipate the democratic form and content of *Leaves of Grass*. Although one is a political manifesto of the Communist League, a group of German émigré workers that linked communists in the cities of Paris, London, Brussels, Cologne, and New York, and the other a searing poetic response to the betrayal of revolutionary ideology inspired by the Compromise of 1850, I want to argue that in the context of the more global crisis of 1848 the philosopher and the poet, the communist and the democrat, the European intellectual and the American worker, are closer than one might think.

The willingness of the Democratic Party and the North to compromise on the issue of slavery led Whitman to compose some of his earliest politically inspired verse. In Whitman's view, the Compromise of 1850 had made slavery rather than freedom the law of the land; and like slavery, it had put the entire revolutionary heritage—rights, freedom, democracy, equality, the dignity of labor, the sovereignty of the people—up for sale. At the center of Whitman's poems on the 1850 Compromise is the contradiction between the republican rhetoric of freedom and the actual commitment to extending slavery into the territory:

> Principle—freedom!—fiddlesticks!
> We know not where they're found.
> Rights of the masses—progress!—bah! (*EPF*, 45)

Each of Whitman's antislavery poems—"Song for Certain Congressmen," "Blood-Money," and "The House of Friends"—also turns on the social practice of selling human bodies—black or white—and the countervailing desire to replace an economy of capital with a cooperative ethos of social love:

> A dollar dearer to them than Christ's blessing;
> All loves, all hopes, less than the thought of gain;
> In life walking in that as in a shroud (*EPF*, 37)

Although Michael Rogin has argued that unlike the European Revolutions of 1848, the American 1848 centered on "slavery and race rather than class,"

Whitman's early political poems reveal the ways the issues of freedom, slavery, race, labor radicalism, capitalism, and imperialism were linked with the more global scene of worker oppression and world revolution in the American 1848.[20] And it is here that Whitman begins to edge toward Marx.

Whitman's impassioned commitment to the struggle of freedom against slavery, labor against capital, in America was fired by his sense that what was happening in America was part of a universal advance from enslavement to freedom. "[N]ot only here, on our own beloved soil, is this democratic feeling infusing itself, and becoming more and more powerful," he wrote in an 1846 editorial on progress. "The lover of his race—he whose good-will is not bounded by a shore or a division line—looks across the Atlantic, and exults to see on the shores of Europe, a restless dissatisfaction spreading wider and wider every day. Long enough have priestcraft and kingcraft stalked over those lands, clothed in robes of darkness and wielding instruments of subjection" (*WJ*, 2: 79). Whitman was engaged in the same religious and political struggle on one side of the Atlantic as Marx was on the other. In fact, among the various national struggles Marx and Engels support in the concluding section of the *Communist Manifesto*, they list "the agrarian reformers in America," an apparent reference to Whitman's own party, the Free Soilers, which advocated the free distribution of small plots of land.[21]

As Whitman wielded the power of the pen against the "instruments of subjection" at home, like Marx he was inspired by the signs of revolutionary ferment he saw spreading in Europe. "In France, the smothered fires only wait the decay of the false one, the deceiver Louis Phillippe [*sic*], to burst forth in one great flame," Whitman wrote in February 1847, a full year before the uprisings in Paris in 1848. "The mottled empire of Austria is filled with the seeds of rebellion—with thousands of free hearts, whose aspirations ever tend to the downfall of despotism; and the numerous petty German states, too, have caught the sacred ardor" (*WJ*, 2: 194–95). For Whitman, as for Marx, the democratic struggle in America was central to both the future of the Republic and the fate of revolution worldwide. In an article on the American union, Whitman wrote: "[T]he perpetuity of the sacred fire of freedom, which now burns upon a thousand hidden, but carefully tended, altars in the old world, waits the fate of our American union. O, sad would be the hour when that union should be dissolved!" (*WJ*, 2: 186).[22]

Like Marx, Whitman found confirmation for his revolutionary reading of history when in 1848 Louis Philippe was dethroned, the Second Republic was declared, and this revolution set off a series of uprisings in Austria, Hungary,

Germany, Italy, and elsewhere throughout Europe. Although these revolutions were defeated, Whitman maintained his belief in the ultimate triumph of liberty, which he celebrated in the poem "Resurgemus," published in the New York *Tribune* on June 21, 1850, two years before Karl Marx began contributing his own weekly columns to the New York *Tribune* on events in Europe for the next decade.[23] Inspired by the revolutions in Europe, and perhaps by the dispatches on these revolutions that Margaret Fuller was sending to the New York *Tribune* from Rome, "Resurgemus" is one of Whitman's earliest experiments with a new free-verse line and the only one of his early poems to be included among the twelve untitled poems of *Leaves of Grass*. As such, it suggests the international frame, the workingmen's movement—perhaps even the communist movement—and the global struggle for democracy out of which Whitman's *Leaves* emerged.

If Whitman's abrupt departure from New York in February 1848 to write for the New Orleans *Daily Crescent* was spurred by his disillusionment with Democratic party politics, his decision to return to Brooklyn just as abruptly a few months later, "large as life . . . and more radical than ever," may have been prompted, not, as was once believed, by a New Orleans romance, but by news of the revolutions in Europe.[24] "God, 'twas delicious!" Whitman wrote at the outset of "Resurgemus":

> That brief, tight, glorious grip
> Upon the throats of kings. (*EPF*, 38)

These lines exude the sense of political and artistic renewal he found in the revolutions of 1848, especially in France.[25]

But why did Whitman wait until 1850 to write his poetic tribute to the revolutionary uprisings in Europe in 1848? Perhaps Whitman found in Europe a more revolutionary version of democratic history than in the United States, where the working people did not rise up in defense of their rights. As early as 1847 in his editorial "American Workingmen, versus Slavery," Whitman issued a call to "the workingmen of the north, east, and west, to come up, to a man, in defence of their rights, their honor, and that heritage of getting bread by the sweat of the brow, which we must leave to our children" (*WJ*, 2: 319). But the workers did not defend their rights: they did not resist the extension of slavery in the territories. As Whitman's "Song for Certain Congressmen" suggests, "young Freedom" was stabbed in America because the people did not rise in defense of their rights. It was not in the New World but in the Old World, in France, Italy, Austria, Switzerland, and elsewhere, that the people arose, and their uprising renewed Whitman's faith in the ultimate triumph of liberty:

> Suddenly, out of its stale and drowsy lair, the lair of slaves,
> Like lightning Europe le'pt forth,
> Sombre, superb and terrible. (*EPF*, 38)

These words—the opening lines of "Resurgemus"—bear an implicit threat to those who cooperated in the defeat of "young Freedom" in America.

While "Resurgemus" may seem very different from the *Communist Manifesto*, the poem's revolutionary sentiment has much in common with Marx's revolutionary pamphlet. "A spectre is haunting Europe—the spectre of Communism," Marx declares in his famous opening to the *Communist Manifesto*, as he sets out to reveal the massive power of a proletarian movement—the fabled "Specter of Communism"—that, as Marx effectively demonstrates, the Old World order of "Pope and Tsar, Metternich and Guizot, French radicals and German police spies" really do have cause to fear. Whitman's "Resurgemus" is also haunted by a phantom presence—a red one:

> Yet behind all, lo, a Shape,
> Vague as the night, draped interminably,
> Head, front and form in scarlet folds;
> Whose face and eyes none may see. (*EPF*, 39)

Like the "spectre of Communism" that Marx invokes at the outset of the *Communist Manifesto* and the spectre of "red" revolution associated with the bloody June days in Paris in 1848 as "the first great battle between proletarian and bourgeoisie,"[26] Whitman's eerie "Shape" in "red robes" augurs the ultimate death and destruction of the oppressive Old World order. As the poem's Latin title "Resurgemus"—we will rise again—affirms, "The People" will rise again despite the fact that "the king struts grandly again," along with an "appalling procession " of state appendages: "Hangman, priest, and tax-gatherer, / Soldier, lawyer, and sycophant" (*EPF*, 38).

For Whitman as for Marx the movement of history is revolutionary, progressive, and the triumph of freedom and the masses is inevitable. Marx's proof is material, economic, grounded in a historical materialist analysis of the determining political and cultural force of the mode of production, class struggle, and Hegelian dialectics. Whitman's proof is affective, visionary, grounded in a quasi-religious faith in the founding ideology, the American and French Revolutions, and the historically violent but just rise of democracy

FIGURE 14. Jean-François Millet, *The Sower* (1850). "The Leaves are really only Millet in another form," Whitman told Horace Traubel in 1888; "they are the Millet that Walt Whitman has succeeded in putting into words" (*WWC*, 1: 7). Courtesy of the Museum of Fine Arts, Boston.

and the masses to take back the self-sovereign power that belongs to them by natural right. While Marx is more scientific and Whitman more romantic, the millennial vision of both has roots in Enlightenment theories of human liberty and natural law.

As in Jean-François Millet's painting *The Sower* (1850), in which Whitman would later see "the long precedent crushing of the masses . . . in abject poverty, hunger . . . yet Nature's force, titanic here, the stronger and hardier for that repression" (Figure 14),[27] Whitman envisions the triumph of liberty as part of the regenerative law of the universe:

Not a grave of those slaughtered ones,
But is growing its seed of freedom,
In its turn to bear seed,
Which the winds shall carry afar and resow,
And the rain nourish. (*EPF*, 39)

Marx uses a similarly regenerative language: "Now and then the workers are victorious, but only for a time. The *real fruit* of their battles lies, not in the immediate result, but in the ever expanding union of the workers" (*CM*, 76; my italics).[28] Both evoke the class struggle as a war between the forces of life and death. Whitman represents violence as generative, dialectical:

Not a disembodied spirit
Can the weapon of tyrants let loose,
But it shall stalk invisibly over the earth
Whispering, counseling, cautioning. (*EPF*, 40)

The collective power of the proletariat "ever rises up again, stronger, firmer, mightier," Marx affirms. For Whitman and Marx, the end—the triumph of the human, of freedom over slavery—is the same, and inevitable. "What the bourgeoisie therefore produces," Marx concludes, "are its own grave-diggers. Its fall and the victory of the proletariat are equally inevitable" (*CM*, 76, 79).

Like Marx, Whitman recognized the relation of local and national struggles to the more global struggle for democratic and human liberation. And in the *Communist Manifesto* it is precisely this transnational perspective that defines communism: "The Communists are distinguished from the other working-class parties by this only," Marx writes: "In the national struggles of the proletarians of the different countries, they point out and bring to the front the common interests of the entire proletariat, *independently of all nationality*" (*CM*, 79; my italics). At another point Marx asserts: "[T]he theory of the Communists may be summed up in the single sentence: Abolition of private property" (*CM*, 80). But as Marx himself evinces when he devotes a full third of the *Communist Manifesto* to describing the actually existing forms of socialism and communism—including the "feudal socialism" of the French and English aristocracy, the "petty-bourgeois socialism" of Sismondi, "German or 'true' socialism," the "bourgeois socialism" of Proudhon, the "Critical Utopian Socialism and Communism" of Saint-Simon, Fourier, Owen and others—"communism" was a contested and fluid term in the context of the political struggles of 1848: Marx is trying to corral the multiple historical forms of communism in the 1840s into a single international party and movement.[29]

Moreover, as David Fernbach observes: "In this period, when the proletarian movement was only just beginning to distinguish itself from the movement of the petty bourgeoisie, the term 'democrat' was generally used in the wide sense to denote all who stood for rule by the people, hence including the Communists."[30] By this definition, Whitman and Marx, the democrat and the communist—far from being the antitheses of each other they would become in Cold War ideology and the founding works of American studies—labored side by side on common ground as democrats "who stood for rule by the people."

Disillusioned with the increasingly centralized and reactionary power of the political state in Europe and America in the years leading up to and following the Revolutions of 1848, Marx and Whitman turned away from the received forms of party, law, and government toward forms of human relation and political community outside the state. Unlike Marx, however, who envisioned the proletariat, or industrial wage laborers, as the primary agents of revolutionary change—"the proletariat alone is a really revolutionary class," he wrote (*CM*, 77), Whitman envisioned a mass revolution and a bottom-up democratic transformation that would be led by workers everywhere, by mechanics, farmers, day laborers, and "every hard-working man" (*WJ*, 2: 319).[31] But, despite differences in their conception of the working-class, Marx and Whitman shared a vision of the power of labor, revolution, and solidarity across the boundaries of the nation-state to reclaim human liberty and the sensuous relation of the individual to the natural and social world that had been given up to constitutions and laws, the capitalist class and the centralized state. As Marx insisted in his Paris manuscripts, in a passage that turned Hegel on his head and anticipated the "Disorderly fleshy and sensual" persona of *Leaves of Grass*: "[M]an [is] a human and natural subject, with eyes, ears, etc., living in society, in the world and in nature" (*EPM*, 398n).

Marx's early writings define the economic conditions and the conditions of political struggle out of which *Leaves of Grass* emerged, and Whitman's 1855 edition of *Leaves of Grass* embodies and materializes the ideal of human liberation—the "corporeal, living, real, sensuous" actualization of both the individual and the species-being—that Marx described in his 1844 Paris manuscripts but rarely elaborated in his later work, which seems more preoccupied with gothic scenes of worker abjection than with giving any substantive vision of what a postcapitalist human and species-world might look like.

Thus, for example, in Whitman's notebook dated 1847 but likely written in 1854, the passage immediately preceding his break into the free-verse line of *Leaves of Grass*—"I am the poet of slaves and of the masters of slaves"—

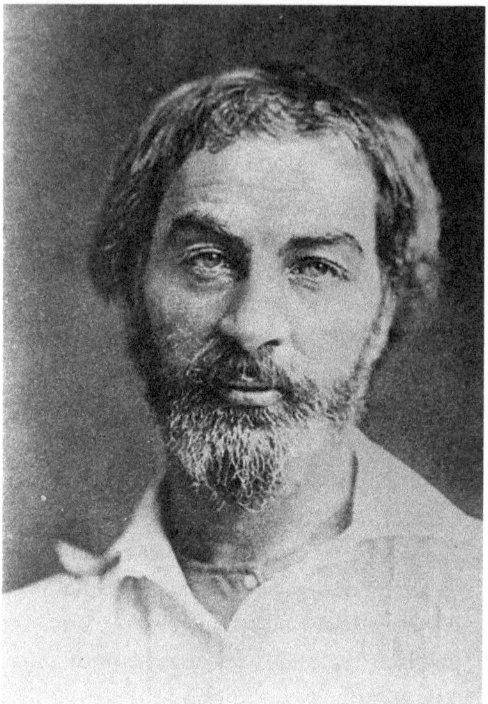

FIGURE 15. Walt Whitman, ca. 1854. The photograph, probably by Alexander Gardner, is known as "the Christ-likeness." "I hear and behold God in every object," Whitman wrote in *Leaves of Grass* around this time. "In the faces of men and women I see God, and in my own face in the glass; / I find letters from God dropped in the street. . . . And I leave them where they are, for I know others will punctually come forever and ever" (*LG* 1855, 83; ellipsis mine). Courtesy of the New York Public Library Rare Books Division and the Walt Whitman Archive.

rejects capitalists and intellectuals in favor of a sensuous human and social being fully in touch with his body, his senses, and the laboring world: "I will not descend among professors and capitalists,—I will turn up the ends of my trousers around my boots, and my cuffs back from my wrists, and go with drivers and boatmen and men that catch fish or work in the field. I know they are sublime" (*NUPM*, 1: 67).

It is this same figure who steps forth in the 1855 *Leaves of Grass* (Figure 15) to celebrate the richness of individual and communal life as an alternative to a capitalist order of money, ownership, and greed, which Whitman evokes in the powerful image of humans blocked from sensuous interaction with the natural and social world by capitalist modes of possession and exchange:

Here and there with dimes on the eyes walking,
To feed the greed of the belly the brains liberally spooning,
Tickets buying or taking or selling, but in to the feast never once going;
Many sweating and ploughing and thrashing, and then the chaff for payment receiving,
A few idly owning, and they the wheat continually claiming.
(*LG* 1855, 73)

These lines poetically embody the more abstract concepts of estrangement, commodification, and objectification that are at the center of Marx's analysis of capitalist political economy in the 1844 Paris manuscripts, in *The German Ideology*, and later in *Capital*. Under capitalism, the worker is "depressed," Marx wrote, "and from being a man becomes an abstract activity and a stomach" (*EPM*, 285). The simultaneously individual and collective voice of Whitman's working-class poet—

I celebrate myself,
And what I assume you shall assume,
For every atom belonging to me as good belongs to you. (*LG* 1855, 25)

—echoes and extends the individual and species-being toward which Marx gestures in his 1844 Paris manuscripts: "My *own* existence *is* social activity," Marx wrote. "Therefore what I create from myself I create for society, conscious of myself as a social being" (*EPM*, 350).

Just as Whitman imagined forms of individual character and social community outside law, government, and the state as the true realization of democracy, so Marx imagined the dissolution of the state as public political power under communism. Communism is not in Marx's view the final "form of human *society*" but a dynamic movement of history and a state of being: "the complete restoration of man to himself as a *social*, i.e. human, being" (*EPM*, 348). As a state of sensuous, corporeal, human being, Marx's vision of communism is, finally, closer to the democratic state of being in relation that Whitman embodies in *Leaves of Grass* than it is to the Soviet Stalinist state that came to define Communism during the Cold War years and beyond.

CHAPTER SEVEN

Insurrection, the Paris Commune, and *Leaves of Grass*

Dim smitten star.
Orb not of France alone, pale symbol of my soul, its dearest hopes,
The struggle and the daring, rage divine for liberty,
Of aspirations toward the far ideal—enthusiast's dreams of brotherhood,
Of terror to the tyrant and the priest.

—Walt Whitman, "O Star of France. 1870–71"

"The spectacle is appalling," Whitman declared in his major reflection on the "complete failure" of democracy in America in *Democratic Vistas* in 1871. "The magician's serpent in the fable ate up all the other serpents," he wrote, "and money-making is our magician's serpent, remaining to-day sole master of the field." While Whitman continued to hope that artists and poets of the future would bring his democracy of the imagination into being in America and worldwide, he also feared that "modern civilization, with all its improvements" was "on the road" to Hell, or what he called "a destiny" "equivalent" in "this real world, to that of the fabled dawned."[1]

And yet, *Democratic Vistas* concludes with a short sequence of "General Notes," in which Whitman lists three global events—"the removal of serfdom in Russia, slavery in the United States, and of the meanest of Imperialisms in France"—that give him hope that "Radical Democracy" and "wondrous armed uprisings of the People" were advancing worldwide (82, 83).

This hope is affirmed by a brief news flash from Europe, received via the Atlantic cable, about the defeat of Napoleon III (Louis-Napoléon) and the popular uprisings of the people in France. And it is with this "wondrous" news of the democratic uprisings in France that Whitman's *Democratic Vistas* concludes:

> LATEST FROM EUROPE—As I send my last pages to press, (Sept. 19, 1870,) the ocean-cable, continuing its daily budget of Franco-German war-news—Louis Napoleon a prisoner, (his rat-cunning at an end)—the conquerors advanced on Paris—the French, assuming Republican forms—seeking to negotiate with the King of Prussia, at the head of his armies—"his Majesty," says the despatch, "refuses to treat, on any terms, with a government risen out of Democracy."
>
> Let us note the words, and not forget them. The official relations of Our States, we know, are with the reigning kings, queens, &c., of the Old World. But the only deep, vast, emotional, real affinity of America is with the cause of Popular Government there—and especially in France. O that I could express, in my printed lines, the passionate yearnings, the pulses of sympathy, forever throbbing in the heart of These States, for sake of that—the eager eyes forever turned to that—watching it, struggling, appearing and disappearing, often apparently gone under, yet never to be abandoned, in France, Italy, Spain, Germany and in the British Islands. (*DV*, 84)

I begin by citing this entire passage because it seems as relevant to the current political moment—and the abandonment of France and Europe "by the official relations of Our States"—as it was to the strained relations between America and Europe at the end of the Civil War. It is also relevant to the founding ideals of the Transatlantic Walt Whitman Association, which was founded in Paris in 2007 and has continued to hold an annual Transatlantic Seminar and Symposium since the first one held at Dortmund University in Germany in 2008. Despite the "official relations" of our various countries, we can still join hands in the values of comradeship, sympathy, and love that Whitman envisioned as the founding ideals not only of the United States and France but of a transatlantic and global democratic community of friends and comrades.

As it turns out, it is not entirely coincidental that the Transatlantic Walt Whitman Association was founded in Paris, France. This chapter focuses on the formative presence of the French people—and the popular insurrections in France—in the democratic language, structure, and vision of *Leaves of Grass* from its earliest formation and first publication in 1855 to the publication of what Whitman thought would be the final edition of *Leaves of Grass* in 1871. This edition contained a new cluster of poems entitled "Songs of Insurrection," which was published in Washington, DC, in September 1870, the same month that Whitman received news of the popular uprisings in France.

The Revolutions of 1848

Whitman's *Democratic Vistas* was not the first time that his call for a democratic uprising of the people in America would be answered by a popular insurrection in France. In "American Workingmen, versus Slavery," which he wrote as editor of the Brooklyn *Daily Eagle* in September 1847, Whitman called upon "*the millions*" of mechanics and farmers throughout the country to—in the words of the popular American musical *Hamilton*—"Rise up, rise up" against a "few thousand rich, 'polished,' and aristocratic owners of slaves" in the South. In a democratic catalogue that anticipates the revolutionary form and content of *Leaves of Grass*, Whitman called "upon every mechanic of the north, east, and west—upon the carpenter, in his rolled up sleeves, the mason with his trowel, the stone-cutter with his brawny chest, the blacksmith with his sooty face . . . and every hard-working man" to annihilate the "little band" who support slavery in America (*WJ*, 2: 318, 319, 320).

This democratic uprising took place not in America, but a few months later in France, when in 1848 King Louis Philippe was overthrown, a second French republic was declared, and this revolution set off a series of uprisings in Austria, Hungary, Germany, Italy, and elsewhere in Europe. As a reporter for the New Orleans *Daily Crescent* between February and May 1848, Whitman experienced firsthand the political euphoria that followed news of the revolutions in Europe. "The whole civilized world is in commotion," Whitman declared in the *Crescent* on April 17, 1848, celebrating the outbreak of revolution in France and the defiance of its writer-hero, Alphonse de Lamartine, in leading the people everywhere to rise up against their oppressors.[2]

Whitman memorialized the Revolutions of 1848—and their failure—in a poem entitled "Resurgemus," published in the New York *Daily Tribune* on June 21, 1850. Despite the failure of the Revolutions of 1848, Whitman links the "Bloody corpses" of the "young men" who died to the image of the grass and the thematic of regeneration that would become central to his democratic poetry. In fact, the shaping presence that the Revolutions of 1848, especially in France, would have on the democratic form and content of Whitman's poetry is suggested by the fact that "Resurgemus" is one of Whitman's earliest experiments with a new free-verse line and the *only one* of his early poems to be included among the twelve untitled poems of the first edition of *Leaves of Grass* in 1855.

As such, "Resurgemus" suggests the international frame, the workingmen's movement—perhaps even the communist movement—and the global struggle for democracy out of which Whitman's *Leaves of Grass* emerged. "God, 'twas delicious! / That brief, tight, glorious grip / Upon the throats of kings," Whitman exclaimed in "Resurgemus," in lines that exude the sense of political and artistic renewal he experienced in response to the Revolutions in Europe (*EPF*, 38). It was not in the New World but in the Old World, in France, Italy, Austria, Switzerland, and elsewhere that the people arose, and their uprising renewed Whitman's faith in the ultimate triumph of liberty: "Suddenly, out of its stale and drowsy lair, the lair of slaves, / Like lightning Europe le'pt forth, / Sombre, superb and terrible," Whitman would exude in the opening lines of "Resurgemus" (*EPF*, 38).

Like the "spectre of Communism" that Marx and Engels invoke at the outset of the *Communist Manifesto* in 1848 and the spectre of "red" revolution associated with the bloody uprising of workers in Paris in June 1848, an uprising Engels described as "the first great battle between proletarian and bourgeoisie" (*CM*, 62), Whitman's "Resurgemus" is also haunted by "a Shape, / Vague as the night, draped interminably / Head, front and form, in scarlet folds; / Whose face and eyes none may see" (*EPF*, 39). Whitman's eerie "Shape" in "red robes" augurs the ultimate death and destruction of the oppressive Old World order. As the poem's Latin title, "Resurgemus," suggests, "The People" *will rise again* despite the fact that "the king struts grandly again," along with an "appalling procession" of state appendages: "Each comes in state, with his train / Hangman, priest, and tax-gatherer, / Soldier, lawyer, and sycophant" (*EPF*, 38).

For Whitman as he embarked on the experimental writing of *Leaves of Grass*, as for the radical republicans in Europe in 1848, "Resurgemus" envisions the triumph of liberty as part of the regenerative law of the universe:

Not a grave of those slaughtered ones,
But is growing its seed of freedom,
In its turn to bear seed,
Which the winds shall carry afar and resow,
And the rain nourish. (*EPF*, 39)

The poet evokes the class struggle as a war between the forces of life and death. Violence is generative, dialectical: "Not a disembodied spirit / Can the weapon of tyrants let loose, / But it shall stalk invisibly over the earth," Whitman writes (*EPF*, 40). The end—the triumph of the *human*, of freedom over slavery—is *inevitable*.

Remembering the Revolution

To the revised and untitled version of "Resurgemus" in the 1855 *Leaves of Grass*, Whitman added the following lines:

> O hope and faith! O aching close of lives! O many a sickened heart!
> Turn back unto this day, and make yourselves afresh. (*LG* 1855, 133)

The lines aptly express the disappointment that Whitman experienced in response to the failure of the Revolutions of 1848. At the same time, the lines beginning "O hope and faith," uttered as both vision and command, suggest the extent to which the Revolutions of 1848, especially the scene of revolution in France, became a source of renewed faith in the ultimate triumph of democracy that catalyzed a new direction in Whitman's work.

Disillusioned with the increasingly centralized and reactionary power of the state in Europe and America in the years leading up to and following the Revolutions of 1848, Whitman turned away from journalism and party politics toward poetry as an alternative means to regenerate the people in the Revolutionary ideals of life, liberty, equality, fraternity, and the pursuit of happiness and the need for collective resistance to the oppressive power of slavery, capitalism, and the state. "The attitude of great poets is to cheer up slaves and horrify despots," Whitman declared in the 1855 preface to *Leaves of Grass* (*LG* 1855, 15), as he sought to embody the true meanings of revolution in a fully free and democratic *being* in touch with the body, the people, nature, and the spirit world.

Like many French radicals in the wake of the brutal military suppression of the June 1848 workers' insurrection and the *coup d'etat* of Louis Bonaparte in December 1851, Whitman shared a vision of the power of labor, revolution, and solidarity across the boundaries of the nation-state to reclaim human liberty and the affective relation to the natural and social world that had been given up to constitutions and laws, capitalist industry and the bureaucratic state. And it is precisely these forms of liberated human *being* and affective *comradeship* outside law, government, and the state that Whitman embodies in the simultaneously individual and collective working-class poet who steps forth in the 1855 *Leaves of Grass* and sings: "I CELEBRATE MYSELF / And what I assume you shall assume, / For every atom belonging to me as good belongs to you" (*LG* 1855, 25).

In subsequent editions of *Leaves of Grass*, Whitman would continue to "[t]urn back" to France and the Revolutions of 1848 to make himself and his readers "afresh" by linking the political struggle in America with the struggle between liberty and slavery throughout the world. In the 1856 edition of *Leaves of Grass*, Whitman highlighted the continuity of the American and European revolutions by changing the title of "Resurgemus" to "Poem of the Dead Young Men of Europe, the 72d and 73d Years of These States" (later "Europe, the 72d and 73d Years of These States"). In another poem inspired by the Revolutions of 1848, entitled "Liberty Poem for Asia, Africa, Europe, America, Australia, Cuba, and the Archipelagoes of the Sea" (later "To a Foil'd European Revolutionaire"), the poet declares to a more international readership a state of ongoing revolution in defense of liberty against tyranny: "COURAGE! my brother or my sister! / Keep on! Liberty is to be subserved, whatever occurs," Whitman asserted: "What we believe in waits latent forever through Asia, Africa, Europe, America, Australia, Cuba, and all the islands and archipelagoes of the sea" (*LG* 1856, 268).

This international focus of the 1856 *Leaves of Grass* continues in "Poem of Salutation"—entitled "Salut au Monde!" in 1860—which may have been inspired by the French poet and participant in the Revolution of 1848, Pierre-Jean de Béranger, whose *chansons* of liberty and internationalism may have inspired Whitman to conceive of himself as a "singer," and entitle several of his major poems "Songs," including most notably "Song of Myself," in the final edition of *Leaves of Grass.*

In the 1856 edition, as in subsequent editions of *Leaves of Grass*, Whitman makes extensive use of the French language to ally his democratic poetry and vision with French revolutionary tradition. "Poem of the Propositions of Nakedness" (later given the old French title "Respondez") begins with the French command, "RESPONDEZ! Respondez!" as if a phantom from the French Revolution had returned from the dead to demand a response to the searingly "naked" and uncannily prophetic vision of a democratic world in negative that the poem presents: "Let the Asiatic, the African, the European, the American and the Australian, go armed against the murderous stealthiness of each other! Let them sleep armed! Let none believe in goodwill!" (*LG* 1856, 320).

In "Poem of the Road" (later "Song of the Open Road"), Whitman makes use of the French refrain "*Allons!*" to enjoin his global readers and comrades to depart with him on the open road of life: "Allons! After the great companions! and to belong to them! / They too are on the road! they are the swift and majestic men! they are the greatest women!" (*LG* 1856, 233). It is here, too, that Whitman first uses the word *adhesiveness*, a phrenological term he would reaccent to express both the intimacy of homoerotic passion and love and non-state forms of community among friends, cities, states, and nations. "Here is adhesiveness—it is not previously fashioned, it is apropos; / Do you know what it is as you pass to be loved by strangers? / Do you know the talk of those turning eye-balls?" (*LG* 1856, 229). The combination of the term *adhesiveness* with the French term *apropos* is—well—*apropos*: first, because *adhesiveness* blends with *fraternité* and other forms of *solidarité* in Whitman's political poetics; and, second, because Whitman looked to the French as a model of greater physical and sexual openness.

The French Reign of Terror and the American Civil War

The formative presence of France in Whitman's work is particularly evident in the 1860 edition of *Leaves of Grass*, as Whitman sought to come to terms with the impending Civil War and the possible death of democracy in the United States. In 1860 Whitman began to organize his poems into clusters that presage the final ordering of *Leaves of Grass*. Of the five clusters in the 1860 *Leaves of Grass*, two bore French titles: "Chants Democratic and Native American" and "Enfans d'Adam." "Chants Democratic and Native American," the longest cluster, comes directly after "Walt Whitman" (later "Song of Myself") and suggests the connection of his songs with the revolutionary traditions of France. "Enfans d'Adam" celebrates amative love, the body, sexuality, and, perhaps most controversially—women's sexuality and desire: "A WOMAN waits for me—she contains all, nothing is lacking, / Yet all were lacking, if sex were lacking, or if the moisture of the right man were lacking / Sex contains all" (*LG* 1860, 302). A third cluster, "Calamus," is connected to France through its emphasis on comradeship and love and its introduction of the French term *ma femme* to signify democracy and lover in their most ideal form.

By giving "Chants Democratic" and "Enfans d'Adam" French titles, Whitman drew explicit attention to the themes of political *and* sexual revolution he associated with France. Whereas "Chants Democratic" locates the crisis of democracy in America within a broader revolutionary struggle for democracy in France and elsewhere, in "Enfans d'Adam" Whitman resists the tendency of nineteenth-century Americans to associate France and the French language with atheism, anarchy, and immorality by giving his poems on sexual love, or *amativeness*, an emphatically French title. Whitman admired the sexual openness and freedom of the French in allowing what he called a "dash of familiarity, even with strangers, (either sex to either sex)," and—however mistaken—he believed that the French way of life would provide a more open atmosphere for people, "either sex to either sex," to express their love for each other.[3]

On the eve of the Civil War, Whitman appeared to long for an uprising against slavery in America analogous to the blood violence of the French Reign of Terror, as instanced by a notebook entry on his 1860 poem "France, the 18th Year of These States."

> (How will it do for figure?)
> *Get a perfect account of the attack and taking of the Bastille*
>   (fire, blood, smoke, death, shouts, attack, desperation)
>   Symbol of the attack on slavery in These States—
> The masses of the north, stern and muscular
> The enthusiasm not only of these lands, but of all lands
> The determined purpose—death does not stop it—it is filled up by others—
> And their death by others still.— (*NUPM*, 4: 1354, ca. 1857–1858)

Comparing the American to the French Revolution in "Notes Left Over" in *Specimen Days and Collect* (1882), Whitman observed: "The French Revolution was absolutely a strike, and a very terrible and relentless one, against ages of bad pay, unjust division of wealth-products, and the hoggish monopoly of a few, rolling in superfluity, against the bulk of the work-people, living in squalor" (*PW*, 2: 528).

"France, the 18th Year of These States" evokes a nightmare vision of the Reign of Terror, linking the birth of freedom in France with the birth of America. The poem justifies the "terrible red birth and baptism" of the Terror as the just retribution for years of oppression and suffering. Invoking the common cause of liberty and revolution in France and America, Whitman declares:

> O Liberty! O mate for me!
> Here too keeps the blaze, the bullet and the axe, in reserve, to fetch them out in case of need,
> Here too, though long deprest, still is not destroyed,
> Here too could rise at last, murdering and extatic,
> Here too would demand full arrears of vengeance. (*LG* 1860, 407)

In the closing section of the poem, the poet sends a "salute over the sea" to Paris and France.

> And I do not deny that terrible red birth and baptism,
> But remember the little voice that I heard wailing — and wait with
> perfect trust, no matter how long,
> And from to-day, sad and cogent, I maintain the bequeath'd cause, as
> for all lands,
> And I send these words to Paris, with my love. (*LG* 1860, 407)

Representing the reign of terror as a source of both fear and desire—as "battues of death" and "terrible red birth"—Whitman locates the political crisis of democracy in America within a broader transatlantic arc of Franco-American history. Allying himself with Paris in particular as the place where worker uprisings had inspired the Revolutions of 1789, 1793, 1830, 1848, and (later) 1871, Whitman seeks to *revive* the shared Revolutionary traditions of America and France and "the bequeath'd cause" of liberty through the power of song.

"France, the 18th Year of These States" is a justification in advance of the American Civil War that anticipates Whitman's later attempt to come to terms with the butchery and unreason of the Civil War in *Drum-Taps* and Abraham Lincoln's reading of the Civil War as the "long-accrued retribution" for the sin of slavery in America in his Second Inaugural Address (1865). By addressing France as fantasy lover and democratic ideal in the final lines of the poem—"I will yet sing a song for you, ma femme"—Whitman signals a change in his democratic poetics (*LG* 1860, 407). On the eve of the American Civil War in the 1860 *Leaves of Grass*, Whitman is no longer singing an actually existing democracy: he is seeking to bring a democratic world into being through the power of song.

The Paris Commune and Late Whitman

In the dark years of scandal, corruption, and capitalist domination that followed the American Civil War, the one bright spot on Whitman's horizon was France, and especially Paris, where throughout the 1860s there had been a series of popular republican uprisings against the authoritarian State, centralized bureaucracy, and Church power under the empire of Napoleon III. These insurrectionary events played a crucial role in the revision and restructuring of the 1871 edition of *Leaves of Grass*, which was published in September 1870, the same month that Whitman received news of the defeat of Napoleon III and the rise of "Republican forms" in France. Although Whitman regarded the 1871 *Leaves of Grass* as the final edition of his *Leaves* and the beginning of a new phase—"My 'Leaves of Grass' I consider substantially finished," he wrote William Michael Rossetti in England (*COR*, 2: 131–32)—this edition has not received the careful critical attention it deserves.

It is in the 1871 edition that Whitman's *Leaves of Grass* moves toward its final form. The volume begins with a sequence of "Inscriptions," drawn from new poems such as "To Thee Old Cause," in which the poet declares "my book and the war are one," older poems such as "To Foreign Lands," in which the poet offers his poems as an embodiment of the "puzzle" of New World democracy, and substantially revised poems such as "One's-Self I Sing," the opening poem in which Whitman defines the dialectics of individual and community, the "separate person" and the "En-Masse," at the center of the drama of democracy in *Leaves of Grass*:

> ONE'S SELF I sing—a simple, separate Person;
> Yet utter the word Democratic, the word *En-masse*. (*LG* 1871, 7)

Only two lines into the poem that would open and frame all subsequent editions of *Leaves of Grass*, Whitman reveals the French signature of the 1871 *Leaves of Grass*, his democratic vistas, and the increased emphasis on democratic communality, both local and global, in his later work. Speaking of the importance of the word *solidarity* to *Leaves of Grass*, "not Philadelphia alone, Camden alone, even New York alone, but all together," Whitman once said: "it is peculiarly a French word: comes naturally from the French . . . their great purpose is human: their purpose is communication, understanding."[4] As Jacques Darras, the contemporary French poet and translator of Whitman, suggests, *Leaves of Grass* might be read as an attempt to add to the literary and political constitution of democracy the word *fraternité* that was left out of the Declaration of Independence: "Democracy is born from precisely this fraternity which is not in the Declaration of Independence but which should be permanently put into action: take the hand of your neighbor, embrace him, put your arm around his neck, in a Christ-like manner."[5]

Although Whitman used the word *en-masse* as early as the 1855 *Leaves of Grass*—"And mine a word of the modern . . . . a word en masse," he declared in the opening poem (later "Song of Myself," 47)—in linking the term "*En-masse*" with the popular masses, the collectivity, in what may have been the first use of the term *en masse* in the English language, Whitman could have been thinking of the 1793 *Levée en Masse*, the call to the French people *en masse* to defend the "unity of the [French] Republic" and "preach the hatred of kings," issued by the Committee on public safety during the French Revolution. This same language of the *en-masse* as a collective army of the people was being used by Republicans against Napoleon III in France in the 1860s and especially after Napoleon III surrendered to the Prussian army in September 1870.

After the chaos of the 1867 *Leaves of Grass*, which registers materially some of the confusion Whitman felt about the unstaunched wounds of the Civil War, the future of democracy, and the role of the democratic poet, Whitman integrated his *Drum-Taps* poems into the body of *Leaves of Grass* so as to rationalize the war both structurally and thematically as part of a saving national and international vision. "My book and the war are one," the poet declares in his 1871 poem "To Thee Old Cause" in words that suggest the ways the meaning of "the war" is extended in the 1871 *Leaves of Grass* to include a broader democratic struggle for the cause of the people and liberty, past, present and future, in nation and world. This more expansive meaning of the "war," is signified textually by the addition of two new groupings, "Marches Now the War is Over" and "Bathed in Wars Perfumes." In "Turn, O Libertad" and the French farewell of "Adieu to a Soldier," the only new poem in the *Marches* cluster, the poet bids "Adieu" to his comrades of the Civil War and turns toward what he calls "fiercer, weightier battles," for democracy in the United States and worldwide.

To keep alive the spirit of revolutionary struggle against what Whitman called the "overweening" power of the nation-state and "the more and more insidious grip of capital," he added a more radical grouping to the 1871 *Leaves* entitled "Songs of Insurrection."

This theme is announced in the opening poem, "Still Though the One I Sing," the only new poem in the cluster:

> STILL though the one I sing,
> (One, yet of contradictions made,) I dedicate to Nationality,
> I leave in him Revolt, (O latent right of insurrection! O quenchless,
> indispensable fire!) (*LG* 1871, 363)

While this cluster appears to be inspired by social conditions in post–Civil War America, it is also addressed to the ongoing scene of republican insurrection in Europe, especially against Napoleon III in France.

This French inscription of "Songs of Insurrection" is evidenced by the fact that of the six poems in the new cluster, the three longest focus on the revolutions in France in 1792–1793, 1848, and 1870. "France, the 18th Year of These States" focuses on the French Reign of Terror; "Europe" focuses on the Revolutions of 1848, especially in France; and "To a Foil'd European Revolutionaire," which focused on the struggle over slavery and bore the more generic title "To a Foiled Revolter or Revoltress" in the 1860 and 1867 editions, is given a French inflection, redirected to European revolutionaries, and heavily revised to link the "war" for democracy in America with the ongoing scene of revolution in France and Europe.

The lines that Whitman added to "To a Foil'd European Revolutionaire" in the 1871 *Leaves of Grass* are almost hysterical as the poet affirms his identification with revolutionaries throughout the world. "Revolt! and still revolt! revolt!" the poet cries, and then adds parenthetically:

> (Not songs of loyalty alone are these,
> But songs of insurrection also;
> For I am the sworn poet of every dauntless rebel, the world over,
> And he going with me leaves peace and routine behind him,
> And stakes his life, to be lost at any moment.) (*LG* 1871, 364)

This ongoing scene of revolution in France also affirms the utopian vision and global reach of "Years of the Modern," which envisions the American Civil War as part of a broader movement toward the racial solidarity and communion of nations in the struggle for democracy: "I see not America only—I see not only Liberty's nation, but other nations preparing, / I see tremendous entrances and exits—I see combinations—I see the solidarity of the races; / I see that force advancing with irresistible power on the world's stage; / . . . / Are all nations communing? is there going to be but one heart to the globe? / Is humanity forming, en-masse?" the poet asks.[6] Originally included in *Drum-Taps* (1865) under the title "Years of the Unperformed," Whitman changed the title to "Years of the Modern," a textual revision that appears to translate his poetic vision into insurrectionary history with the popular uprisings in France between 1868 and 1871. "Years of the Modern" was published in "Songs of Parting," a new cluster of poems that would conclude the 1871 and final 1881 editions of *Leaves of Grass*.

Although the title page bears the date 1871, this edition of *Leaves of Grass* was, in fact, published in September 1870, the same month that Napoleon III was captured by the Germans. Five months later, Whitman's call for "Revolt! and still revolt, revolt!" would be answered with the overthrow of Napoleon III, the declaration of a Third Republic, the siege of Paris, the defeat

FIGURE 16. Bruno Braquehais, postcard with his photograph of *Voltaire Lenoir Barricade of the Paris Commune*, 1871. In his 1871 elegy, "O Star of France!," Whitman mourned the bloody defeat of the Paris Commune as the simultaneously "crucified" and "sacred" star and symbol of his hopes for the future of democracy worldwide. Courtesy of the Musée de l'Histoire Vivante, Montreuil, France.

of France by the Germans, a worker insurrection in Paris, the formation of the Paris Commune between March and May 1871, and its bloody suppression during what has come to be known as *la Semaine Sanglante*, the Bloody Week. This uprising of the Paris communards has been described by modern historians as "the biggest popular insurrection in modern European history" and the epitome of "'revolution' as a spontaneous popular act" (Figure 16). In the words of Marxist historian David Harvey, the Commune was "the greatest class-based communal uprising in capitalist history." It was also the last of the major uprisings that spread from Paris as "a collective sovereign" that decided the fate of the French nation in 1789, 1792, 1830, and 1871.[7]

Despite their bloody suppression and defeat, the worker uprisings that led to the formation of the Paris Commune in the spring of 1871—known among the French as *le Temps des Cerises*, the Time of Cherries—also played a shaping role in Whitman's plans for a new volume of poems centered around what he called "Democratic Nationality" in his 1872 preface to *As a Strong Bird on Pinions Free*. In his magnificent elegy, "O Star of France!," which was published in the New York *Galaxy* in June 1871, shortly after news of *la Semaine Sanglante* reached the United States, Whitman mourns the defeat of the Paris commune at the same time that he invokes France as the simultaneously "crucified" and "sacred" star and symbol of his hopes for the future of democracy worldwide:

> Dim, smitten star!
> Orb not of France alone—pale symbol of my soul, its dearest hopes.
> The struggle and the daring—rage divine for liberty,
> Of aspirations toward the far ideal—enthusiast's dreams of
> brotherhood,
> Of terror to the tyrant and the priest.[8]

In 1872 Whitman published "O Star of France!" in *As a Strong Bird on Pinions Free and Other Poems*, a new volume of seven poems focused on themes of democratic and spiritual union. The role that the insurrection of workers and the formation of the Paris Commune may have played in inspiring a new direction—and democratic faith—in Whitman's later work is suggested by the fact that it was in the preface to *As a Strong Bird on Pinions Free* that Whitman first announced his intent to turn away from the "song of a great composite Democratic Individual, male or female" in *Leaves of Grass* toward a new volume of poems focused on democratic communality, or what he called "an aggregated, inseparable, unprecedented, vast composite, electric Democratic Nationality" (*LGC*, 746). Although critics have tended to read this as a reference to the nation-state, what he means by "Democratic Nationality" appears to reference the forms of affective union and comradeship—or *fraternité*—among individuals, cities, states, and nations that exist outside the official structures of law, constitutions, and government.

Although Whitman suffered a paralytic stroke in 1873 that made it impossible for him to write a new volume of poems focused on "Democratic Nationality" at a time when he, like Karl Marx, was wrestling with what he called "the immense problem" of "Labor" and "Capital" looming over the United States and threatening "to overshadow all" (*PW*, 2: 753), it is once again in France rather than in Gilded Age America that he finds the "symbol" of his "dearest hopes" for democracy and the dream of "brotherhood" in the future and worldwide.

But Whitman's embrace of France did not end with his poem "O Star of France!" in 1871. In 1881, when he was in Boston giving his annual Lincoln lecture, all his comradely identification with the French people was reawakened when he saw an exhibit of paintings by the French painter Jean-François Millet. He was especially moved by *The Sower*, a pictorial tribute to the regenerative power of labor painted shortly after the Revolutions of 1848 (Figure 14). "I stood long and long before 'the Sower,'" Whitman wrote. "Never before have I been so penetrated by this kind of expression . . . To me [it] told the full story of what . . . necessitated the great French revolution—the long precedent crushing of the masses of a heroic people . . . every right denied . . . yet Nature's force, titanic here . . . and the bursting at last—the storming of the Bastil[l]e . . . the tempest of massacres and blood. Yet who can wonder" (*PW*, 1: 267–68; ellipses mine). "The Leaves are really only Millet in another form—," he would later tell Horace Traubel in 1888; "they are the Millet that Walt Whitman has succeeded in putting into words."[9]

Here as elsewhere toward the close of his life Whitman would continue to affirm the revolutionary alliance and indeed the familial relation between America and France: "(We grand-sons and great-grand sons do not forget your grand-sires)," Whitman wrote in "Bravo, Paris Exposition!" in a final *salut* and declaration of love for France on the occasion of the Paris Exposition of 1889, which featured the exhibition of the Eiffel Tower: "Add to your show, before you close it, France," he wrote, "America's applause, love, memories and good-will" (*LGC*, 544–45).

And France, or at least later French writers, would return the favor not only in absorbing Whitman as one of their own—"Whitman nous est parent," Philéas Lebesgue would write of Whitman and modern French poetry in 1911—but also in producing the champagne that would ease the final years of Whitman's life.[10] Shortly before his death in 1892, Whitman would find literal French comfort in belly and head as he drank the champagne that eased and soothed his aching and aging body. As Whitman wrote in one of his last poems, "Champagne in Ice" (ca. 1891–1892):

> No use to argue temperance, abstinence only,
> I've had a bad spell 40 hours, continuous
> 'Till now a heavy bottle of good champagne wine in my thirst,
> Cold and tart-sweet drink'd from a big white mug half fill'd with ice,
> It is started me in stomach and in head,
> As I slowly drink, thanking my friend,
> Feeling the day, and in myself, freedom and joy. (*LGC*, 684–85)

As Whitman's decision to make poets rather than politicians the ambassadors of the democratic future in *Democratic Vistas* suggests, despite the failure of political leadership and vision at the top, the shared traditions and connections between Whitman and the French, France and America, have been kept alive through the power of artistic exchange and song.

PART FOUR

DEMOCRATIC VISTAS

CHAPTER EIGHT

Whitman, Melville, and the Tribulations of Democracy

The very hill made sacred by the blood of freedom's earliest martyrs, is sold and trafficked for.

—Walt Whitman, New York *Aurora* (1842)

But the Declaration of Independence makes a difference.

—Herman Melville to Evert Duyckinck (1849)

Walt Whitman and Herman Melville were both born in the state of New York in 1819, within two months of each other. In the year of their birth, the United States was entering the first of the periodic depressions that would characterize the modern industrial world. In the same year, James Tallmadge Jr., a representative from New York, introduced an amendment to prohibit the extension of slavery into Missouri and to provide for the emancipation of those slaves who were already there. Although the immediate issue of slavery in Missouri was resolved by the Missouri Compromise of 1820, which admitted Missouri as a slave state but prohibited slavery in the remainder of the Louisiana territory "forever," the debate over the Tallmadge amendment provoked a conflict between North and South so bitter and far-reaching that even Thomas Jefferson was led to predict disaster for the American republic: "All, I fear, do not see the speck in our horizon which is to burst on us as a tornado, sooner or later. The line of division lately marked out between different portions of our confederacy, is such as will never, I fear, be obliterated."[1] The conflict between North and South was intensified by the conflict between rich and poor, capital and labor, brought by the Panic of 1819. Emerging in the year that Whitman and Melville were born, these signs of division on the horizon of the American republic would become sources of major political struggle in the lives and works of both writers and in the ensuing conflict over the very meaning of democracy not only in the Americas but throughout the world.

A Revolutionary Formation

Melville and Whitman came of age during the 1830s, a decade of intensified conflict and crisis over the revolutionary ideals of the founding and the American "experiment" in democracy. As the man who named the era before the Civil War, Andrew Jackson rose to power as a military hero who had defeated the Creek Indians and won the Battle of New Orleans against the British in the War of 1812. Jackson was elected president in 1828 on a Democratic platform that emphasized "the people," democracy, states' rights, free enterprise, and expansion westward. And yet, for all Jackson's rhetoric of equality and the common man, as later historians have demonstrated, the Age of Jackson led to an increase rather than a close in the gap between labor and capital, an Indian Removal Act that displaced or sought to destroy Native peoples, and an ideological commitment to America as a *white male* republic based on patriarchal paternalism and theories of innate racial and sexual difference.

As mariner and renegade ship worker and as journalist and Democratic party radical, Melville and Whitman were both raised on the Revolutionary ideals of the founding. Melville's paternal grandfather, Thomas Melville, was a member of the Boston Tea Party, and his maternal grandfather, General Peter Gansevoort, had successfully defended Fort Stanwix against British and Indian attack during the Revolution. Although Melville's father, Allan Melville, allied himself with Federalism and the business classes against what he called the "scurvy and ungrateful" masses,[2] his uncle Peter Gansevoort was elected to the state legislature as a Jacksonian Democrat in 1829, and in 1844 his oldest brother, Gansevoort, stumped throughout the west for Democratic presidential candidate James Polk on a platform of western expansion and Texas annexation.

Whitman's family had similarly deep roots in the Revolution and democratic party in the Age of Jackson. "They all espoused with ardor the side of the 'rebellion' in 76," Whitman said of his father's side of the family (*NUPM*, 1: 6). In his daybooks, Whitman recorded instances of patriotism and heroism on both the maternal and paternal sides of his family during the British occupation of Long Island.[3] Whitman's father, Walter Whitman Sr., was a free thinker and a radical Thomas Paine democrat who subscribed to the *Free*

Enquirer, edited by the socialists Frances Wright and Robert Dale Owen, who sought through the rhetoric of a "war of class" to unite the grievances of New York City workers in an anticapitalist and anticlerical platform.[4]

Although Melville came from a patrician and Whitman from a working-class family, both families suffered losses as the result of an increasingly volatile capitalist marketplace. Melville's father lost his import business in 1827 through overinvestment and died suddenly in 1832 depressed and half-mad. During the severe economic panic of 1837, which lasted for seven long years, Melville's brother Gansevoort suffered financial losses that reduced the entire family to genteel poverty. As a carpenter, Whitman's father mortgaged house after house as the Whitman family moved from country to city and back again in search of work. As a result, neither Whitman nor Melville had much formal schooling beyond their early years. Like whaling for Ishmael, journalism and politics for Whitman and the life of a seaman and adventurer for Melville became their Harvard and their Yale.

Whitman learned his politics as a journalist and editor in the bustling and rumble-tumble world of New York party politics; Melville learned his as a common sailor on merchant ships and whalers bound for the Pacific, where the democratic mixture of races and classes among ordinary sailors starkly contrasted with the authoritarian and rigidly hierarchical structures of life aboard ship in the nineteenth century. Although Whitman and Melville both retreated from some of the more radical political movements of the time—including Abolition and Reconstruction—at their most utopian they were also the most visionary and democratic of nineteenth-century canonical writers. For both, democracy was at once a national, global, and family affair. But while they were raised on similar Revolutionary traditions and shared a similarly utopian ideal of democracy grounded in homoerotic comradeship, labor, and love, they are also representative of the contradictory, antithetical, and at times conservative and at other times radically alternative views of democracy that marked the political crisis of the nation before, during, and after the Civil War.

Body Politics

Whitman and Melville began their literary careers as popular writers. Like "The Child's Champion" (1841), Whitman's popular temperance novel, *Franklin Evans; or The Inebriate: Tale of the Times* (1842), was published by the *New World*, a mass-circulation newspaper. Written "*for the mass*," not "for the critics but for THE PEOPLE," and framed by the language of sentimentalism and "Temperance Reform," *Franklin Evans* seeks to teach the value of a "prudent, sober, and temperate course of life" as part of a broader movement of national republican regeneration (*EPF*, 127, 128). And yet, as Michael Moon and Michael Warner have argued, in Whitman's early temperance tales, the rhetoric of temperance reform functions as a fluid medium for voicing, at the same time that it condemns, a seductive urban underworld of male desire, pleasure, cruising, dissipation, same-sex eroticism, fluid identities, and border crossing that erode the illusory boundaries of class and identity, sex and blood.[5]

Melville's popular novel *Typee: A Peep at Polynesian Life* (1846) gives voice to a similarly potent intermingling of sex and democracy, bodily desire and fear. Both narratives suggest the fear of the excesses of the unruly body—the wayward and perverse passions and impulses—that lay just beneath the strident political rhetorics of liberty and equality during the Jacksonian era. The massive social and reformist zeal to control the excesses of the "savage" and unruly body during the Age of Jackson is reflected not only in the campaigns against the Indians, but in the appeals to self-mastery and social control that underwrote the male purity movement, the antimasturbation tracts, the temperance movement, the public education movement, and Protestant missions to such places as the South Pacific and the Hawaiian Islands.

Whereas Whitman made use of the temperance genre and the languages of personal and national regeneration to give voice to erotically charged fantasies of bodily excess and dissipation among men, Melville transformed the travel adventure narrative into an X-rated story of the Typee Valley as a realm of pure freedom and bodily pleasure that satirizes the political and religious pieties of the Age of Jackson. Beginning with the narrator's revolt against the arbitrary authority of a tyrannical ship captain, *Typee* is full of erotic images of naked and sexually inviting women, sparsely clad Native men who drink, smoke, and commune with each other at the Ti, a place that the narrator calls "a sort of Bachelor's Hall," and a sensuous rhythm of life organized by the pleasures and desires of the body rather than the "civilized" virtues of labor, capital, religion, marriage, family, laws, and government (*MT*, 157).

If Whitman's *Franklin Evans* is an urban fantasy of erotic abandon among men that masquerades as a Jacksonian temperance tract, *Typee* is a Rousseauesque fantasy of pure sex and pure democracy—of "freedom from all restraint," "equality of condition," and "fraternal feeling" among the Typee islanders (*MT*, 185, 203)—that doubles as a trenchant political critique of the failures of democracy not only in America but worldwide. Linking the extermination of the Indigenous inhabitants of North America with the future of "disease, vice, and premature death" that awaits the Typee Natives when Christian missionaries arrive within the next "few years" to "civilize" them, the narrator complains: "The Anglo-Saxon hive have extirpated Paganism from the greater part of the North American continent; but with it they have likewise extirpated the greater portion of the Red race. Civilization is gradually sweeping from the earth the lingering vestiges of Paganism, and at the same time the shrinking forms of its unhappy worshippers" (*MT*, 195).

Unlike Melville, whose experiences in England, the South Pacific, and South America enabled him to see firsthand the dehumanizing global effects of the spread of capitalist industrialism and European and American imperialism, Whitman was more sanguine in his vision of westward expansion as part of a universal democratic advance toward liberation from the tyrannical orders of the past. Embracing the notions of "manifest destiny" set forth in the July 1845 issue of John O'Sullivan's *Democratic Review*, Whitman looked upon "the boundless democratic free west!" as the ultimate site of America's democratic experiment and a means of resolving the increasing conflict between labor and capital in the cities of the East (*WJ*, 2: 237). As editor of the Brooklyn *Daily Eagle*, Whitman—unlike Melville, but like Melville's brother Gansevoort—supported the expansionist politics of Polk, which resulted in the annexation of Texas in 1845, the acquisition of Oregon in 1846, and an illegal "executive" war in Mexico in 1846–1847.

Slavery and the Compromise of 1850

"But seriously something great is impending," Melville wrote in an 1846 letter to his brother Gansevoort, describing the Mexican war as "a little spark" that would kindle "a great fire." Envisioning the specter of mass carnage and a second American Revolution, "when the Battle of Monmouth will be thought child's play" (*MC*, 41), Melville's words proved prophetic. The debate over the extension of slavery into the territories acquired by the United States through the conquest of Mexico led to a political crisis and breakdown as the linked issues of race, class, gender, labor, industry, capitalist expansion, and war exposed major contradictions in the ideology of the American republic. These contradictions and the ensuing struggle over the legitimacy of the Constitution and the meaning of American democracy culminated in a Civil War not only between individual, state, and national government but also between brother and brother, sister and sister, on the common ground of the American republic itself.

A few weeks after the Treaty of Guadalupe Hidalgo was signed with Mexico on February 2, 1848, a Revolutionary uprising of workers and students in Paris resulted in the abdication of King Louis Philippe, the declaration of a second French republic, and the spread of the revolution throughout Europe. These 1848 revolutions combined with the ongoing political struggle over freedom and slavery in the United States to intensify the more global dimensions and aspirations of the American 1848. Although the American 1848 did not manifest itself in an immediate act of violence against the state, this revolution would be deferred until 1861, when it erupted into a scene of mass carnage and internecine Civil War more bloody than any before in history.

Under Whitman's editorship, the Brooklyn *Daily Eagle* was the first of the New York dailies to support Congressman David Wilmot's 1846 proposal that slavery be forbidden in any new territory acquired by the United States. "Set Down Your Feet, Democrats!" Whitman declared in the December 21, 1846, issue: "let the Democratic members of Congress, (and Whigs too, if they like,) plant themselves . . . fixedly and without compromise, on the requirement that *Slavery be prohibited in them forever*" (*WJ*, 2: 153; ellipsis mine). At a time when wage labor was becoming a new form of slavery, Whitman's antislavery editorials bear the traces of labor movement radicalism in stressing the danger of the slave system to the rights and dignity of all laborers. In "American Workingmen, versus Slavery," he called upon workers to defend their rights so "that their calling shall *not* be sunk to the miserable level of what is little above brutishness—sunk to be like owned goods, and driven cattle!" (*WJ*, 2: 319).

The political crisis over labor and slavery in America and Europe marked a turning point in the life and work of Melville and Whitman, as each began to experiment with a variety of literary voices, modes, and forms as a prelude to writing what would become *Moby-Dick* (1851) and *Leaves of Grass* (1855). By the summer of 1849, when the Barnburners returned to the Democratic party fold, Whitman began to move away from journalism and party politics toward poetry and oratory as the most effective means of reaching and radicalizing the American people in the democratic ideals of the founding. As the talk of secession mounted, Henry Clay of Kentucky introduced into the Senate a series of compromise resolutions, proposing the admission of California as a free state, a stricter Fugitive Slave Law, the extension of slavery into the new territory, and a prohibition of congressional interference with the interstate slave trade. The willingness of the Democratic party, the North, and especially Daniel Webster to support this 1850 Compromise on the issue of slavery sent Whitman literally raging into verse.

Whitman's first free-verse poems, "Blood Money," "The House of Friends," and "Resurgemus," which were published in 1850, emerged out of the political passions aroused by slavery, free soil, and the European revolutions. Like "Blood Money" and "The House of Friends," Whitman's celebration of the ultimate triumph of liberty in "Resurgemus" breaks the pentameter and turns on the images of slavery and freedom. "Not a grave of those slaughtered ones, / But is growing its seed of freedom," Whitman wrote, linking the democratic struggle for freedom with the fluid, eternal processes of nature (*EPF*, 39). In an early notebook, dated 1847 but probably written in 1854, Whitman also began to experiment with the idea of using poetry as a form of political action. When in his notebook Whitman broke into lines approximating the free verse of *Leaves of Grass*, the lines bear the impress of the slavery issue:

> I am the poet of slaves, and of the masters of slaves
> I am the poet of the body
> And I am (*NUPM*, 1: 67)

The lines join or translate within the representative figure of the poet the conflicting terms of master and slave that threaten to split the Union. And yet, even in these trial lines, the poet's grammar of democratic union appears to be short-circuited, like the political union itself, by the fact of an economy of masters and slaves within the body of the republic.

Although Melville's novel *Mardi and a Voyage Thither* (1849) began as another sea narrative in the popular mode of *Typee* and *Omoo*, following the Revolutions of 1848, and perhaps under the influence of the democratic and nationalist aspirations of the Young America movement and the example of his own family's active involvement in the American Revolution and the political crisis of the time, Melville transformed his "adventures in the Pacific" into an experimental quest narrative that anticipates the multilayered symbolics of *Moby-Dick* and his later works in its mixture of voices, modes, and perspectives—satirical and metaphysical, American and global, historical and literary, political and self-reflexively aesthetic. Melville's declaration of imaginative independence also freed him to become a romancer of contemporary politics by incorporating into *Mardi*, which was dedicated to his brother Allan, an extensive political allegory on the Revolutions of 1848 and the crisis of democracy in America and Europe.

The failure of *Mardi* to sell forced Melville to return to his semiautobiographical sea narratives in his next two novels, *Redburn: His First Voyage* (1849) and *White-Jacket; or, The World in a Man-of-War* (1850). Although he regarded writing these books as forms of "forced" labor "done for money" (*MC*, 138), he continued to experiment with ways of conjoining a saleable adventure story with his desire to speak truth about the world, including the world of contemporary politics and the bonds of affection between men. "But the Declaration of Independence makes a difference," he wrote his friend Evert Duyckinck in the spring of 1849, associating the Declaration not only with political rights and a break from England but with imaginative and bodily freedom—a break away from the "muzzle" that "intercepted Shakespeare's full articulations" and the fear of democratic sociality and the body ("belly") that prevents Emerson from "munching a plain cake in company of jolly fellows, & swiging off his ale like you & me" (*MC*, 122).

Redburn, which Melville dedicated to his brother Thomas, gives voice to an affirming vision of democracy, commerce, and world union that echoes the Jacksonian politics of the Melville family, at the same time that it reveals the intertwined rhetorics of democratic idealism and capitalist imperialism that have marked and continue to mark the domestic and foreign policies of the United States. In *White-Jacket* the ideals of democracy and the bonds of affection between men are set against the feudal practice of flogging in the American Navy as a violation of the "broad principles of political liberty and equality" set forth in the Declaration of Independence and the Constitution (*MWJ*, 144). For the common sailor, "stripped like a slave" and "scourged worse than a hound" for "all degrees of transgression" in accord with the Navy's *Articles of War*, says the protagonist White Jacket, "our Revolution was in vain; to him our Declaration of Independence is a lie" (*MWJ*, 138, 139, 144). Although *White-Jacket* focuses on the humiliating and life-scarring practice of flogging aboard a "Man-of-War," at a time when the struggle over slavery in the United States was threatening to rend the Union, the whip also serves as a politically charged symbol, not only of slavery, but of all forms of arbitrary authority that oppress sailors, slaves, laborers, women, colonials, the body, and—perhaps most significantly for Melville and Whitman—men who love men.

White-Jacket comes closer to advocating revolution than any other novel that Melville wrote. Citing Blackstone and Justinian in support of the higher "Law of Nature," White Jacket asserts: "Every American man-of-war's-man would be morally justified in resisting the scourge to the uttermost; and, in so resisting, would be religiously justified in what would be judicially styled 'the act of mutiny' itself" (*MWJ*, 145). When White Jacket is himself about to be unjustly flogged by Captain Claret, he feels an instinct to rebel against "an insulted and unendurable" existence by killing both the captain and himself—a murder and suicide that are only averted by the intervention of two of the crew members on his behalf.

In the end, the isolation and loneliness of the individual are overcome by the comradeship White Jacket finds with Jack Chase and other main-top-men, a comradeship that White Jacket associates with the Christian and democratic millennium of world peace and justice: "We main-top-men are all aloft in the top; and round our mast we circle, a brother-band, hand in hand, all spliced together" (*MWJ*, 396). But while this "brother-band" resists the structures of bodily and sexual discipline signified by the captain's determination to shave their beards and hair—an attack on their very "manhood," Jack Chase proclaims—in the end they all "succumb" (*MWJ*, 361, 360). Perhaps afraid to offend his readers with a novel that appears to affirm the right of revolution and an alternative social order grounded in communality and love between men, Melville, too, succumbs in the end by having his narrator assert that salvation is individual rather than collective. "Whatever befall us," White Jacket urges at the end of the novel, "let us never train our murderous guns inboard; let us not mutiny with bloody pikes in our hands" (*MWJ*, 400). Rather than righting "unredressed" wrongs through collectivity and resistance, the man-of-war world must await the interposition of God as "Our Lord High Admiral" (*MWJ*, 400). Whereas Whitman's political poems of 1850 urge resistance to slavery and the Fugitive Slave Law in the United States and resistance to all forms of tyranny and enslavement throughout the world, even in his most radical novel Melville appears to support the Democratic politics of his family in urging patience and compromise on the issues of both slavery and resistance in order to preserve the authority of law against "an unbounded insurrection" he appears to fear in both body and body politic (*MWJ*, 359).

Epics of Democracy

"Whitman rode through the years undisturbed by such deep and bitter truths as Melville had found," F. O. Matthiessen asserted in his influential study *American Renaissance: Art and Expression in the Age of Emerson and Whitman* (179). And yet, in the early 1850s when Melville and Whitman turned toward the work of writing their prose and poetic epics of American democracy, both shared an essentially tragic vision of the slave system as a trope for America itself, the sign of a culture of abundance propelled not by the revolutionary dream of freedom but by the economics of market capitalism. The scholarly emphasis on the essential difference between Melville and Whitman has kept us from recognizing the similarly democratic and dystopian impulses out of which their work emerged, and the ways their imaginative writings overlap and intersect in their struggle to come to terms with the political and economic tribulations of democracy in the mid-nineteenth century.

"While we are rapidly preparing for that political supremacy among nations, which prophetically awaits us at the close of the present century; in a literary point of view, we are deplorably unprepared for it," Melville complained in an 1850 review of Nathaniel Hawthorne that reveals his own aspiration to become "the literary Shiloh of America" (*PTP*, 248, 252). Melville calls on Americans "to carry republican progressiveness into Literature, as well as into Life," in words that echo the nationalist rhetoric of the Young American movement that he shared with Whitman (*PTP*, 245). "The Americans of all nations at any time upon the earth have probably the fullest poetical nature," Whitman declared in the 1855 preface to *Leaves of Grass*. "Here are the roughs and beards and space and ruggedness and nonchalance that the soul loves" (*LG* 1855, 5).

Melville's effort to become part of what he called the "shared" literary "fullness and overflowing" of his times was hindered by his experience of genteel poverty and enslavement to the capitalist marketplace. "Dollars damn me," he confessed to Hawthorne while he was completing *Moby-Dick*. "What I feel most moved to write, that is banned,—it will not pay. Yet, altogether, write the *other* way I cannot" (*MC*, 191). In *Moby-Dick; or, The Whale* (1851), Melville seeks to straddle the contradiction between capitalist marketplace and democratic art by conjoining the popularity of *Typee* with the experimental poetics of *Mardi*. Like the voyage of the *Pequod*, *Moby-Dick* is propelled by a double impulse: it is both whaling adventure and metaphysical quest, epic of democracy and work of high art.

The narrative fluidity of *Moby-Dick*, the ways the first-person narrator floats in and out of view, sometimes surfacing as the voice of Ishmael and sometimes submerged in the voice of an apparently omniscient narrator, creates a doubleness of perspective and an ironic inflection that counters the more specifically nationalist, democratic, and affirming dimensions of the narrative. In the "Knights and Squires" chapters of the book (chapters 26 and 27), for example, Ishmael appears to give voice to Melville's defense of whaling and the whaleman as the "aesthetically noble" subject of his democratic epic: "But this august dignity I treat of, is not the dignity of kings and robes, but that abounding dignity which has no robed investiture. Thou shalt see it shining in the arm that wields a pick or drives a spike; that democratic dignity which, on all hands, radiates without end from God. . . . The centre and circumference of all democracy! His omnipresence, our divine equality!" (*MD*, 117; ellipsis mine). On the nether side of Ishmael's voice, however, looms a less sanguine and more critical omniscient narrator who appears to undermine and ironize the contemporary rhetorics of Jacksonian democracy, labor radicalism, millennial Christianity, literary nationalism, and global revolution that the passage exudes.

Ishmael's democratic excess and its potentially ironic inflection are particularly evident in his subsequent epic invocation to the "great democratic God":

> If, then, to meanest mariners, and renegades and castaways, I shall hereafter ascribe high qualities, though dark; weave round them tragic graces . . . if I shall touch that work-man's arm with some ethereal light . . . then against all mortal critics bear me out in it, thou just Spirit of Equality, which hast spread one royal mantle of humanity over all my kind! Bear me out in it, thou great democratic God . . . Thou who didst pick up Andrew Jackson from the pebbles; who didst hurl him upon a war-horse; who didst thunder him higher than a throne! (*MD*, 117; ellipses mine)

Ishmael invokes the "just Spirit of Equality" in support of a democratic poetics that weaves "tragic graces" around workers and renegades and celebrates the myth of democratic possibility represented by Andrew Jackson's rise from commoner, to warrior, to president. But the passage also reveals a problem with the imperial will unleashed by democracy. If Jackson came to power by defeating the British at New Orleans, his heroism was also grounded in a policy of war, violence, and subjugation of Native Americans. Hurled "higher than a throne" by a democratic God whose own acts seem less "just" than warlike and imperial, the figure of Jackson suggests that the problem with democracy may lie inside rather than outside democratic ideology itself: the unencumbered self at the heart of liberal democratic theory leads not to liberation but enslavement, the subjection of the many to the totalitarian will of the one—as signified by the imperial rise of Napoleon Bonaparte in Europe and Andrew Jackson as new monarch in America. Or, as Ishmael's invocation to democracy appears to forewarn, Ahab as totalitarian master/monster aboard the *Pequod*.

As a fictional embodiment of the best and the worst in liberal democratic ideology, Ahab is at once a heroic and a tragic figure. "Who's over me?" he declares, in his Promethean quest to conquer evil and find out the meaning of the universe (*MD*, 164). Although Ahab has his "humanities"—he sees the values of home and hearth in Starbuck's eyes, and he takes hold of Pip's hand in an act of sympathetic identification with the outcast slave—he ends by destroying not only the ship of America as ship of the world but the very possibility of liberal freedom represented by its global and multiracial crew of "mariners, and renegades and castaways."

As the symbolism of the doubloon as "naval" of the *Pequod* suggests, for Melville as for Karl Marx, the logic of democracy is inextricably bound up with the imperial logic of capital. The specter of imperial capital that haunts the revolutionary dream of freedom in *Moby-Dick* receives its fullest articulation in "Fast-Fish and Loose-Fish," a chapter in which Ishmael's description of the two laws that govern the American whaling industry—"A Fast-Fish belongs to the party fast to it" and "A Loose-Fish is fair game for anybody who can soonest catch it"—leads to a reflection on *the law of possession* as fundamental to "all human jurisprudence." "What are the sinews and souls of Russian serfs and Republican slaves but Fast-Fish, whereof possession is the whole of the law?" Ishmael asks at the outset of what is, in effect, Melville's most sustained critique of a contemporary political world in which slaves, widows, waifs, starving families, "hundreds of thousands of broken-backed laborers," "poor Ireland," and "Texas" are no more than "Fast-Fish" within a capitalist order of "Possession" (*MD*, 397–98).

Turning to the "kindred" but more "internationally and universally applicable" "doctrine of Loose-Fish," Ishmael concludes by locating the rise of the American republic and the "Rights of Man" within a more global economy of imperialist *possession*:

> What was America in 1492 but a Loose-Fish . . . ? What was Poland to the Czar? What Greece to the Turk? What India to England? What at last will Mexico be to the United States? All Loose-Fish?
>
> What are the Rights of Man and the Liberties of the World but Loose-Fish? What all men's minds and opinions but Loose-Fish? . . . What is the great globe itself but a Loose-Fish? And what are you, reader, but a Loose-Fish and a Fast-Fish, too? (*MD*, 398)

Without any mediating forms of social community, attachment, or love, the autonomous individuals liberated and empowered by Lockean theory and the Revolutionary enlightenment become symbolic Ishmaels—orphans and outcasts of a universe whose rights, liberties, and very thoughts are both "Loose-

Fish" and "Fast-Fish, too" within a global order of capitalist and imperial dominance in which "Possession" is "the whole of the law" (*MD*, 397).

This grim reading of the imperial logic of unleashed individualism is set against the promise of democratic community bodied forth in the interracial, cross-cultural, and same-sex "marriage" of Ishmael and Queequeg and the utopian vision of erotic comradeship in "A Squeeze of the Hand." In this chapter the "business" of sperm squeezing merges into a fantasy of baptismal deliverance as Ishmael imagines crew members squeezing sperm and each other in communal and masturbatory acts of labor and love:

> Squeeze! squeeze! squeeze! all the morning long; I squeezed that sperm till I myself almost melted into it; I squeezed that sperm till a strange sort of insanity came over me; and I found myself unwittingly squeezing my co-laborers' hands in it, mistaking their hands for the gentle globules. Such an abounding, affectionate, friendly, loving feeling did this avocation beget. (*MD*, 416)

Like the similarly masturbatory fantasy at the center of Whitman's "Song of Myself," the sexually fluid and masturbatory image of men merging and coming together—"let us all squeeze ourselves into each other; let us squeeze ourselves universally into the very milk and sperm of kindness"—is at the very center of Melville's vision of social community and the possibility of democracy in *Moby-Dick* (*MD*, 416).

"Would that I could keep squeezing that sperm for ever!" Ishmael exclaims in a passage that sets the "attainable felicity" of domestic life and wife against the fantasy of squeezing sperm "eternally":

> I have perceived that in all cases man must eventually lower, or at least shift, his conceit of attainable felicity; not placing it anywhere in the intellect or the fancy; but in the wife, the heart, the bed, the table, the saddle, the fire-side, the country; *now that I have perceived all this*, I am ready to squeeze case eternally. In thoughts of the visions of the night, I saw long rows of angels in paradise, each with his hands in a jar of spermaceti. (*MD*, 416; my italics)

Although this passage is usually read as a scene of renunciation in which Ishmael—and implicitly Melville—gives up his love for men in favor of the safer normative life of the shore, as my italicization suggests, the passage appears to say just the opposite: *Now* that Ishmael has "perceived" the social need to "lower, or at least shift" his erotic desire from man to woman, fantasy to reality, open sea to domestic shore, *now* that he has *perceived all this*, he is even more "ready" to "keep squeezing that sperm for ever" in loving union with his co-laborers and fellow seamen—with the pun on *semen* obviously intended!

As "A Squeeze of the Hand" suggests, at his most democratic and utopian, Melville sounds uncannily like Whitman. In fact, Ishmael's sentimental fantasy of workers "universally" squeezing "hands all around" in "the very milk and sperm of kindness" anticipates Whitman's baptismal vision of naked sleepers flowing "hand in hand over the whole earth from east to west as they lie unclothed" in "The Sleepers" (*LG* 1855, 114). And yet here, as elsewhere in Melville's work, dreams of erotic comradeship are always momentary rather than enduring. "This 'all' feeling, though, there is some truth in it," Melville wrote Hawthorne in one of his most Whitmanian passages: "You must often have felt it, lying on the grass on a warm summer's day. Your legs seem to send out shoots into the earth. Your hair feels like leaves upon your head. This is the *all* feeling. But what plays the mischief with the truth is that men will insist upon the universal application of a temporary feeling or opinion" (*MC*, 194). Whereas Whitman's homoerotic "*all* feeling" became the base of his democratic faith and vision, Melville's dream of erotic comradeship is itself immersed in the flow of capital and slavery, as instanced by the fact that Ishmael's vision of homoerotic community is produced by and within labor for capital. The possibility of democratic, bodily, and erotic freedom signified by "A Squeeze" (chapter 94) is set against the phallic power of the whale's penis in "The Cassock" (chapter 95) and the satanic "hell-fired" quest of Ahab, who drives both the dream of democracy and the ship of the world toward destruction in the concluding pages of the novel.

Or not. Ishmael survives on the coffin life-buoy of his comrade and literal *life boy* Queequeg. As a biblical descendant of Abraham's servant Hagar and thus at least a figurative slave, Ishmael may represent some renewed possibility of liberation and democracy. But Ishmael also bears the burden of the crew's failure to revolt and thus the failure of revolutionary tradition and the collective will of the workers in the present. Like the failure of the American people to revolt against either the spread of slavery into the territories or the imperial will of capitalism in its advance across the country to the Pacific and beyond, Ishmael survives the failure of the revolutionary dream in the "Epilogue," but "only" as "another orphan." We do not know the meaning of that survival, and neither did Melville or America. In fact, the original publication of *Moby-Dick* in England was entitled *The Whale* and did not include the seemingly magical "Epilogue."

Like *Moby-Dick*, Whitman's *Leaves of Grass* also emerged out of a sense of apocalyptic gloom about the prospect of democracy in America. "Nations sink by stages, first one thing and then another," Whitman wrote in one of his antislavery lectures while he was working on the first edition of *Leaves of Grass*. By the summer of 1854, the capture and return of the fugitive slave Anthony Burns in the Revolutionary city of Boston—an event Whitman satirized in his 1855 poem "A Boston Ballad"—was only one of a number of signs that the American republic had become "cadaverous as a corpse" (*NUPM*, 1: 216).

Whereas Melville located the problem of democracy within the logic of democratic freedom itself, Whitman, like Lincoln and the newly emergent Republican Party, called for a return to the Declaration of Independence and a more revolutionary commitment to the ideals of democracy. The publication of *Leaves of Grass* on or about July 4, 1855, represented an act of revolution, an attempt to regenerate nation and world in the ideals of liberty and social union on which the American republic had been founded. The poet's experience of the "*all*-feeling" of homoerotic union at the outset of the initially untitled "Song of Myself," the first and longest poem in the 1855 *Leaves*, is not "temporary," as in Melville's *Moby-Dick*, but at the very center of the vision of democracy that would inform all of Whitman's work:

> I mind how we lay in June, such a transparent summer morning;
> You settled your head athwart my hips and gently turned over upon me,
> And parted the shirt from my bosom-bone, and plunged your tongue
>   to my barestript heart,
> And reached till you felt my beard, and reached till you held my feet.
> Swiftly arose and spread around me the peace and joy and knowledge
>   that pass all the art and argument of the earth. (*LG* 1855, 28–29)

The democratic knowledge that the poet receives and gives of a universe bathed in an erotic force that joins God, men, women, and the natural world is linked with the ecstasy of same-sex love among and between men.

Like Whitman, Melville identified himself as a "social plebeian." In a letter written to Hawthorne at the time he was completing *Moby-Dick*, he declared his belief in "political equality," that "a thief in jail is as honorable a personage as Gen. George Washington." But he also admitted the patrician limits of what he called "my ruthless democracy on all sides": "It seems an inconsistency to assert unconditional democracy in all things, and yet confess a dislike to all mankind—in the mass" (*MC*, 190, 191). Whereas Melville fears the unleashed energies of the masses, Whitman merges with the turbulent and unruly masses in his act of poetic self-naming:

> Walt Whitman, an American, one of the roughs, a kosmos,
> Disorderly fleshy and sensual . . . . eating drinking and breeding,
> No sentimentalist . . . . no stander above men and women or apart from them . . . . no more modest than immodest. (*LG* 1855, 48)

By naming himself as "one of the roughs" and by celebrating his disorderly and sensual nature in an unpunctuated sequence that mirrors the unruly flow of the senses, Whitman's poet encompasses those very qualities of disorder and intemperance most feared by the critics of democracy. "I speak the password primeval . . . . I give the sign of democracy," Whitman announces, linking the democratic "sign" that the poet gives with giving public voice to the socially marginalized and sexually repressed (*LG* 1855, 48).

At the center of Whitman's democratic epic is a scene of masturbation that associates self-touching with same-sex love and other forms of nonreproductive sexuality between men:

> Is this then a touch? . . . . quivering me to a new identity,
> Flames and ether making a rush for my veins,
> Treacherous tip of me reaching and crowding to help them,
> My flesh and blood playing out lightning, to strike what is hardly different from myself,
> On all sides prurient provokers stiffening my limbs,
> Straining the udder of my heart for its withheld drip. (*LG* 1855, 53)

Stimulated and stiffened by the "treacherous" fingertips of himself, or another who is "hardly different from myself," the poet loses bodily balance and the balance between self and other, body and soul, that is part of his democratic persona. Whereas "A Squeeze of the Hand" represents a moment of democratic and visionary bliss amid scenes of gothic terror and maniacal revenge, Whitman's touch sequence is presented in the politically charged language of a mass insurrection in which touch, as the "red marauder," usurps the governance of the body:

> No consideration, no regard for my draining strength or my anger,
> Fetching the rest of the herd around to enjoy them awhile,
> Then all uniting to stand on a headland and worry me.
>
> The sentries desert every other part of me,
> They have left me helpless to a red marauder,
> They all come to the headland to witness and assist against me.

I am given up by traitors;
I talk wildly . . . . I have lost my wits . . . . I and nobody else am the greatest traitor,
I went myself first to the headland . . . . my own hands carried me there. (*LG* 1855, 53–54)

At a time of widespread fear of mass insurrection, slave revolt, and civil war, the poet's "worry" in this passage is both personal and political. The entire sequence links the turbulence of a sexually unruly body with the danger of what Melville called "ruthless democracy on all sides." And it is on the level of sex and the body that the poem tests the democratic theory of the American republic.

Whitman symbolically resolves the bodily crisis of his protagonist by linking the onslaught of touch—as a sign of unruliness in body and body politic—with the regenerative energies of the universe:

You villain touch! what are you doing? . . . . my breath is tight in its throat;
Unclench your floodgates! you are too much for me.

Blind loving wrestling touch! Sheathed hooded sharptoothed touch!
Did it make you ache so leaving me?

Parting tracked by arriving . . . . perpetual payment of the perpetual loan,
Rich showering rain, and recompense richer afterward.

Sprouts take and accumulate . . . . stand by the curb prolific and vital,
Landscapes projected masculine full-sized and golden. (*LG* 1855, 54)

The moment of sexual release is followed by a restoration of balance as the ejaculatory flow merges with and is naturalized as the regenerative flow of the universe. Within this regenerative economy (homo)erotic touching is safe and natural, quivering the poet not to a new and marginal identity as sunken-eyed onanist in heteronormative America but toward an experience of cosmic generativity—"masculine full-sized and golden."

The drama of self and community, the one and the many, is completed in images of Christlike triumph over scenes of human suffering, injustice, and defeat in the history of nation and world: "I troop forth replenished with supreme power, one of an average unending procession," the poet declares, spreading the hope of democratic regeneration "over the whole earth" (*LG* 1855, 69).

Whereas Melville worries about the tragedy of the imperial will at the very sources of American democracy (Is Whitman Ahab?), Whitman celebrates the "supreme power" and "unending procession" of a democratic and erotic will that flows up to Canada and down to Mexico in its desire to "pass the boundaries" and encompass the whole world.

And yet even in the final celebratory passages of "Song of Myself," Whitman's poet registers some of Melville's doubts about the future of democracy as he imagines humanity, liberated from classical restraint and Christian humility, blinded and desecrated by a capitalist orgy of "buying or taking or selling":

> Here and there with dimes on the eyes walking,
> To feed the greed of the belly the brains liberally spooning,
> Tickets buying or taking or selling, but in to the feast never once going;
> Many sweating and ploughing and thrashing, and then the chaff for
> payment receiving,
> A few idly owning, and they the wheat continually claiming.
> (*LG* 1855, 73)

As in Melville's "Fast-Fish and Loose-Fish" chapter, the specter of a newly oppressive reign of capitalist "possession"—with "A few idly owning" and the "Many sweating and ploughing and thrashing, and then the chaff for payment receiving"—is at the root of a more tragic vision of the future of democracy Whitman shared with Melville, and, one might note, with Karl Marx.

"Do I contradict myself?" Whitman asks in the concluding sequence of the poem, "Very well then . . . . I contradict myself; / I am large . . . . I contain multitudes" (*LG* 1855, 85). His words sum up his effort to "contain" signs of dissension, contradiction, and doubt within the expansive body of the poet in order to affirm the poem's final message of democratic hope and progress:

> Do you see O my brothers and sisters?
> It is not chaos or death . . . . it is form and union and plan . . . . it is
> eternal life . . . . it is happiness. (*LG* 1855, 85)

Unlike Melville, whose democratic epic concludes with the specter of shipwreck and apocalypse, Whitman's epic poet bequeaths the final power of democratic creation to the *you* of the reader and the open road of a future he appears to signify textually by the absence of any mark of punctuation after "I stop some where waiting for you" at the poem's end.[6]

The Fractured State

Melville returned to the scene of Revolution in his novels and short stories of the mid-1850s, not, like Whitman, to regenerate nation and world in the possibilities of democracy, but to explore the nagging ironies, contradictions, and delusions of the Revolutionary heritage. In *Pierre; or, The Ambiguities* (1852), he imagines the tragic consequences for an idealistic young man—"a thorough-going Democrat"—who seeks to live in accord with the principles of Revolutionary and Christian virtue embodied by a putatively heroic but in fact savage tradition of fathers whose aristocratic and class pretensions—grounded in the conquest of Natives, enslavement of Africans, and sexual philandering in the New World—have given rise to the religious and political hypocrisies of the present. Melville carried on this critique of the failure of Revolutionary and Christian idealism in a series of short stories that present a bleak vision of worker alienation on Wall Street ("Bartleby, the Scrivener"), dehumanized and desexualized women enslaved to machines in a New England factory ("The Tartarus of Maids"), and the origins of the Americas in scenes of colonization and violence ("The Encantadas").

In "Benito Cereno," which was published in 1855, the same year as the first edition of *Leaves of Grass*, Melville extended his critique of the economic, racial, sexual, and class ideologies that undermined the possibilities of democracy to the transatlantic commerce in human bodies that linked Africa, Europe, and the Americas in the eighteenth and nineteenth centuries. Based on Amasa Delano's published account of a slave revolt that took place aboard the Spanish slave trader *Tryal* in 1805, "Benito Cereno" is haunted by the spectral presence of other slave revolts in the Americas, including the insurrection led by Toussaint L'Ouverture in San Domingo in 1791–1804 and more recent slave rebellions aboard the *Amistad* in 1839 and the *Creole* in 1841. Melville locates his story of slave revolt aboard the *San Dominick* within the commercial and imperial networks of the international slave trade and the proslavery ideologies and racist psychology that made this horrendous trade in "living freight" possible.

The story turns on the ironic failure of the American Amasa Delano to read the signs of slave revolution because he is blinded by the socially imposed taxonomies of racial and sexual difference: the Anglo-Saxon race is, in his view, superior to Africans who are ideally suited to be slaves, "negresses" who make natural mammies, and Spaniards who are by nature effeminate and treacherous. As the leader of the revolt, the physically slight Babo counters proslavery and racist ideologies of black "docility," "unaspiring contentment," and "blind attachment" with the intellectually imposing presence of a black man who, even in defeat and death, projects a revolutionary will to overthrow white mastery in the New World: "The body was burned to ashes; but for many days, the head, that hive of subtlety, fixed on a pole in the Plaza, met, unabashed, the gaze of the whites" (*PTP*, 84, 116).

Like Melville's stories of the 1850s, which seek to raise the veil of history on the common men, women, and slaves betrayed by the American Revolution, Whitman's 1856 edition of *Leaves of Grass* is shaped by a similar desire to recall the people to the ideals of the Revolution. "Remember the organic compact of These States! / Remember the pledge of the Old Thirteen thenceforward to the rights, life, liberty, equality of man!" Whitman wrote in "Poem of Remembrance for a Girl or a Boy of These States" (*LG* 1856, 275). But beneath the affirmation of a "simple, compact, well-joined scheme" in "Sun-Down Poem" (later "Crossing Brooklyn Ferry") and the global democratic embrace of "Poem of Salutation" (later "Salut au Monde!") is a barely concealed hysteria that self and world may be coming apart at the seams (*LG* 1856, 211). The sources of the poet's anxiety surface in "Poem of the Propositions of Nakedness" (later "Respondez!"), the only new poem to directly address the political landscape of 1856. Like Melville in his works of the mid-1850s, Whitman tears away the veils of the republican myth to expose a world in negative in which the virtuous American republic envisioned by the Revolutionary founders reveals its true state as a mass of historical contradictions:

> Let freedom prove no man's inalienable right! Every one who can
> tyrannize, let him tyrannize to his satisfaction!
> . . . .
> Let there be money, business, railroads, imports, exports, custom,
> authority, precedents, pallor, dyspepsia, smut, ignorance, unbelief!
> . . . .
> Let the white person tread the black person under his heel! (Say! which
> is trodden under heel, after all?) (*LG* 1856, 318, 319, 321)

"O seeming! seeming! seeming!" Whitman exclaimed toward the close of the poem as he edged ever closer to Melville's ambiguities and the nihilistic vision of *The Confidence-Man: His Masquerade*. In this 1857 novel, Melville evokes man and nation as part of an absurd drama of fraud and masquerade presided over not by Ishmael's "great democratic God" but by God as cosmic joker and con man. "Life is a pic-nic *en costume*," declares the cosmopolitan at the center of the novel: "one must take a part, assume a character, stand ready in a sensible way to play the fool."[7]

As *The Confidence-Man*, "Respondez!," and other works by Melville and Whitman suggest, both experienced a period of intense depression in the late 1850s. While the sources of this depression were personal and financial, it also corresponded with a deepening political crisis over democracy, slavery, and union and another severe economic depression in 1857, which lasted for two years. During these years, Melville stopped writing and sought unsuccessfully to earn a living as a public lecturer. Although he wrote poems in "private," he did not publish another book until after the Civil War. With the exception of *Billy Budd*, which was published posthumously, he turned away from fiction writing for the remainder of his life.

During these same years of political and economic crisis, Whitman, too, flirted with the idea of withdrawal from the public political sphere. In a small sheaf of twelve unpublished poems written between 1858 and 1859 entitled "Live Oak, with Moss," he expressed his desire to give up his role as democratic poet in order to pursue a personal love affair with a man: "I can be your singer of songs no longer—," he writes; "I am indifferent to my own songs—I am to go with him I love, and he is to go with me" (*LOM*, 17, 19).

But unlike Melville, Whitman chose not to withdraw from public political engagement. Rather, in the 1860 edition of *Leaves of Grass* he sought to resolve the political crisis of democracy through an appeal to the body, sex, and homosexual love. The new role that Whitman conceived for himself as the evangel-poet of democracy and love receives its fullest articulation in the 1860 "Calamus" poems, in which he represents himself and his poems as the embodiment of "a new friendship" that will "twist and intertwist" the "States" in bonds of comradeship and love: "The dependence of Liberty shall be lovers, / The continuance of Equality shall be comrades. / These shall tie and band stronger than hoops of iron" (*LG* 1860, 351).

The Union War

With the election of Lincoln to the presidency in 1860, the focus of national politics shifted away from the controversy over slavery to the battle to preserve the federal Union. On February 7, 1861, the Confederate States of America was formed, and by the end of the month, seven states of the lower South had left the Union. When the Palmetto Guard of South Carolina fired on Fort

Sumter on the morning of April 12, 1861, no one imagined that the Civil War would last for another four years or that the war that had begun bloodlessly would be one of the bloodiest in history.

"They said . . . great deeds were done no more / . . . But battle can heroes and bards restore," Melville wrote in his elegy "On Sherman's Men" (*BP*, 131; ellipses mine). For Melville as for Whitman, the Civil War, which began as a struggle to save the Union rather than to end slavery, became a simultaneously tragic and exhilarating source of personal and political renewal. Whereas for Whitman the war became a means of testing the American experiment in democracy by realizing the capacity of the American people for self-sacrificial virtue, citizenship, and community, for Melville the war appears to have inspired new forms of public political commitment in imitation of both his real and his figurative Revolutionary fathers (Figure 17).

In December 1862 Whitman went to the army camp at Falmouth, Virginia, in search of his brother George, who had been wounded in the battle of Fredericksburg. "One of the first things that met my eyes in camp, was a heap of feet, arms, legs &c. under a tree in front a hospital," he wrote (*COR*, 1: 59). The sight continued to haunt him as a sign of both the massive carnage of the Civil War and the dismembered body of the American republic. At the camp at Falmouth, Whitman discovered the role he would play during the war: he would minister literally to the wounded body of the republic by visiting some 100,000 wounded, sick, and dying soldiers in the hospital wards of Washington, DC (Figure 18). It was ironically during the war years, and especially in the hospitals, that Whitman came closest to realizing the republican dreams of the founders: "the War, to me, *proved* Humanity, and proved America and the Modern," he wrote.[8]

Although Melville's knowledge of the war came mainly through newspapers, the telegraph, and *The Rebellion Record* (1862–1865), in 1864 he too experienced the war firsthand when he went to visit his cousin Colonel Henry Gansevoort on the battlefront in Virginia. Here Melville participated in a two-day cavalry scout against the Confederate colonel John S. Mosby and his Partisan Raiders, which became the base of his wartime ballad "The Scout toward Aldie." Melville's pursuit of the malevolent and elusive Mosby appears to have shaped his later poetic evocation of the war not only as a heroic battle to save the Union and liberate the republic from the incubus of slavery, but also as an epic and fateful struggle against the destructive force of evil in the cosmos.

FIGURE 17. Herman Melville, 1861. For Melville, the Civil War became a simultaneously tragic and exhilarating source of personal and political renewal. "They say . . . great deeds were done no more / . . . But battle can heroes and bards restore," he wrote in his elegy "On Sherman's Men" (*BP*, 131). Courtesy of the Hawthorne Graphics Collection, Phillips Library, Peabody Essex Museum, Salem, Massachusetts.

At the close of the war, Whitman published *Drum-Taps* (1865) and *Sequel to Drum-Taps* (1865–1866), and Melville published *Battle-Pieces and Aspects of the War* (1866). In these two retrospective poetic accounts of the war, both writers seek to locate the apparent unreason, carnage, and tragedy of the fratricidal war between North and South within some larger pattern of history. Unlike Melville, however, who draws on the Bible and *Paradise Lost* in the complex allusive structure of *Battle-Pieces*, Whitman rejects the epic models of the past for his *Drum-Taps* poems. Whereas Melville assumes a posture of

FIGURE 18. Photograph of Walt Whitman, Washington, DC, 1863 or 1864, by Alexander Gardner. During the Civil War, Whitman ministered literally to the wounded body of the American republic by visiting some 100,000 wounded, sick, and dying soldiers in the hospital wards of Washington, DC. Courtesy of the Alderman Library at the University of Virginia and the Walt Whitman Archive.

ironic detachment, organizing his poems around public events, major battles, and the triumphs and defeats of northern (and some southern) generals, like Winslow Homer's sketches of the Civil War, Whitman's point of view is democratic and engaged (Figure 19). He enters his poems personally in the figure of the common soldier, presenting the war in lyric rather than epic terms: his war scenes could be anywhere, North or South; his heroes are the masses of ordinary soldiers, particularly the unknown soldiers whose graves he marks

FIGURE 19. *Infantry Column on the March* (1862), drawing by Winslow Homer during the Civil War. Like Homer's sketches of the Civil War, Whitman's *Drum-Taps* poems are insistently democratic, told from the point of view of the masses of ordinary soldiers, as in his poem "An Army Corps on the March." Courtesy of the Cooper-Hewitt Museum, Smithsonian Institution/Art Resource, New York.

with his own poetic inscription: "*Bold, cautious, true, and my loving comrade*" (*DTS*, 58). Eschewing the biblical and epic analogy of Melville's *Battle-Pieces*, Whitman finds his symbolic and mythic structure closer to the democratic ground of America: in the makeshift hospitals of camp and field; in an army corps on the march; in the death of an unknown soldier; in the recurrent image of red blood consecrating "the grass, the ground"; and in the figure of the poet as wound-dresser and comrade.

But despite underlying differences between Melville's more conventionally literary and patrician and Whitman's more insistently democratic approach to the war, at their most optimistic, both poets envisioned the war as a reaffirmation of the ideals of the founding and thus a struggle to preserve the American experiment in democracy as what Melville called "the world's fairest hope" ("Misgivings," *BP*, 7). Amid the capitalist, materialist, and corrupting influences of the time, both poets place particular emphasis on the republican acts of "patriotic passion" displayed by young men who are willing to fight and die for an ideal—whether southern or northern, states' rights or national union—grounded in a common revolutionary history ("Supplement," *BP*, 184).

And yet, beneath these self-sacrificial acts of republican manhood and virtue, there is also in the poems of *Drum-Taps* and *Battle-Pieces* an underlying melancholia and a desire to mourn. Like Melville's dedication of *Battle-Pieces* "TO THE MEMORY OF THE THREE HUNDRED THOUSAND

FIGURE 20. Dead of the 24th Michigan Infantry, Gettysburg, photographed by Tim O'Sullivan. In his dedication of the Gettysburg National Cemetery on November 9, 1863, Abraham Lincoln said: "We here highly resolve that these dead shall not have died in vain; that this nation, under God, shall have a new birth of freedom." Courtesy of the Brady-Handy Collection, Library of Congress Prints and Photographs Division.

WHO IN THE WAR FOR THE MAINTENANCE OF THE UNION FELL DEVOTEDLY UNDER THE FLAG OF THEIR FATHERS," the pathos and shadowy ambiguity of Melville's poems suggests that the war may be an absurd scene of butchery visited upon the idealistic sons by the sins—and political bad faith—of the Revolutionary founders (Figure 20). While Melville and Whitman both emphasize themes of compassion, brotherhood, and reconciliation between North and South, their poetry also registers anxiety that the war to save the Union may have made any future union impossible. In "Reconciliation" Whitman, like Lincoln in his Second Inaugural Address, attempts to bind up the wounds of the nation by encouraging a spirit of reconciliation, but the reconciliation he envisions occurs not in life but in death. As in Melville's "Magnanimity Baffled," in which the northern conqueror reaches out to a southern hand only to find it dead, so in "Reconciliation" the enemy that the poet bends down to touch with his lips is a corpse.

If for Melville the victory of the Union meant the triumph of the institutions of democracy, what he called "the principles of democratic government" ("Supplement," *BP*, 187), for Whitman the victory of the Union meant the triumph of the American people in the non-state forms of comradeship, compassion, and love exhibited by common soldiers on both sides during the war (Figure 21). Whereas in Whitman's "A March in the Ranks Hard-Prest, and the Road Unknown," the "half-smile" of a "dying lad" intimates a sustaining gesture of comradeship, love, and hope for both soldiers and citizens as they march in darkness along the unknown roads of the future; in Melville's "The Scout toward Aldie," a moment of erotic camaraderie between girlish-looking boys from both North and South during the war is cut short by the icy figure of Captain Cloud. His act of vengeance anticipates the central drama of *Billy Budd* in evoking the Civil War as a fateful sacrifice of innocence, comradeship, and love to an increasingly empowered—and seemingly necessary—reassertion of patriarchal, military, and national authority and law (*BP*, 154–55).

Democratic Vistas

"The years of the war tried our devotion to the Union; the time of peace may test the sincerity of our faith in democracy," Melville wrote in his "Supplement" to *Battle-Pieces*, a prose meditation on the political urgency of "the times" in which he addresses "his countrymen" directly on "the work of Reconstruction" and the challenges facing democracy and national reunification in the post–Civil War period. Amid debates about the Fourteenth Amendment, which would guarantee black civil rights and citizenship and exclude former secessionists from public office, Melville urged a political policy of "common sense and Christian charity" in allowing for the speedy reentry of the South into full participation in the "Re-establishment" of the Union (*BP*, 187, 181). Like Whitman, Melville opposed the Radical Republican effort to penalize and exclude former secessionists from public office as contrary to the cause of union and "those cardinal principles" of "democracy" and "representative government." "It is enough," he wrote, "if the South have been taught by the terrors of civil war to feel that Secession, like Slavery, is against Destiny; that both now lie buried in one grave; that her fate is linked with

FIGURE 21. Calling card presented to Whitman by George B. Field, in the Armoury Square Hospital, Washington, March 12, 1865. "During those three years in hospital, camp or field, I made over six hundred visits or tours, and went . . . among from eighty thousand to a hundred thousand of the wounded and sick, as sustainer of spirit and body . . . in time of need" (*PW*, 1: 112–13; ellipses mine). Courtesy of the Charles Feinberg Collection, Library of Congress.

ours; and that together we comprise the Nation." "And yet," Melville added, "it is right to rejoice for our triumph, so far as it may justly imply an advance for our whole country and for humanity" ("Supplement," *BP*, 186, 182, 184).

But while Melville invokes fraternal sentiment and Whitman the bonds of comradeship and love as the ground for political reunion and the means of securing the advance of democracy worldwide, as in Melville's "A Meditation," in which the northern speaker asks, "Can Africa pay back this blood / Spilt on Potomac's Shore?," in the post–Civil War period, remorse about the "Horror and anguish" of "the civil strife" began to manifest itself as anger against the African race for causing the war between the "natural" kith and kin of the white Republic (*BP*, 170–71, 170). "Emancipation has ridded the country of the reproach, but not wholly of the calamity" of black slavery, Melville wrote, citing Lincoln in support of the "grave evil" represented by the "co-existence of the two races in the South" ("Supplement," *BP*, 186).

Although Whitman shared Melville's fears about the future of black and white relations and its effects on the American republic in the years following the Civil War, his 1867 poem "Ethiopia Saluting the Colors" suggests that there was also something "strange and marvellous" about the emancipation of black slaves at the end of the Civil War. Originally published with the subtitle "(*A Reminiscence of* 1864)" in the 1871 edition of *Leaves of Grass*, "Ethiopia" is written from the point of view of a soldier in "doughty" Sherman's conquering army as it marches through the Carolinas "toward the sea." "Who are you, dusky woman, so ancient, hardly human," the soldier asks when he sees a "dusky woman" "rising by the roadside" to greet "the colors" as she "curtseys to the regiments, the guidons moving by" (*LG* 1871, 357, 358). Like Melville, who represents "the negro," whether "bond or free," as an "alien" African presence who threatens the stability of the American republic and the future of democracy with the specter of race war (*BP*, 186), Whitman's "Ethiopia" might be read as an exotic alien and possibly ominous presence who will affect the country's destiny in uncertain ways.

But the concluding lines of the poem associate Ethiopia with wonder and fate and a broader movement of political and spiritual liberation:

> What is it, fateful woman—so blear, hardly human?
> Why wag your head, with turban bound—yellow, red and green?
>
> Are the things so strange and marvelous, you see or have seen?
> (*LG* 1871, 358)

Identified with the origins of civilization, "so ancient, hardly human," and nobility, with her "high-borne turban'd head," Ethiopia recounts her experience of being "*sunder'd*" from her "*parents*" by her "*master*," who "*caught me as the savage beast is caught*" and forced her to suffer the terrors of the middle passage on "*a cruel slaver*" a hundred years ago (*LG* 1871, 357).

Ethiopia's name and her story link her with Africa, African people, and the prophetic figure of Ethiopia in biblical Psalms: "Princes shall come out of Egypt; Ethiopia shall soon stretch out her hands to God" (Psalms 68.31). Identified with spiritual and political liberation from Egyptian captivity, this biblical figure has been embraced by African American slaves from Phillis Wheatley, who used the term "Ethiopia" to refer to herself, Africa, and the African diaspora, to Frederick Douglass, who cites the Biblical prophecy "Ethiopia shall stretch out her hand unto God" as part of his call for a new era "the wide world o'er" of "rights," "human brotherhood," and "freedom's reign" at the end of his 1852 oration "What to the Slave Is the Fourth of July?"[9] In fact, Phillis Wheatley herself was "caught" in Africa as a child of seven or eight and arrived in America on a "cruel slaver" in 1761, about the same time as Whitman's Ethiopia.

The speaker's allusion to "things strange and marvellous" transpiring in America suggests that the final lines of the poem may be uttered by Whitman rather than by the soldier, who seems puzzled and troubled by Ethiopia's "rising," "saluting," and "lingering all the day" as the "guidons" of Sherman's liberating army float by. It is Whitman who would recognize the marvel and miracle of this "ancient," formerly enslaved, and *now* emancipated African woman stepping "forth" from her "hovel door" in her African turban of "yellow, red and green" and "saluting the colors" of "doughty Sherman" and his "regiments" that have emancipated her from one hundred years of slavery. The poet's concluding words emphasize that there is indeed something "fateful," "strange and marvellous" about the "things" Ethiopia has seen and is seeing in the emancipation of slaves and the apparent "Union" of the colors of black and white, Africa and America, at the end of the Civil War.

Written in 1867, and published in the 1871 edition of *Leaves of Grass*, "Ethiopia Saluting the Colors" enacts the same vision of "the solidarity of the races" that Whitman imagined in "Years of the Unperform'd," a poem that was first published in *Drum-Taps* in 1865: "I see tremendous entrances and exits—I see new combinations—I see the solidarity of the races," Whitman wrote. "I see Freedom, completely arm'd, and victorious, and very haughty, with Law by her side, both issuing forth against the idea of caste; / . . . / Are all nations communing? is there going to be but one heart to the globe? / Is humanity forming, en-masse?" the poet asks (*DTS*, 53, 54). Not coincidentally, "Ethiopia Saluting the Colors" was published in the same 1871 edition of *Leaves of Grass* to which Whitman added a cluster of poems entitled "Songs of Insurrection," which was inspired by the ongoing scene of Revolution in the United States and in France.

But the Civil War, which was fought on one side to preserve the union of the republic and on the other to preserve the republican tradition of local and state sovereignty, became a springboard away from the republican and essentially agrarian order of the past toward the centralized, industrialized nation-state of the future. In Whitman's view, the "most deadly portending" change in the post–Civil War period was the emergence, under the pressures of a wartime economy, of a leviathan state. In his poem "The Conflict of Convictions," Melville also foresaw the irony that in using national power to quell a local rebellion, the ultimate victim of the Civil War might be the "Founders' dream." Out of the Union victory a new power state would emerge, symbolized by the iron dome that replaced the original wooden dome of the Capitol during the Civil War:

> Power unanointed may come—
> Dominion (unsought by the free)
> And the Iron Dome,
> Stronger for stress and strain,
> Fling her huge shadow athwart the main;
> But the Founders' dream shall flee. (*BP*, 10)

Unlike Whitman's "Pioneers! O Pioneers!" and other postwar poems which continue to hail the advance of America across the continent and beyond as part of the advance of democracy worldwide, Melville is less sanguine about the newly empowered and imperial figure of "America" that emerges from the war: "Law on her brow and empire in her eyes. / So she, with graver air and lifted flag" (*BP*, 121).

And yet despite the desire of both writers to retreat from the pathology of what Whitman called a country "coil'd in evil times" (*LGC*, 399), in Whitman's *Democratic Vistas* (1871) and Melville's *Billy Budd, Sailor*, each wrote an enduring meditation on the Revolutionary origins of the American republic and the problems, contradictions, and future of democracy not only "for our whole country," as Melville had said, but "for humanity" (*BP*, 184). Written in response to Thomas Carlyle's critique of democracy and universal enfranchisement in "Shooting Niagara: And After?," the question Whitman poses in *Democratic Vistas* is whether democracy is possible under the conditions of laissez-faire capitalism. "Must not the virtue of modern Individualism," he asked, "continually enlarging, usurping all, seriously affect, perhaps keep down entirely, in America, the like of the ancient virtue of Patriotism, the fervid and absorbing love of general country?" (*PW*, 2: 373).

To this "serious problem and paradox in the United States" (*PW*, 2: 373),

Whitman responded with the visionary and utopian force of erotic, or adhesive, love. Countering the revolutionary movement away from the feudal structures of the past toward the sovereign power of the individual, he envisions a universal Hegelian force that binds and fuses humanity: There is "not that half only, individualism, which isolates. There is another half, which is adhesiveness or love, that fuses, ties and aggregates, making the races comrades, and fraternizing all" (*PW*, 2: 381). It is to these "threads of manly friendship" running through the "worldly interests of America" that Whitman looks for the "counterbalance" and "spiritualization" of "our materialistic and vulgar American democracy" (*PW*, 2: 414). "I say democracy infers such loving comradeship, as its most inevitable twin or counterpart, without which it will be incomplete, in vain, and incapable of perpetuating itself" (*PW*, 2: 415).

Although *Democratic Vistas* addresses the problems and contradictions of democracy in the United States in the post–Civil War period, the future—or vistas—it imagines are global and transnational. Unlike Whitman, who declares the "latent right of insurrection" as a "quenchless, indispensable fire" at the outset of "Songs of Insurrection" (*LG* 1871, 363) and celebrates the bloody insurrection of the Paris Commune as part of the ongoing "struggle and the daring, rage divine for liberty" in "O Star of France. 1870–71" (*LGC*, 396), Melville's *Clarel: A Poem and Pilgrimage in the Holy Land*, which he began writing at the very time of the popular uprisings in France in 1870–1871, gives voice to the right of revolution at the same time that it registers terror of the bloody and anarchic consequences of proletarian or slave revolt. Beyond a first stage of rights and a second stage of material progress and wealth, Whitman's *Democratic Vistas* theorizes a future public culture of democracy that will be achieved not by law, government, or the market but by the democratizing force of adhesive, or manly, love, which "alone can bind . . . all nations, all men, of however various and distant lands, into a brotherhood, a family" (*PW*, 2: 381; ellipsis mine).

In the post–Civil War years, Melville too looked to non-state forms of democratic affection and community as a means of countering the increasing use of military force and law to achieve social order. At the close of the war, he observed that the "kind of pacification, based upon principles operating equally all over the land, which lovers of their country yearn for," can never be achieved by the force of arms or by "law-making" itself, "however anxious, or energetic, or repressive." But, he added, a just and equitable peace between North and South "may yet be largely aided by *generosity of sentiment public and private*" (*BP*, 185; my italics). "Benevolence and policy—Christianity and Machiavelli—dissuade from penal severities toward the subdued," he wrote in words that suggest the ways "the terrible historic tragedy of our time"—the blood sacrifice of the Civil War and its apparent failure to restore either the union or democracy—would continue to loom over the tragedy of human passion and law that is enacted aboard the man-of-war world of *Billy Budd*, which was written in the years before Melville's death in 1891 (*BP*, 185, 188).

Dedicated to Jack Chase, "that great heart" and one of Melville's *chums* aboard the US frigate *United States* in 1843, the "inside narrative" of *Billy Budd* turns backward toward the ship, the sea, and the Revolutionary era in an attempt—like Whitman's *Democratic Vistas*—to come to terms with the democratic paradox of revolution and social order, liberty and law, through the affective force of homoerotic attraction, community, and love inspired by the Handsome Sailor. Whereas the dialectics of individual and community in *Democratic Vistas* is propelled by the conservative and radical figures of Carlyle and Hegel and focused primarily on the disintegrative force of capitalist greed and laissez-faire individualism, the historical dialectics between individual liberty and state-enforced military authority in *Billy Budd* is underwritten by Edmund Burke's *Reflections on the Revolution in France* (1790) and Thomas Paine's *The Rights of Man* (1791) and focused on the threat to the Revolutionary heritage, individual rights, and the future of democracy represented by the rise of the imperial state.

This historical dialectics is suggested at the outset when Billy Budd is impressed from the merchantman of *The Rights of Man* into "the King's service" on the *Bellipotent*, a British naval ship threatened not only by the specter of "unbridled and unbounded revolt" in its own ranks, but by the "flame" of the French Revolution and the "conquering and proselytizing armies of the French Directory" at the beginning of the Napoleonic wars (*BB*, 12, 11). On the simplest level *Billy Budd* is an allegory of Billy's good nature and Claggart's natural depravity mediated by the seemingly rational but in fact ambiguous figure of patriarchal authority and law represented by Captain Vere. Set in the year 1797, against the backdrop of ongoing Revolutionary struggle between an Old World hierarchical order of subjection to God, Church, and King and a New World ethos of individual freedom, rights, and agency proclaimed by both the American, French, and Haitian Revolutions, *Billy Budd* meditates on the problems of revolution, democracy, and the rise of the imperial state represented by France and Britain in the late eighteenth century and by a newly empowered United States—with "Law on her brow and empire in her eyes"—in the late nineteenth century ("America," *BP*, 121).

The man-of-war world of the *Bellipotent* is regulated by an Old World order of military law, discipline, duty, and subjection to the imperial will of the King in his pursuit of empire, war, and national glory. The sailors aboard a warship like the *Bellipotent* are not only "the least influential class of mankind," but like Billy Budd they are also in effect slaves who have been impressed into the King's service against their will—sometimes even "by drafts culled direct from jails" (*BB*, 21). Through a subtle allusive structure that links the fictional events of the inside narrative with actual events in American history—including the controversial execution of three sailors as mutineers aboard the USS *Somers* in 1842—the question *Billy Budd* poses is, Will the United States follow the imperial order of the past, signified by Britain and France, Nelson and Napoleon, or will it, can it, be the "budd" or bloom of an alternative democratic order?

This alternative order is adumbrated by the "Handsome Sailor," "a common sailor" associated from the outset of the story with "natural regality," "strength and beauty," proficiency as a laborer, comradely affection, a "moral nature" to match his physical "comeliness and power," and the "honest homage" of his shipmates (*BB*, 3, 4). At a time when the United States was retreating from the egalitarian ideals of the founding and the more radical possibilities of what W. E. B. Du Bois called "Black Reconstruction" into the compromised politics of Jim Crow, lynching as social ritual, and the terrors of the Ku Klux Klan, what is perhaps most significant about the Handsome Sailor as a comment on the failure to achieve black equality and civil rights in the post–Civil War period is the fact that in his most ideal, democratic, and hopeful form, the Handsome Sailor is first fully embodied not by the welkin-eyed Anglo-Saxon Billy Budd but by "a common sailor so intensely black that he must needs have been a native African of the unadulterated blood of Ham" (*BB*, 3). This black Handsome Sailor is a model of democratic personality and affection—of love freely given—as the base of democratic community. At "the centre of a company of his shipmates," who "were made up of such an assortment of tribes and complexions as would have well fitted them to be marched up by Anacharsis Cloots before the bar of the first French Assembly as Representatives of the Human Race" (*BB*, 3), he is also the herald of a new global order of democracy grounded in the ideals of *liberté, egalité, fraternité* promised by the French Revolution.

Like the black Handsome Sailor, Billy Budd also represents the possibility of an alternative democratic order: he is a figure of republican virtue, manliness, and labor not merely for survival but as form of self-realization. He embodies the traditionally "feminine" values of the heart above the head, of feeling above the law, of love and compassion against the invasiveness of the state. This state power is expressed through the "police surveillance" of Claggart as master-at-arms and enforced by the "uncompanionable" patriarch Captain Vere in the name of reason, discipline, duty, and the "martial law operating through" officers of the King who have, in Vere's words, "ceased to be natural free agents" (*BB*, 42, 55). Against this regime of "brute Force" presided over by Vere and his subordinates aboard the *Bellipotent*, Billy, like Whitman's comrades of the open road, exhibits the power of erotically charged feeling, of homoerotic affect, as a political force that binds men together in democratic community.

Billy embodies the values of affection and "charity for all" that Lincoln had invoked in his Second Inaugural Address (1865) and Melville had seconded in his "Supplement" to *Battle-Pieces* as a means "to bind up the nation's wounds" and create "a just and lasting peace, among ourselves, and with all nations."[10] It is not the power of arms, law, or punishment but Billy's power to model and draw forth social affection and love that orders the previously disordered society of *The Rights of Man*: "Before I shipped that young fellow, my forecastle was a rat-pit of quarrels," says the captain of *The Rights*. "But Billy came; and it was like a Catholic priest striking peace in an Irish shandy." "A virtue went out of him" and "they all love him," he says. "Anybody will do anything for Billy Budd; it's the happy family here" (*BB*, 6). Even Claggart, who is driven by the passions of "envy and antipathy" to accuse Billy of mutiny, is sexually aroused by him, as suggested symbolically by his desire "to ejaculate something hasty" at the sight of Billy's "spilled soup" (*BB*, 29, 25). His "melancholy expression" sometimes betrays "a touch of soft yearning, as if Claggart could even have loved Billy but for the fate and ban" of his "evil nature" (*BB*, 38).

Captain Vere must also resist the promptings of his heart and love in condemning Billy to hang for striking Claggart dead when the latter falsely accuses him of mutiny. Comparing the "the clash of military duty with moral scruple—scruple vitalized by compassion" with an "upright judge" being "waylaid by some tender kinswoman of the accused," Vere tells his illegally assembled drumhead court: "the heart here, sometimes the feminine in man, is as that piteous woman, and hard though it may be, *she must here be ruled out*"

(*BB*, 54, 55; my italics). Billy's putatively capital crimes of mutiny and homicide appear to be intricately bound up with the civil crime of disrupting sexual boundaries—of bringing out the "piteous woman" in man and men loving men. Even after Billy's death, the ship's chaplain is drawn by overpowering emotion to "an act strange" of sexual, political, and spiritual transgression: "Stooping over, he kissed on the fair cheek his fellow-man, a felon in martial law" (*BB*, 63).

For Billy's shipmates, as for the chaplain, Billy's death is an incitement to forms of democratic community, collective resistance, and love against "the martial discipline" of the imperial state. These acts of democratic remembrance are signified by the ongoing circulation among sailors of the "chips" of the spar from which Billy was hung in memory of the "image" of human goodness he represents; and by the bottom-up world of sensual pleasure and companionship evoked by the "tarry hand" of one of Billy's shipmates, who transforms Billy's life into the ballad "Billy in the Darbies," which circulates "among the shipboard crews for a while" before it is "rudely printed" and closes the narrative of *Billy Budd.*

"With mankind," Captain Vere proclaims, "forms, measured forms are everything," as he seeks to reassert the "measured forms" of discipline at the first sign of possible revolt among "the multitude" following Billy's death (*BB*, 68). "Toned by music and religious rites subserving the discipline and purposes of war" (*BB*, 68), Vere's attempt to dissolve the multitude and the threat of revolution by reasserting the martial rhythms of the state is an uncanny enactment of what Walter Benjamin would later describe as the aestheticization of politics in the Fascist state. Vere's decision to condemn Billy despite or perhaps because of the homoerotic promptings of his heart is not only an attempt to control the multitude and "the disruption of forms" associated with the French Revolution and its aftermath through a reassertion of the power of the state and law; it is also a reassertion of the power of new medical and scientific discourses of the body and eroticism that would contain sexuality and the body within the "measured forms" of male and female spheres and the patriarchal family.

Against the invasive mechanisms of the state, Melville's *Billy Budd*, like Whitman's *Democratic Vistas*, suggests the potential power of democratic personality, of non-state forms of feeling and love between men, and of artistic creation in bringing an alternative democratic order and ethos into being. Whatever Billy's last charitable words—"God bless Captain Vere!"—mean (*BB*, 64), a mournfulness or nostalgia for the very forms of erotic comradeship

Whitman affirms hangs over Melville's final work, suggesting the extent to which "intense and loving comradeship, the personal and passionate attachment of man to man" also shapes the most politically utopian moments in Melville's work (*PW*, 2: 414). For Melville as for Whitman, political freedom was inseparable from freedom of written expression and freedom of sexual expression, and all three would be at the constitutive center of any new democratic order of the future. Or as Melville put it in his 1849 letter to Duyckinck: "the Declaration of Independence makes a difference" (*MC*, 122). And so does poetry, as instanced by the ballad "Billy in the Darbies" at the close of *Billy Budd*. It is here that Melville, like the sailor poet who transforms Billy's comradely world into democratic art, bids "adieu" to what he called, in an early draft of "Billy in the Darbies," "my last queer dream."

CHAPTER NINE

Public Love

Whitman and Political Theory

> Gaze, loving and thirsting eyes, in the house or street or public assembly!
> Sound out, voices of young men! loudly and musically call me by my nighest name!
>
> —Walt Whitman, *Leaves of Grass* (1856)

In 1783, at the close of the American Revolutionary War, George Washington broke into tears as he silently embraced, kissed, and said good-bye to each of his officers at the Fraunces Tavern in New York. As it was remembered and circulated in the American cultural imaginary, this revolutionary scene of public emotion and tears, which Whitman later recast as part of the simultaneously homoerotic and democratic dream fantasy of "The Sleepers" in 1855, came to signify the new forms of antipatriarchal authority imagined by the American republic: the commander in chief and later president of the United States as sentimental friend. Publicly divesting himself of authority as commander in chief through speechless acts of physical affection, mutuality, and exchange, George Washington symbolically embodied the republican ideal of military authority returning to the self-sovereign citizen soldiers of the American republic and the Continental army dissolving into an affectionate union among friends.

This ideal of republican union is, of course, very far from the realities of violence and blood that have marked and continue to mark American and democratic history. Although the preamble to the Constitution of the United States makes its appeal to "justice," "domestic tranquility," "the blessings of liberty," and the creation of a "more perfect union" in the name of "We, the people," the Constitution was in fact an illegal document put together in secret by an elite group of property-holding white men who literally feared for their lives in the wake of the rebellion of debtors led by Daniel Shays in Massachusetts in 1786–1787 and other turbulent signs—inside, outside, and on the borders of the American republic—that the "Union" was on the verge of collapse into anarchy and blood.

At the center of the struggle over the Constitution as it was defended by Alexander Hamilton, James Madison, and John Jay in the *Federalist Papers* (1786–1787) was the problem and paradox of liberty and union: how to reconcile the ideal of an American republic grounded in liberty and the self-sovereign rights of the individual with the need for order, law, and government. "Among the difficulties encountered by the convention," wrote Madison in *Federalist* No. 37, "a very important one must have lain in combining the requisite *stability and energy in government* with the inviolable attention due to *liberty and the republican form*" (my italics).[1] The founders sought to resolve the problem of the passions and self-interest of human nature, states, and nations legally through a written constitution, representative government, the separation and balance of powers, and "the *federal principle*" of power divided between state and nation (No. 51, 293). This liberal model of government was grounded in conflict, in what Madison called "contending interests" (No. 37, 198); it left unresolved when it did not overtly repress or privatize the role that passion, eroticism, sympathy, and love might play in bringing about what Whitman would later call democracy as "a living union" among people (*PW*, 2: 471). It is the relations among public emotion, homoeroticism, political union, and democratic theory that I want to explore in this essay.

In recent years, Whitman's work has received increasing attention from political theorists and philosophers of democracy. Taking Whitman "seriously as a social scientist," the former Harvard professor of the science of government Samuel H. Beer compares Whitman's model of the state as an organic union held together by a diversity of interests to Émile Durkheim's argument in *The Division of Labor in Society* (1893) that in modern industrial society the diversities of the division of labor are "the principal source of cohesion."[2] Poems such as "Song of Myself" and "Crossing Brooklyn Ferry," Beer argues, "confirm Whitman as a master of the sociological imagination" (377).

Whereas Beer emphasizes Whitman's "nation-centered purpose," in "Walt Whitman and the Culture of Democracy" the political theorist George Kateb contends that Whitman "is perhaps the greatest philosopher of democratic culture" as the setting for the development of "democratic individuality" (545). Reading "Song of Myself" as a "work in political theory" (548), Kateb argues that Whitman's notion of the individual as composite, multiple, and "strange" becomes the means through which individuals are connected to each other in a democratic rights-based polity: "To admit one's compositeness and ultimate unknowability," Kateb writes, "is to open oneself to a kinship to others that is defined by receptivity or responsiveness to them. It intensifies the mutuality between strangers that is intrinsic to the idea of rights based-individualism in a democracy" (556).

While Beer and Kateb have pioneered in opening a space for public discussion of Whitman as a serious philosopher and theorist of democracy, their work is also characteristic of a long tradition of liberal literary and political criticism that has bracketed or erased the collective, adhesive, and homoerotic dimensions of Whitman's theory of democracy.[3] Like social philosophers from Plato to Edmund Burke, to Durkheim, and to Herbert Marcuse, Beer recognizes the erotic nature of the bonds that attach individuals to each other and to the state, but he does not elaborate on this insight; nor does he make any allusion to the specifically homoerotic sources of Whitman's notions of adhesiveness, comradeship, and love.

Like Hannah Arendt, Kateb in his turn sees democratic individualism as a form of resistance to various forms of statism, from nationalism to totalitarianism or communitarianism. He explicitly rejects the importance of American nationality, "group identity," and adhesiveness to Whitman's theory of democracy (547). "Connectedness" as Kateb understands it, is an ideal of "receptivity and responsiveness" *within* the individual that "is not well illustrated by Whitman's notion of adhesive love, or love of comrades." He writes:

> Adhesiveness threatens to suffocate the very individualism of personality that Whitman is trying to promote, while it despiritualizes and falsifies the superior idea of oneself as composite, and hence as indefinite, and hence not properly amenable to an all-enfolding merger. It does not go with the spirit of rights-based individualism. It also serves the sinister project of nationalism. The comradely side of Whitman is not his most attractive because it is not the genuinely democratic one. (563–64)

As I have argued elsewhere, it is simply not possible to take Whitman seriously as a philosopher of democracy without taking seriously the importance of the collectivity and the en-masse to his theory of democracy; the centrality of Whitman's concept of *adhesiveness*—or affectionate and usually same-sex love—to his political thinking; and the inseparability of his erotic and sexual experience as a man who loved other men (sometimes strangers) to his poetic, visionary, and, I would argue, theoretical writings about the future of democracy in America and worldwide.[4]

I want to use the work of one of the major democratic theorists of our time, Jürgen Habermas, as a means of reflecting on the relations among sex, tears, politics, poetry, and public love that underwrite Whitman's theory of democracy. In *The Structural Transformation of the Public Sphere: An Inquiry into a Category of Bourgeois Society* (1962), Habermas describes the public sphere as a space between civil society (the family and the market) and the state (government) in which private persons engage in public talk about issues of common interest to all. As it emerged out of the privacy of the family and the intimacy of letters as the "containers for the 'outpourings of the heart'" in the eighteenth century, the public sphere of letters became the base for political criticism and resistance to public and state authority.[5] Habermas's concept of a public sphere of political dialogue separate from the state provides a useful model for understanding Whitman's theory of democracy and its inseparability from his effort to resist liberal privatization—the increasing distinction between a private sphere of intimacy, sex, women, and the family and a public sphere of politics, reason, men, and the state under liberal capitalism.

As it developed in the United States in the nineteenth century, the public sphere of speech, print, and popular assembly—protected by the Constitutional guarantees of freedom of speech, press, and assembly—became the space where those social and sexual outsiders excluded by the Constitution or marginalized by society might find public voice through non-state forms of participation, citizenship, and resistance.[6] As a popular writer, journalist, and poet, Whitman participated in this movement toward giving public and written voice to the masses of common men and women who made up the American people. He was also at the origins of a movement to resist sexual oppression and liberal privatization by publicly naming the taboo subjects of sex and the body and by giving public and print expression to the multiple—and sometimes secret and forbidden—forms of erotic attraction, pleasure, desire, and love that bring and hold people together not only in forms of social and political union but in all forms of daily life.

Whitman came of age at a time when the racial, sexual, economic, and class contradictions that were left unresolved at the time of the founding were beginning to tear the American union apart at the seams. At the center of Whitman's effort to address the problem of political union and, in effect, to make public love the role of print, publication, and literature. Like "The Child's

Champion" (1841), Whitman's popular temperance novel *Franklin Evans; or The Inebriate: Tale of the Times* (1842) was published by *The New World*, a mass-circulation newspaper which, as Whitman wrote, gave him the power of reaching and shaping "mighty and deep public opinion" by "diffusing" his story "by every mail to all parts of this vast republic" (*EPF*, 126–27). Written "*for the mass*"—not "for the critics, but for THE PEOPLE"—and framed by the language of sentimental and "Temperance Reform," *Franklin Evans* seeks to teach the value of "a prudent, sober, and temperate course of life" as part of a broader movement of national republican regeneration (*EPF*, 127, 128). "Victory! victory! The Last Slave of Appetite is free, and the people are regenerated!" (*EPF*, 223), the multitudes proclaim in a Washingtonian dream sequence that is one part temperance meeting and one part national revival. But as Michael Moon and Michael Warner have argued, in Whitman's early temperance tales, the rhetoric of temperance reform functions as a fluid medium for voicing at the same time that it condemns a seductive urban underworld of male desire, pleasure, cruising, dissipation, same-sex eroticism, fluid identities, and border crossings that erode the illusory boundaries of class and identity, sex and blood.[7]

Whereas in *Franklin Evans* the desire to name and tell the "seductive enchantments" and erotic pleasures available to young men in the new urban space of the city exists in uneasy tension with the republican ideal of personal and national regeneration, by the time Whitman published the first edition of *Leaves of Grass* in 1855, he is determined to give public voice to hitherto unnamed sexual, erotic, and homoerotic urges that in effect tie individuals, the body politic, and the entire universe together. "And . . . a kelson of the creation is love," the poet declares, in a mystical vision that literally comes out of the erotic and homoerotic union at the outset of the long opening poem (later entitled "Song of Myself"):

> I mind how we lay in June, such a transparent summer morning;
> You settled your head athwart my hips and gently turned over upon me,
> And parted the shirt from my bosom-bone, and plunged your tongue
> to my barestript heart,
> And reached till you felt my beard, and reached till you held my feet.
>
> Swiftly arose and spread around me the peace and joy and knowledge
> that pass all the art and argument of the earth;
> And I know that the hand of God is the elderhand of my own,
> And I know that the spirit of God is the eldest brother of my own,

And that all men ever born are also my brothers . . . . and the women
my sisters and lovers,
And that a kelson of the creation is love;
And limitless are leaves stiff or drooping in the fields,
And brown ants in the little wells beneath them,
And mossy scabs of the wormfence, and heaped stones, and elder and
mullen and pokeweed. (*LG* 1855, 28–29)

Here as in the "Twenty-eight young men" (34), "Thruster holding me tight" (45), and "Is this then a touch?" (53) sequences, scenes of sexual and orgasmic pleasure with another man, with twenty-eight young men, with the "voluptuous coolbreathed earth," or with oneself, become the source of political and spiritual vision—the ideal of "form and union and plan" toward which the poem moves (*LG* 1855, 34, 45, 53, 85).

The democratic knowledge that the poet receives and gives of a universe bathed in an erotic force that links God, men, women, and the natural world is not only linked with the ecstasy of same-sex union among and between men. The democratic "sign" that the poet gives is also linked with giving public voice to the socially marginalized and sexually repressed. "I speak the password primeval . . . . I give the sign of democracy," Whitman writes:

Through me many long dumb voices,
Voices of the interminable generations of slaves,
Voices of prostitutes and of deformed persons,
Voices of the diseased and despairing, and of thieves and dwarfs,
. . . .
Through me forbidden voices,
Voices of sexes and lusts . . . . voices veiled, and I remove the veil,
Voices indecent by me clarified and transfigured. (*LG* 1855, 48)

Although Whitman's reference to clarifying and transfiguring "indecent" voices has been read as a capitulation to bourgeois propriety, the lines suggest just the opposite. "Sexes and lusts" are not "indecent" because they are bad but because they are socially "forbidden." In accord with the Habermassian principle of publicity, the poet clarifies and transfigures "sexes and lusts" by removing the veils of bourgeois decorum and liberal privacy, by making them public and common.

As Robert K. Martin, Gary Schmidgall, and other gay critics have shown, Whitman's poems might be read as a virtual handbook of the multiplicity of sexual and erotic pleasures men find with each other.[8] In fact, as I want to elaborate in this essay, it is in daring to structure his poetry and his political vision around a sexual and specifically "homosexual" symbolics that Whitman is at his most radical as a democratic theorist.[9] Having said this, however, it is also important to recognize that the social and political force of erotic attraction in Whitman's work is not always sexual—or genital; and it is not always—though it is mostly—between men.

In the 1855 poem later entitled "The Sleepers," for example, Whitman presents two historical scenes of Washington weeping in a public display of affection for his troops. The first is at "the defeat at Brooklyn." Standing "amid a crowd of officers," Washington "cannot repress the weeping drops" as "He sees the slaughter of the southern braves confided to him by their parents" (*LG* 1855, 110). In the second, Washington stands in "the old tavern" at the close of the war as "the wellbeloved soldiers all pass through":

> The officers speechless and slow draw near in their turns,
> The chief encircles their necks with his arm and kisses them on the
> cheek,
> He kisses lightly the wet cheeks one after another . . . . he shakes hands
> and bids goodbye to the army. (*LG* 1855, 110)

By incorporating these scenes from the beginning and end of the American Revolution into the seemingly private homoerotic dream fantasy of "The Sleepers," Whitman gives to the private, the sexual, and the imaginary, a public, democratic, and national inflection. He embodies in the figure of Washington himself the public and political role that emotion, tears, and bodily affection between men will play in creating new and more democratic forms of leadership, citizenship, and friendship as the foundation of the new American nation.

This founding scene of public affection and love is immediately paired in "The Sleepers" with Whitman's account of his mother's "remembrance" of the bodily attraction and love that she felt for an Indian woman—a "stranger"—"when she was a nearly grown girl living home with her parents on the old homestead":

> My mother looked in delight and amazement at the stranger,
> She looked at the beauty of her tallborne face and full and pliant limbs,
> The more she looked upon her she loved her,
> Never before had she seen such wonderful beauty and purity.
> (*LG* 1855, 111)

Here as in the "Twenty-eight young men" sequence in "Song of Myself," in which a socially repressed woman (along with Whitman himself) fantasizes a scene of group sex with twenty-eight male bathers, Whitman imagines democratic culture as the broadest possible opening up of society to the energies of erotic and homoerotic attraction and love in all their various social and sexual forms.[10] The erotic force of love becomes a democratizing power that erodes the traditional boundaries of sex, race, class, family, and propriety and gives rise to alternative forms of social and sexual relations: between a highborn woman and twenty-eight working-class men, between Whitman himself as the "unseen hand" and twenty-eight young men, between a "nearly grown girl" and an Indian woman of exquisite "beauty," or anonymously between "strangers."

Inseparable from Whitman's democratizing desire to make public love is the Adamic process of naming anew—of finding alternative ways of publicizing and saying what the culture had silenced or banned as onanism, sodomy, or the sin that has no name. Although critics have tended to treat Whitman's use of the phrenological term *adhesiveness* to describe "manly love" or "the passion of friendship for man"[11] as a term that came into being in the 1860 "Calamus" poems and then disappeared or was sublimated later, Whitman first used the term *adhesiveness* in the 1856 "Poem of the Road" to suggest the sexual and bodily "yearnings" that arouse and draw strangers to each other amid the potentially alienating spaces of the modern world:

> Here is adhesiveness—it is not previously fashioned, it is apropos;
> Do you know what it is as you pass to be loved by strangers?
> Do you know the talk of those turning eye-balls?
> . . . .
> Why are there men and women that while they are nigh me the sun-light expands my blood?
> Why when they leave me do my pennants of joy sink flat and lank?
> . . . .
> What is it I interchange so suddenly with strangers?
> What with some driver as I ride on the seat by his side?
> What with some fisherman, drawing his seine by the shore, as I walk by and pause? (*LG* 1856, 229, 230)

Far from being "too literal an application" of "overt, acted-out connectedness" as Kateb argues, adhesiveness is the "not previously fashioned" but "apropos" term that Whitman uses to describe the very qualities of responsiveness and receptivity that Kateb regards as Whitman's most important contribution to the theory of democracy. "Here is the profound lesson of reception, neither preference or denial," Whitman writes; "The black with his wooly head, the felon, the diseased, the illiterate person, are not denied" (*LG* 1856, 224). Rather than emanating from democratic individuality, as Kateb argues, the lesson of reception, equality, and sympathy that grounds "overt, acted-out connectedness" in Whitman's democratic theory emanates from the "fluid and attaching character" of adhesiveness as the erotic and bodily force, or "efflux of the soul," that attracts people—including men and strangers—to each other (*LG* 1856, 230). As Rorty observes in *Achieving Our Country*, "Whitman's image of democracy was of lovers embracing" (25). It is this "shuddering longing ache of contact" (*LG* 1856, 231) that, to quote Kateb against himself, "gradually build[s] up the overt connectedness of a democratically receptive culture: its tolerance, its hospitableness, and its appetite for movement, novelty, mixture, and impurity" ("Walt Whitman," 563).

By using the French term "*Allons!*," Whitman links his call to the open road of adhesiveness and comradeship to the democratizing energies of the French Revolution, the Revolutions of 1848, and the greater bodily openness and fraternity that he associated with French culture:

> Allons! out of the dark confinement!
> It is useless to protest—I know all, and expose it!
>
> Behold through you as bad as the rest!
> Through the laughter, dancing, dining, supping, of people,
> Inside of dresses and ornaments, inside of those washed and trimmed
> faces,
> Behold a secret silent loathing and despair! (*LG* 1856, 237)

Here again, Whitman's call to the "public road" of democratic freedom and adhesiveness is inseparable from publication and public expression as part of an ongoing emancipatory struggle against the oppressive social and sexual codes of the past—the "limits and imaginary lines" that keep private persons locked in "a secret silent loathing and despair" (*LG* 1856, 226, 237).

This impulse toward public expression of adhesive love received renewed impetus by two events that coalesced in Whitman's personal and political life in the late 1850s: Whitman appears to have had an intense love affair with a man, which he recorded in an unpublished sheaf of twelve poems entitled "Live Oak, with Moss"; and the political union on which he staked his identity as the poet of democracy began to dissolve under the pressure of slavery and other contradictions in the body politic of the American republic. In his unpublished political pamphlet entitled "The Eighteenth-Presidency!" and in his journals and notebooks of the time, Whitman was so gloomy about the state of national and party politics, the slavery crisis, and increasing economic hardship that he appears to have contemplated taking his "voice" directly to the people either as a public lecturer or by seeking political office himself (*NUPM*, 6: 2120–35).[12] In a notebook entry for April 24, 1857, he imagines himself as a public advocate for the people in Washington or elsewhere, darting "hither or thither, as some great emergency might demand": "*Not* to direct eyes or thoughts to any of the usual avenues, as of official appointment, or to get such any way— To put all those aside for good.— But always to keep up living interest in public questions,—and *always to hold the ear of the people.* —" (*NUPM*, 4: 1554).

In the love poems of "Live Oak, with Moss," which were written between 1858 and 1859, he also appears to have flirted with the idea of taking the path pursued by Emily Dickinson around the same time—of retreating from the public sphere of print and publicity. "I can be your singer of songs no longer," Whitman announces in poem V of the sequence (later "Calamus" 8):

> I have found him who loves me, as I him, in perfect love,
> With the rest I dispense—I sever from all that I thought would suffice
> me, for it does not—it is now empty and tasteless to me,
> I heed knowledge, and the grandeur of The States, and the examples of
> heroes, no more,
> I am indifferent to my own songs—I am to go with him I love, and he
> is to go with me,
> It is to be enough for each of us that we are together—We never
> separate again.— (*LOM*, 17–19)

But Whitman chose against the path of public renunciation. Rather, and in some sense quite extraordinarily, he turned in the 1860 edition of *Leaves of Grass* toward an effort to resolve the political crisis of the Union—the paradox of liberty and union, the one and the many—on the level of the body, sex, and homosexual love.

This effort at personal and national resolution is evident in "Proto-Leaf" (later "Starting from Paumanok"), the long opening poem that would serve as a kind of preface to the 1860 and future editions of *Leaves of Grass*. Rather than allowing himself to be personally consumed by the passion of his love for men, Whitman avows to give open expression to the "burning fires" of this passion as the affective and political force that will hold "These States" together:

I will sing the song of companionship,
I will show what alone must compact These,
I believe These are to found their own ideal of manly love, indicating it
in me;
I will therefore let flame from me the burning fires that were
threatening to consume me,
I will lift what has too long kept down those smouldering fires,
I will give them complete abandonment,
I will write the evangel-poem of comrades and of love,
(For who but I should understand love, with all its sorrow and joy?
And who but I should be the poet of comrades?) (*LG* 1860, 10–11)

Believing, as he wrote in the manuscript of "Proto-Leaf," that "the main purport of America is to found a new ideal of manly friendship, more ardent, more general," Whitman presents the 1860 *Leaves of Grass* as the "New Bible" of the American republic and himself as the evangel-poet and embodiment of a new democratic gospel of "manly love."[13] He envisions the "burning fires" of "manly" passion as both the affective foundation of political "Union" and a radically democratizing force that will level distinctions between sexes and classes, "vices" and "virtues":

O my comrade!
O you and me at last—and us two only;
O power, liberty, eternity at last!
O to be relieved of distinctions! to make as much of vices as virtues!
O to level occupations and the sexes! O to bring all to a common
ground! O adhesiveness!
O the pensive aching to be together—you know not why, and I know
not why.
. . . .
O hand in hand—O wholesome pleasure—O one more desirer and
lover,
O haste, firm holding—haste, haste on, with me. (*LG* 1860, 22)

As the preface poem to the 1860 *Leaves*, "Proto-Leaf" reveals a poet newly articulate about his public role as the evangel-poet of those sexual offenders and social outsiders who were—and still are—among the least visible and most oppressed within the putatively liberating but in fact heteronormatizing structures of the liberal state.[14]

The new role that Whitman conceived for himself as the evangel-poet of democracy and love receives its fullest articulation in the "Calamus" poems. In the opening poem (later "In Paths Untrodden"), Whitman resolves to publish and give voice to the "not yet published" standard of manly love as a form of resistance to the traditional "pleasures, profits, conformities" of public culture and the marketplace:

> Escaped from the life that exhibits itself,
> From all the standards hitherto published—from the pleasures,
> profits, conformities,
> Which too long I was offering to feed to my Soul;
> Clear to me now, standards not yet published—clear to me that my
> Soul,
> That the Soul of the man I speak for, feeds, rejoices only in comrades.
> . . . .
> I proceed, for all who are, or have been, young men,
> To tell the secret of my nights and days,
> To celebrate the need of comrades. (*LG* 1860, 341–42)

Although the "Calamus" poems are frequently treated as Whitman's most private sequence of poems, they are also his most public and politically engaged. Framed by an appeal to publicity, the "Calamus" sequence seeks to express, enact, and incite new "types" of "manly attachment" and "athletic love" as the source and ground of a fully realized democratic culture.

This emphasis on publicity and public exhibition is evident even in the seemingly more "private," separatist, and renunciatory poems of "Live Oak, with Moss": "Publish my name and hang up my picture as that of the tenderest lover," Whitman declares in poem VII (*LOM*, 25; later "Recorders Ages Hence"). Although Alan Helms, Herschel Parker, and others have argued that Whitman's decision to publish his "Live Oak, with Moss" poems as part of the "Calamus" sequence represents a corruption of some originary purity of homosexual feeling and art, their argument has the effect of reprivatizing both homosexuality and art in a way that is contrary to Whitman's brave homoerotic, democratic, and insistently public and political purpose.[15] Drawing on multiple sources—from Plato's concept of the ethical and political force of erotic love and the erotically charged relation between teacher and pupil in the Greek space of the *Paideia* to the Gospels of Jesus Christ, artisan republicanism, the culture of sentiment, and the radical reform energies of the antebellum United States—Whitman tells "the secret" of his "nights and days" not for sensation or sublimation but as an emancipatory act of sexual, political, and artistic liberation.

Whitman's public and liberatory focus and the relation between sexual "secrets" and political union, between manly love and democratic theory, might be effectively illustrated by any one of the "Calamus" poems. In this essay, I want to focus in particular on "Calamus" 5 (later "For You O Democracy"), "Calamus" 15 (later "Trickle Drops"), and "The Base of All Metaphysics," a poem that Whitman added to the "Calamus" sequence after the Civil War in the 1871 *Leaves of Grass.*

In "Calamus" 5 Whitman seeks to resolve the paradox of liberty and union and the political crisis of the nation not through an appeal to law, the Constitution, or the courts or "by arms," but through the erotic force of physical love and intimacy between men. How can this be? "Affection shall solve every one of the problems of freedom," Whitman writes, representing himself and his poems as the embodiment of "a new friendship" that will "twist and intertwist" the "States" in bonds of comradeship and love:

> Those who love each other shall be invincible,
> They shall finally make America completely victorious, in my name.
>
> One from Massachusetts shall be comrade to a Missourian,
> One from Maine or Vermont, and a Carolinian and an Oregonese, shall be friends triune, more precious to each other than all the riches of the earth.
>
> . . . .
>
> The most dauntless and rude shall touch face to face lightly,
> The dependence of Liberty shall be lovers,
> The continuance of Equality shall be comrades.
>
> These shall tie and band stronger than hoops of iron. (*LG* 1860, 349–51)

Whitman's "new friendship" seeks to intervene in a Constitutional imaginary grounded in reason, self-interest, contract, and the marital bond between male and female. His appeal to "manly affection" as the basis of democratic liberty, equality, and union seeks to retrieve the passions of love, sympathy, fraternal feeling, and bodily desire that were, in effect, written out of the Constitution. While Madison subscribed to the "republican theory" that "the people are the only legitimate fountain of power," he feared "the public passions" that would be aroused by referring "constitutional questions" to their power (*Federalist* No. 49, 283–84). "It is the reason, alone, of the public, that ought to control and regulate the government," he asserted in *Federalist* No. 49. "The passions ought to be controlled and regulated by the government" (285). Especially following the French Revolution in 1789 and the Reign of Terror in the 1790s, the Federalists sought to secure the American nation against the effects of passion, sympathy, and fraternal feeling at home and abroad. "No entangling alliances," Washington had warned in his Farewell Address in 1796 in an effort to isolate the United States from the more fraternal, egalitarian, and global forms of sympathy, passion, love, and republican citizenship associated with the French Revolution.[16]

But what exactly does Whitman mean by his assertion that "Affection shall solve every one of the problems of freedom" and how does it relate to his theory of democracy? Whitman's vision of adhesiveness or erotic attachment—especially between men—refigures ideas of sympathetic attachment, identification, and affection that were regarded as the base of political community by conservative eighteenth-century philosophers such as Edmund Burke and by Scottish moral sense philosophers such as Adam Smith. In Smith's view, human society is held together by moral sympathy, "an internal monitor activated by the sympathetic attachments."[17] It is through the power of sympathetic identification that one can enter into another's body and feel his pain. "By the imagination we place ourselves in his situation," Smith writes in *The Theory of Moral Sentiments* (1759); "we conceive ourselves enduring all the same torments, we enter as it were into his body, and become in some measure the same person with him, and thence form some idea of his sensations."[18] Smith's theory of sympathetic identification adumbrates the fluid interchange of self and other that underwrites Whitman's theory of democracy. Refigured in Whitman's writings as "this never satisfied appetite for sympathy, and this boundless offering of sympathy—this universal democratic comradeship," sympathy or what Whitman calls "this old, eternal yet ever-new interchange of adhesiveness, so fitly emblematic of America" (1876 preface; *PW*, 2: 471) creates the fluid conditions for an equitable, just, and democratic society.

Unlike Smith, who excludes erotic love from the moral sentiments, Whitman rewrites eighteenth-century sympathy as "this terrible, irrepressible yearning," a "living, pulsating" desire for "love and friendship" that is at once sexual appetite and democratizing force (1876 preface; *PW*, 2: 471). The same erotic force that draws the poet to his male lovers also draws him to being in general, through sympathetic identification with women, blacks, workers, the poor, the outcast, and the oppressed. "Agonies are one of my changes of garments," Whitman asserts as he enters into the body of the "hounded slave": "Hell and despair are upon me . . . . crack and again crack the marksmen / I clutch the rails of the fence . . . . my gore dribs thinned with the ooze of my skin" (*LG* 1855, 62). This imaginative identification with the feeling of others becomes the affective base for justice, equity, and democratic union and the ground for resistance to injustice and oppression on behalf of oneself and others worldwide.[19]

Whereas the Constitutional founders sought to regulate and control passion, Whitman wants to let it "flame out" as the affective foundation of political union and the public culture of democracy. He seeks to fill public space with the "new signs" of male passion and love—with men kissing, holding hands, embracing, and touching "face to face." "I will plant companionship thick as trees along all the rivers of America, and along the shores of the great lakes, and all over the prairies, / I will make inseparable cities, with their arms about each other's necks." Beyond the law, the military, and the abstract and disembodied language of democratic rights, Whitman begins to formulate the notion of a public culture of men loving men as a model of the non-state forms of democratic affection that will unite America and the world in ties "stronger than hoops of iron" (*LG* 1860, 351).

Like the poetic figure of Washington weeping, hugging, and kissing his soldiers, these public displays of physical affection and love between men are also part of Whitman's effort to challenge the male and female marital structures of the Revolutionary and post-Revolutionary imaginary. During the age of the transatlantic revolutions in America, France, and Haiti, transformations in the concept of the subject and citizenship and in the relations between citizens and the state were inseparable from a reconceptualization of men and women and the relations between them. Renouncing models of patriarchal authority associated with the old world, monarchy, and the feudal past, American patriots represented the affectionate bond of love and friendship between husband and wife as the model of republican relations in family, society, and state. As Jan Lewis argues: "Marriage was the very pattern from which the cloth of republican society was to be cut," and "friendship" was the word most frequently used to describe ideal republican marriage.[20]

The extent to which the male and female couple came to dominate not only literature but all aspects of American life in the post-Revolutionary period is suggested by the essay "From the Genius of Liberty," which appeared in *The Key* on April 14, 1798: "That MAN who resolves to live without WOMAN, or that WOMAN who resolves to live without MAN are ENEMIES TO THE COMMUNITY in which they dwell, INJURIOUS TO THEMSELVES, DESTRUCTIVE TO THE WORLD, APOSTATES TO NATURE, AND REBELS AGAINST HEAVEN AND EARTH."[21]

The naturalness of the relation between MAN and WOMAN that the "Genius of Liberty" encodes is not only a sexual order: it is also a politics and a metaphysics. The "Genius" of American "Liberty," the perpetuation of human community, and the metaphysical order of things come to depend on the naturalness of the union between MAN and WOMAN.

As early as the 1840s, Whitman challenged this metaphysics of male and female marital love in such tales as "The Child's Champion" and *Franklin Evans* by circulating the countermodel of a *real* though subaltern culture of male affection and love. In the 1856 *Leaves of Grass,* he avows his intent to write against the forms of male and female love that have dominated the literature and culture of democracy: "This tepid wash, this diluted deferential love, as in songs, fictions, and so forth, is enough to make a man vomit; as to manly friendship, everywhere observed in The States, there is not the first breath of it to be observed in print" (*LG* 1856, 356). In Whitman's view, it was the historically patriarchal and unequal relationship between man and woman that made "manly friendship" a more appropriate because more egalitarian model of democracy than the "diluted deferential love" of popular fiction and songs. At the same time, Whitman's commitment to making both *male and female* sex public—"that the body is to be expressed, and sex is" (*LG* 1856, 356)—was part of the historical process of achieving political equality between men and women.[22]

As "Calamus" 5 suggests, in the 1860 *Leaves*, and especially in the "Calamus" poems, Whitman's political and democratic project becomes inseparable from his desire to resist both the privatization of sex and the naturalization of male-female marriage as the fundamental means of organizing sexuality and social space: "It shall be customary in all directions, in the houses and streets, to see manly affection, / The departing brother or friend shall salute the remaining brother or friend with a kiss" (*LG* 1860, 350). Whitman infuses his poems and democratic culture with forms of "manly affection" that are neither private nor always sexual and genital but public, erotic, and multiple—a practice of everyday life that is visible and pervasive. Acts of physical affection and love between men not only take place in public, they take place *only* in public.

Whitman fills his poems and the public space of print with forms of manly love that include images of himself as "the new husband" and "comrade," the poet-lover of his readers and teacher of élèves. He is the "suffering" lover who gives voice to the "anguish and passion" of unreturned love between men ("Calamus" 9), and he is the man who joyously sleeps with his lover outdoors "under the same cover in the cool night" ("Calamus" 11). He is the urban cruiser, who celebrates Manhattan's "frequent and swift flash of eyes offering me love" ("Calamus" 18). "Lovers, continual lovers, only repay me," he avows in lines that subvert notions of the couple and monogamy as the only forms of sexual pleasure and love ("Calamus" 18). He is the American comrade who publicly kisses and is kissed by "a Manhattanese" ("And I, in the public room, or on the crossing of the street, or on the ship's deck, kiss him in return"; "Calamus" 19). He is the lover of strangers ("Passing stranger! you do not know how longingly I look upon you") and of "other men in other lands . . . in Germany, Italy, France, Spain—Or far, far away, in China, or in Russia or India—talking other dialects" ("Calamus" 22, 23; ellipsis mine). He is the "unremarked" person who silently holds hands with "a youth who loves me, and whom I love" amid "a crowd of workmen and drivers in a bar-room" ("Calamus" 29). He is the recorder of "two simple men . . . on the pier, in the midst of the crowd": "The one to remain hung on the other's neck, and passionately kissed him, / While the one to depart, tightly prest the one to remain in his arms" ("Calamus" 32; ellipsis mine). He is the dreamer who dreams of a city of "robust love": "It was seen every hour in the actions of the men of that city, / And in all their looks and words" ("Calamus" 34). And he is the poet of a future culture of public love: "Now it is you, compact, visible, realizing my poems, seeking me" ("Calamus" 45).

In *The Structural Transformation of the Public Sphere*, Habermas argues that the appearance of John Stuart Mill's *On Liberty* in 1859 marked a shift away from the revolutionary conceptualization of the public sphere as a site of democratic opinion formation toward a strengthening of the legal and administrative power of the state and an increasing distinction between a private sphere of home, family, and economics and a public sphere of government and politics. Not surprisingly, Mill's *On Liberty* appeared in the same year that Whitman began to theorize the public role of the "secret" culture of male love in securing the future of democracy worldwide. Whereas "Calamus" 5 emphasizes manly love as a force for political union and a practice of everyday life, "Calamus" 15 (later "Trickle Drops") seeks to publicize the private, to make the passions of the heart, the body, and the blood of male love public by bleeding—or more properly, hemorrhaging—into print:

O DROPS of me! trickle, slow drops,
Candid, from me falling—drip, bleeding drops,
From wounds made to free you whence you were prisoned,

From my face—from my forehead and lips,
From my breast—from within where I was concealed—Press forth,
red drops—confession drops,
Stain every page—stain every song I sing, every word I say, bloody
drops. (*LG* 1860, 361)

Whitman writes against a disembodied public sphere of reason and print and a nineteenth-century medical discourse that locates nonreproductive sexualities, associated with onanism, intemperance, and other forms of bodily excess, outside the realms of political citizenship and human community.[23]

As in "Calamus" 2 (later "Scented Herbage of My Breast"), Whitman resolves to "unbare" his "broad breast" by giving voice to the private or "concealed" as a source of sexual guilt, pain, and repression in an amative order of things. As a nineteenth-century version of "Don't ask, don't tell," privacy is in fact a prison that keeps male and female bodies separate and distinct and nonamative sexualities "secret" and oppressed. The poet's wounds—whether self-inflicted or socially imposed—become a source of freedom by bleeding openly into speech, print, and song. The conjunction of tears and blood flowing out of a body without bounds poetically enacts the breakdown of the boundaries between private and public, sex and print, wound and voice, female and male, that the poem encodes. Male tears and blood flow into the public sphere in images that associate the poet's body with both the male onanist and the female hysteric as they were being constituted by nineteenth-century medical discourse.[24]

"[A]ll ashamed and wet," Whitman also draws on the medical theory of semen as a form of blood to represent his poems as a kind of masturbatory flow into print and publicity:

Let them know your scarlet heat—let them glisten,
Saturate them with yourself, all ashamed and wet,
Glow upon all I have written or shall write, bleeding drops,
Let it all be seen in your light, blushing drops. (*LG* 1860, 361)

Saturating a "them" that encompasses the printed page, "every song I sing," and the public he addresses with the blood, semen, and tears of homosexual passion, Whitman's poetic act of making the private public is part of a political struggle for freedom and justice. As the political theorist Seyla Benhabib observes: "All struggles against oppression in the modern world begin by redefining what had previously been considered private, nonpublic, and nonpolitical issues as matters of public concern, as issues of justice, as sites of power that need discursive legitimation."[25]

Rather than representing a sublimation or retreat from the homoerotic politics of the 1860 *Leaves of Grass*, as some have argued, the Civil War reaffirmed and extended Whitman's democratic vision of the love between men as a force for social, political, and ultimately ethical and religious union. The eroticism of male-male physical contact and love pervades Whitman's Civil War poems, including the more public and political space of "When Lilacs Last in the Dooryard Bloom'd," Whitman's elegy on the death of President Lincoln in which Lincoln, like Washington, is evoked as comrade and lover. The centrality of physical and public acts of affection between men to Whitman's historical understanding of the Civil War is further suggested by the fact that he later incorporated most of "Calamus" 5—"The dependence of Liberty shall be lovers / The continuance of Equality shall be comrades"—into his effort to come to terms with the blood and carnage of the Civil War in his 1865 *Drum-Taps* poem "Over the Carnage Rose Prophetic a Voice."

Whitman envisioned adhesiveness not as a sexual relation only but as a social relation, a politics, and a metaphysics.[26] It is this metaphysics of male-male love that is the subject of "The Base of All Metaphysics," the only poem that Whitman added to the "Calamus" sequence in the post–Civil War period. Rather than sublimating, diluting, or silencing Whitman's celebration of homosexual love, the poem invokes "the new and antique" systems of philosophy—of Plato and Socrates, of Christ and the Christian Church, of Kant, Fichte, Schelling, and Hegel—as the base for alternative forms of male passion and love outside the patriarchal, property-based, and reproduction-centered marriage of man and woman.[27] Perhaps influenced by a recent reading of Plato, "whose whole treatment," Whitman wrote, "assumes the illustration of love" by "the passion inspired in one man by another man, more particularly a beautiful youth" ("it is astounding to modern ideas," he added), Whitman represents "[t]he dear love of man for his comrade, / the attraction of friend to friend" as the model of an erotic "attraction" that binds man to man, friend to friend, husband to wife, city to city, and land to land (*NUPM*, 5: 1882).[28] In "The Base of All Metaphysics," a pervasive and seemingly natural male-female metaphysics of hierarchy and oppression is displaced and denaturalized by an egalitarian and more democratic metaphysics of male-male love.[29]

It was not until after the Civil War in *Democratic Vistas* that Whitman sought to synthesize the relations among individualism, political union, and public love into a major theory of democracy. Published as a pamphlet in 1871,

Democratic Vistas begins by acknowledging the seedy, greedy corruptions of Gilded Age America. "[W]ith unprecedented materialistic advancement—society, in these States, is canker'd, crude, superstitious, and rotten," Whitman writes. "Never was there, perhaps, more hollowness at heart than at present, and here in the United States" (*PW*, 2: 369):

> The depravity of the business classes of our country is not less than has been supposed, but infinitely greater. The official services of America, national, state, and municipal . . . are saturated in corruption, bribery, falsehood, mal-administration. . . . The great cities reek with respectable as much as non-respectable robbery and scoundrelism. . . . In business, (this all-devouring modern word, business,) the one sole object is, by any means, pecuniary gain. The magician's serpent in the fable ate up all the other serpents; and money-making is our magician's serpent, remaining to-day sole master of the field. (*PW*, 2: 370; ellipses mine)

Whitman presents the specter of a disunited states—a democratic society disintegrated by the forces of capitalist individualism that were supposed to be its salvation. Democratic individualism had reached a dead end in what Whitman calls "the increasing aggregation of capital in the hands of a few," "the advent of new machinery, dispensing more and more with hand-work," "the growing, alarming spectacle of countless squads of vagabond children," "the hideousness and squalor of certain quarters of the cities," and the "advent of late years . . . of these pompous, nauseous, outside shows of vulgar wealth" (*PW*, 2: 753; ellipsis mine). The world of "pride, competition, segregation, vicious willfulness, and license beyond example" (*PW*, 2: 422) that Whitman describes is, in effect, the world of late capitalism that we know today, only now the serpent's field is corporate and global rather than individual and national.

The question Whitman finally poses in *Democratic Vistas* is whether or not democracy is possible under the conditions of laissez-faire capitalism. Democracy, Whitman argues, cannot be "held together merely by political means": it needs poets to aid in the political creation of a democratic culture that will take "firm and . . . warm . . . hold in men's hearts, emotions and belief" (*PW*, 2: 368; ellipses mine). Like the political theorist Hannah Arendt in the twentieth century, Whitman expresses concern that the expansion of the economic sphere will replace the common concern for political community—for the *res publica*—in the hearts and minds of the people.[30] While Whitman believed that "the ulterior object of political and all other government" was "to develop, to open to cultivation, to encourage the possibilities of all beneficent and manly outcroppage, and of that aspiration for independence, and the pride and self-respect latent in all characters" (*PW*, 2: 379), he also feared that unleashed individualism—or what he called "Selfism"—would undermine the common good of the American republic. "Must not the virtue of modern Individualism," he asked, "continually enlarging, usurping all, seriously affect, perhaps keep down entirely, in America, the like of the ancient virtue of Patriotism, the fervid and absorbing love of general country?" (*PW*, 2: 373).[31]

To this "serious problem and paradox in the United States" (*PW*, 2: 373), Whitman responded with the visionary and utopian force of erotic, or adhesive, love. Countering the revolutionary movement away from the feudal structures of the past toward the sovereign power of the individual, he envisions a universal Hegelian force that binds and fuses humanity: There is "not that half only, individualism, which isolates. There is another half, which is adhesiveness or love, that fuses, ties and aggregates, making the races comrades, and fraternizing all" (*PW*, 2: 381). Far from being "too literal" or threatening "to suffocate" "rights-based individualism" in "an all-enfolding merger," as Kateb argues, it is to the "threads of manly friendship" running through the "worldly interests of America" that Whitman looks for the "counterbalance" and "spiritualization" of "our materialistic and vulgar American democracy" (*PW*, 2: 414): "I say democracy infers such loving comradeship, as its most inevitable twin or counterpart," he writes, "without which it will be incomplete, in vain, and incapable of perpetuating itself" (*PW*, 2: 414–15).

Whereas *Democratic Vistas* opens with a tribute to the "lessons" of individual "variety and freedom" affirmed by John Stuart Mill's *On Liberty*, it closes with a homoerotic rewriting of Hegel's *Introduction to the Philosophy of History*, with what Whitman calls "the Hegelian formulas" or spirit manifesting itself historically in democratic community (*PW*, 2: 421).[32] In the concluding section of *Democratic Vistas*, as Whitman leaps ahead in "fond fantasy" to imagine what a fully realized democratic culture might look like on the second centennial of the republic in 1976, the only future he can imagine is one in which "the development, identification, and general prevalence" of homoerotic love, "carried to degrees hitherto unknown," will pervade "individual character" and "general politics": "*Intense and loving comradeship, the personal and passionate attachment of man to man*—which, hard to define, underlies the lessons and ideals of the profound saviours of every land and age, and which seems to promise, when thoroughly develop'd, cultivated and recognized in manners and literature, the most substantial hope and safety of the future of these States, *will then be fully express'd*" (*PW*, 2: 414; my italics).

It is in "intense and loving comradeship, the personal and passionate attachment of man to man" that Whitman finds the affective base for the non-state forms of political community that will take "hold in men's hearts, emotions and belief" and receive fullest public expression in "the average, the bodily, the concrete, the democratic, the popular, on which all the superstructures of the future are to permanently rest" (*PW*, 2: 426).

The bonds of loving comradeship that Whitman imagines are the base not only of political union in the United States but of a new metaphysics of democracy worldwide. Although *Democratic Vistas* addresses the problems and contradictions of democracy in the United States in the post–Civil War period, the future—or vistas—it imagines are transnational and global. Like Karl Marx and like C. L. R. James in a later period, Whitman saw the outbreak of the American and French Revolutions and the 1848 Revolutions in Europe as part of a broader popular democratic revolution that would eventually spread to the entire world. The empowering of the masses and the structures of law, government, and rights put into place following the American and French revolutions were only the first stage of a more global revolution. "The great word Solidarity has arisen," Whitman declared in *Democratic Vistas* (*PW*, 2: 382). Whereas Marx imagines the will of the people becoming the state, like C. L. R. James and recent theorists of what Nancy Fraser has called counter or *subaltern* public spheres, Whitman imagines a collective popular will that exists apart from the authority of the state. The state is the legal structure of democracy; the people are its base and its future. Beyond a first stage of rights and a second stage of material progress and wealth, Whitman theorizes a future public culture of democracy that will be achieved not by law, government, or the market but by the democratizing force of adhesive, or manly love, which "alone can bind, and ever seeks to bind, all nations, all men, of however various and distant lands, into a brotherhood, a family" (*PW*, 2: 381).[33]

As "Calamus" 23 (later entitled "This Moment Yearning and Thoughtful") suggests, it was through the open road of his feeling for other men—sometimes strangers—that Whitman was able to imagine forms of democratic community outside law and government and beyond the nation-state:

> This moment as I sit alone, yearning and thoughtful, it seems to me
> there are other men in other lands, yearning and thoughtful;
> It seems to me I can look over and behold them, in Germany, Italy,
> France, Spain—Or, far, far away, in China, or in Russia or
> India—talking other dialects;

And it seems to me if I could know those men better, I should become attached to them, as I do to men in my own lands;

. . . .

O I know we should be brethren and lovers,
I know I should be happy with them. (*LG* 1860, 367)

In Whitman's homoerotic vistas, the love of strangers models the public culture of male love that he imagines as the future of democracy: the stranger exists as an unknown figure, a foreigner in public space, outside the prescribed intimacies of home, marriage, and family. Rather than serving what Kateb calls "the sinister project of nationalism," Whitman's erotic experience of desire for, sympathetic attachment to, and identification with strangers—the swift and fluid exchange of glances, bodies, and love in the streets, bars, buses, theatres, and public spaces of the modern metropolis—enables him to imagine a fully democratic world of strangers loving strangers worldwide.

Returning to Plato's evocation of love between men as a simultaneously erotic, ethical, and political force, Whitman challenges the rhetorics of male and female romance that have ordered sex, society, and politics in the West. Seeking to displace what he calls "the amative love hitherto possessing imaginative literature," Whitman envisions "adhesive love" as the "base of all metaphysics," the model of alternative forms of social affection and political community, and the erotic base for the future of democracy not only in the United States but worldwide:

Camerado, I give you my hand!
I give you my love more precious than money,
I give you myself before preaching or law;
Will you give me yourself? will you come travel with me? (*LGC*, 159)

NOTES

Introduction: The Whitman Revolution

1. On the bulging-crotch version of the 1855 engraving, see Ted Genoways, "'One Goodshaped and Wellhung Man': Accentuated Sexuality and Uncertain Authorship of the Frontispiece to the 1855 Edition of *Leaves of Grass*," in *Leaves of Grass: The Sesquicentennial Essays*, ed. Susan Belasco, Ed Folsom, and Kenneth M. Price (Lincoln: University of Nebraska Press, 2007), 87–123.

2. Gay Wilson Allen, "Walt Whitman—Nationalist or Proletarian?" *English Journal* 26 (1937): 51–52.

3. Walt Whitman, *Leaves of Grass*: *An Exact Copy of the First Edition 1855* (New York: Eakins Press, 1966), n. pag.

4. Whitman regarded Thomas Paine as one "of the superber characters of my day or America's early days" who was "much maligned" and "much misunderstood." "I swore when a young man [to] do public justice" to him, Whitman later told Horace Traubel (*WWC*, 2: 205–6). He carried out his resolve in 1877 when he gave a speech entitled "In Memory of Thomas Paine" at a gathering to celebrate Paine's 140th birthday at Lincoln Hall in Philadelphia. As M. Wynn Thomas observes, Whitman's real tribute to Paine "was not in the feeble, yet touchingly loyal lectures he delivered in his old age, but in the gloriously radical vigor of the early *Leaves of Grass*" (*The Lunar Light of Whitman's Poetry* [Cambridge, MA: Harvard University Press, 1987], 31).

5. Thomas Paine, *Collected Writings*, ed. Eric Foner (New York: Library of America, 1995), 52–53.

6. In "A Pact," Ezra Pound wrote: "It was you that broke the new wood / Now is a time for carving" (*Personae* [New York: New Directions, 1926], 89). On Whitman's international legacy as a poet, see *Walt Whitman: The Measure of His Song*, ed. Jim Perlman, Ed Folsom, and Dan Campion (Duluth, MN: Holy Cow! Press, 2019), and its superb introduction by Ed Folsom, "Talking Back to Walt Whitman," 1–63.

7. *Putnam's Magazine*, September 1855, in facsimile of *Leaves of Grass* (1855; see n. 3), n. pag.

8. Whitman's language experiment did not go unnoticed by the genteel literary establishment. Whitman, said Oliver Wendell Holmes, "takes into his hospitable vocabulary words which no English dictionary recognizes as belonging to the language" (Oliver Wendell Holmes, *Works* [Boston: Houghton Mifflin, 1892], 4: 234).

9. George Kateb, "Walt Whitman and the Culture of Democracy," *Political Theory* 18 (November 1990), 563, 564. For a more extensive discussion of Whitman and political theory, see chapter 9, "Public Love: Whitman and Political Theory."

10. Arthur Rimbaud, in his famous "Lettre du Voyant," written to Paul Demeny in 1871; in *Correspondance inédite* (1870–1875), ed. Roger Gilbert-Lecomte (Paris: Éditions des Cahiers Libres, 1929), 49–61. For a discussion of the ways Whitman's democracy is inextricably linked with French *fraternité*, see Jacques Darras, "Walt Whitman, poète de l'utopie américaine: Entretien avec Jacques Darras," *Esprit* (October 2002): 58. See also Betsy Erkkila, *Walt Whitman Among the French: Poet and Myth* (Princeton, NJ: Princeton University Press, 1980).

11. Charley Shively's comment on this passage was made in response to James E. Miller's insistence on Whitman's "omnisexuality" at the 1992 Centennial Conference at the University of Iowa; see also Shively's pioneering book *Calamus Lovers: Walt Whitman's Working Class Camerados*, ed. Charley Shively (San Francisco: Gay Sunshine Press, 1987), 31.

12. Whitman said he "deliberately and insultingly ignored all the other, the cultivated classes as they are called, and set himself to write 'America's first distinctive Poem,' on the platform of these same New York Roughs, firemen, the ouvrier class, masons and carpenters, stagedrivers, the Dry Dock boys, and so forth" (*NUPM*, 1: 333–34). This was the same disaffected class of artisans who, like Whitman's father, belonged to societies dedicated to the freethinking and anticlerical legacy of Thomas Paine.

13. The Latin phrase *E pluribus unum* (Out of many, one) was adopted as the Great Seal of the United States by an act of Congress in 1782.

14. On Whitman as a personal and mystical poet, see James E. Miller, Jr., "'Song of Myself' as an Inverted Mystical Experience," in *A Critical Guide to Leaves of Grass* (Chicago: University of Chicago Press, 1957), 636–61; and Malcolm Cowley, "Introduction," in *LG* 1855, vii–xxxvii.

15. Allen Ginsberg, *Howl and Other Poems* (San Francisco: City Lights Books, 1956), 23.

16. F. O. Matthiessen, *American Renaissance: Art and Expression in the Age of Emerson and Whitman* (New York: Oxford University Press, 1941), ix, vii.

17. Robert K. Martin, *The Homosexual Tradition in American Poetry* (Austin: University of Texas Press, 1979).

18. Paul Jay, ed., *Selected Correspondence of Kenneth Burke and Malcolm Cowley, 1915–1981* (New York: Viking, 1988), 273.

19. Cowley, "Introduction," *LG* 1855, xii.

20. "For Dickinson, the private life, intense, domestic, microcosmic; for Whitman, the 'kosmos,' the 'democratic vistas' of the panorama, the open road," Rich writes, in "Beginners," *The Kenyon Review* 15 (Summer 1993): 13.

21. See also *Whitman and Dickinson: A Colloquy*, ed. Éric Athenot and Cristanne Miller (Iowa City: University of Iowa Press, 2018), where this essay first appeared.

22. Matthiessen, *American Renaissance*, ix; Samuel H. Beer, "Liberty and Union: Walt Whitman's Idea of the Nation," *Political Theory* 12 (1984): 361–86; Kateb, "Walt Whitman and the Culture of Democracy," 545–71. See also John E. Seery, ed., *A Political Companion to Walt Whitman* (Lexington: University Press of Kentucky, 2011).

23. William Douglas O'Connor, *The Good Gray Poet: A Vindication* (New York: Bunce and Huntington, 1866), 5.

24. See Whitman to William Douglas O'Connor, November 12, 1882: "The more I think of it, the more I am convinced that [it] is Comstock's game," Whitman wrote in response to the attempt to ban the publication and circulation of his poems in Boston (*COR*, 3: 295); Oliver Stevens's letter to Osgood is reprinted in the Walt Whitman Archive at https://whitmanarchive.org/biography/correspondence/tei/loc.05596.html.

25. Carroll Smith-Rosenberg, *Disorderly Conduct: Visions of Gender in Victorian America* (New York: Knopf, 1985), 181.

26. On Tobey's refusal to circulate a lecture in defense of *Leaves of Grass* that lay preacher George Chainey published in his weekly journal *This World* because it cites "To a Common Prostitute," which violates the federal law prohibiting the circulation of "obscene" literature by US mail, see William Douglas O'Connor, "Tobey or Not Tobey? That Is the Question," initially written in September 1882, and later published in Horace Traubel's *Conservator*, as "Another Recovered Chapter in the History of 'Leaves of Grass,'" September 7, 1896, 99–102.

27. W. Graham Robertson, *Time Was: Rossetti, Oscar Wilde, Ellen Terry* (Philadelphia: R. West, 1931), 70; cited in Richard Ellmann, "Oscar Meets Walt," *New York Review of Books*, December 3, 1987, 44.

28. Gavin Arthur, *Gay Sunshine* 35 (Winter 1975): 29.

29. Betsy Erkkila, *Whitman the Political Poet* (New York: Oxford University Press, 1989).

See also Ed Folsom, "'A Yet More Terrible and More Deeply Complicated Problem': Walt Whitman, Race, Reconstruction, and American Democracy," *American Literary History* 30 (Fall 2018): 531–38; Doris Sommer, "The Bard of Both Americas," in *Approaches to Teaching Whitman's Leaves of Grass*, ed. Donald D. Kummings (New York: MLA, 1990), 159–67; and Walter Grünzweig, "Noble Ethics and Loving Aggressiveness: The Imperialist Walt Whitman," in *An American Empire: Expansionist Cultures and Policies, 1881–1917*, ed. Serge Ricard (Aix-en-Provence: Université de Provence, 1990), 151–65.

30. Thomas Paine, *Letter to the Abbé Raynal* (1782) in *Complete Writings of Thomas Paine*, ed. Philip S. Foner (New York: Citadel Press, 1945), 2: 243.

Chapter One

1. Cited in Kenneth Silverman, *A Cultural History of the American Revolution* (New York: T. Y. Crowell, 1976), 575.

2. For a discussion of the psychological sources of Whitman's familial images, see Edwin Haviland Miller, *Walt Whitman's Poetry: A Psychological Journey* (Boston: Houghton Mifflin, 1968).

3. Jefferson to Roger C. Weightman, June 24, 1826, in Thomas Jefferson, *Writings*, ed. Merrill D. Paterson (New York: Library of America, 1984), 1517.

4. Freneau, "On Mr. Paine's Rights of Man," in *Poems of Freneau*, ed. Harry Hayden

Clark (New York: Harcourt, Brace, 1960), 125. For an earlier use of Columbia as a figure of America, see Phillis Wheatley's "To His Excellency General Washington" (1775), in *The Poems of Phillis Wheatley*, ed. Julian D. Mason, Jr. (Chapel Hill: University of North Carolina Press, 1966), 166.

5. Annette Kolodny discusses the conflict in American literature between the pastoral vision of a feminine landscape and the "aggressively destructive masculine orientation of history," in *The Lay of the Land: Metaphor as Experience and History in American Life and Letters* (Chapel Hill: University of North Carolina Press, 1975), 38.

6. Whitman, *The Uncollected Poetry and Prose*, ed. Emory Holloway (Garden City, NY: Doubleday, Page, 1921), 1: 51.

7. "Walt Whitman and His Poems," in *The United States Review*, reprinted in Whitman, *Leaves of Grass: An Exact Copy of the First Edition 1855*, n. pag.

8. For a discussion of the relation between Whitman's attitude toward women, particularly mothers, and some of the social and sexual ideologies of his time, see Harold Aspiz, *Walt Whitman and the Body Beautiful* (Urbana: University of Illinois Press, 1980); and Myrth Jimmie Killingsworth, "Whitman and Motherhood: A Historical View," *American Literature* 54 (March 1982): 28–43.

9. Whitman, *The Complete Writings of Walt Whitman*, ed. Richard Maurice Bucke, Thomas B. Harned, and Horace L. Traubel (New York: G. P. Putnam's Sons, 1902), 9: 11.

10. "America" also exists in a 36-second wax cylinder recording that appears to be the voice of Whitman reading the last four lines of the poem. See Ed Folsom, "The Whitman Recording," *Walt Whitman Quarterly Review* 9 (Spring 1992): 214–16.

11. In conceiving of motherhood not in relation to the isolate family nor as a biological function only, but as a social principle and a creative and intellectual force, Whitman comes close to the mother-centered utopian vision of Charlotte Perkins Gilman's *Herland* (1915).

Chapter Two

1. Edith Wharton, *A Backward Glance* (New York: Appleton-Century, 1934), 186.

2. Matthiessen, *American Renaissance*, 530.

3. Roger Asselineau, *The Evolution of Walt Whitman* (Cambridge, MA: Belknap Press of Harvard University Press, 1962), 2: 267; Larzer Ziff, *Literary Democracy: The Declaration of Cultural Independence in America* (New York: Viking Press, 1981), 246. For further discussion of Whitman's French usage, see also Louise Pound, "Walt Whitman and the French Language," *American Speech* 1 (May 1926): 421–30; and K. H. Francis, "Walt Whitman's French," *Modern Language Review* 51 (October 1956): 493–506. Pound's article is descriptive, presenting a partial inventory of Whitman's French usage. K. H. Francis is more critical of Whitman: Whitman, he argues, used French words "with absolute confidence (even though some of them are wrongly employed), and with the dogmatic ebullience which is so typical of his whole output" (494).

4. Reverend John Witherspoon, *Pennsylvania Journal and the Weekly Advertiser* (1781), in M. M. Mathews, ed., *The Beginnings of American English* (Chicago: University of Chicago Press, 1931), 16.

5. Adams, in Mathews, *Beginnings*, 42.

6. Adams, in Mathews, *Beginnings*, 41.

7. Noah Webster, *Dissertations on the English Language* (1789; Gainesville, FL: Scholars' Facsimiles and Reprints, 1951), 20.

8. John Pickering, *A Vocabulary or Collection of Words and Phrases Which Have Been Supposed to Be Peculiar to the United States of America* (Boston: Cummings and Hilliard, 1816), in Mathews, *Beginnings*, 72. On Benjamin Franklin, see H. L. Mencken, *The American Language: An Inquiry into the Development of English in the United States* (New York: Knopf, 1936), 11.

9. Edgar Allan Poe, "Dream-Land," in *Poe: Poetry, Tales, and Selected Essays*, ed. Patrick F. Quinn and G. R. Thompson (New York: Library of America, 1984), 79.

10. Ralph Waldo Emerson, *Nature* (1836), in *Emerson: Essays and Lectures*, ed. Joel Porte (New York: Library of America, 1983), 20.

11. Emerson, "The Poet," in *Emerson's Essays and Lectures*, 450.

12. Sir William Craigie, *The Study of American English* (Oxford: Clarendon Press, 1927), 203.

13. Whitman cited by Horace Traubel, in *DN* 3: 729n.

14. Herbert Croft, *A Letter, From Germany, to the Princess Royal of England; on the English and German Languages* (Hamburg: Fauche, 1797), 8n.

15. Howard Mumford Jones, *America and French Culture: 1750–1848* (Chapel Hill: University of North Carolina, 1927), 200.

16. For an excellent study of the often hostile response to the revolutions of 1848 in France and elsewhere in Europe among mid-nineteenth-century American writers, see Larry J. Reynolds, *European Revolutions and the American Literary Renaissance* (New Haven, CT: Yale University Press, 1988).

17. *Walt Whitman of the New York Aurora*, ed. Joseph J. Rubin and Charles H. Brown (State College, PA: Bald Eagle Press, 1950), 2.

18. Whitman, *Uncollected Poetry and Prose*, 1: 213.

19. Whitman, in *New York Dissected*, ed. Emory Holloway and Ralph Adimari (New York: R. R. Wilson, 1936), 56.

20. Whitman, in *New York Dissected*, 61.

21. On Whitman and Chaucer, see Michael Dressman, "Whitman, Chaucer, and French Words," *Walt Whitman Review* 23 (June 1977): 82.

22. Whitman, *Uncollected Poetry and Prose*, 1: 243.

23. In the Charles E. Feinberg Collection, Library of Congress.

24. C. Carroll Hollis, "Whitman and Swinton: A Cooperative Friendship," *American Literature* 30 (January 1959): 443.

25. William Swinton, *Rambles among Words: Their Poetry, History, and Wisdom* (New York: Scribner, 1859), 291, 288.

26. Swinton, *Rambles*, 290.

27. For a study of Whitman and French literature, see Erkkila, *Walt Whitman Among the French.*

28. "Letter to Ralph Waldo Emerson," *LG* 1856, 346–58.

29. Traubel, in *WWC* 4: 223.

30. On Whitman's self-censorship in the 1860 *Leaves of Grass*, see Joseph Cady, "Not Happy in the Capitol: Homosexuality and the 'Calamus' Poems," *American Studies* 19 (Fall 1978): 5–22; and Hershel Parker, "The Real 'Live Oak, with Moss': Straight Talk about Whitman's 'Gay Manifesto,'" *Nineteenth-Century Literature* 51 (September 1996): 145–60. For essays that challenge this argument about Whitman's self-censorship, see chapters 4 and 9.

31. "Inscription," *Leaves of Grass* (New York: n.p., 1867), 5; and "One's-Self I Sing," *Leaves of Grass* (Washington, DC: n.p., 1871), 7; reprinted in *The Walt Whitman Archive*, ed. Ed Folsom and Kenneth M. Price, https://whitmanarchive.org.

32. Robert E. Spiller, "The Cycle and the Roots: National Identity in American Literature," in *Toward a New American Literary History*, ed. Louis J. Budd, Edwin H. Cady, and Carl L. Anderson (Durham, NC: Duke University Press, 1980), 15.

33. Spiller, "The Cycle and the Roots," 15. See also Matthiessen, *American Renaissance*; Robert E. Spiller et al., eds., *A Literary History of the United States* (New York: Macmillan, 1948); and Perry Miller, *The New England Mind: The Seventeenth Century* (New York: Macmillan, 1939) and *The New England Mind: From Colony to Province* (Cambridge, MA: Harvard University Press, 1953).

Chapter Three

1. Whitman, *Walt Whitman's Memoranda during the War and Death of Abraham Lincoln*, ed. Roy P. Basler (Bloomington: Indiana University Press, 1962), 65.

2. Cited in Carl Sandburg, "Introduction," *Leaves of Grass*, ed. Carl Sandburg (New York: Modern Library, 1921), vii.

3. See for example, O. S. Fowler, *Amativeness: Or, Evils and Remedies of Excessive and Perverted Sexuality Including Warning and Advice to the Married and Single* (New York: Fowler and Wells, 1844).

Chapter Four

1. Cowley to Burke, in Jay, *Selected Correspondence*, 273.

2. Cowley, "Introduction," *LG* 1855, xii.

3. In letters to his lover, Russell Cheyney, F. O. Matthiessen had also drawn sympathetic attention to Whitman's erotic attachments to men. But in his influential book *American Renaissance*, he dismissed the "vaguely pathological and homosexual" quality of Whitman's work and sought to reclaim him for serious national and international attention by an insistently formalist approach to *Leaves of Grass* as a "language experiment" with analogues in oratory, opera, the ocean, and the visual arts (535). For a review of Whitman criticism and homosexuality, see Martin, *The Homosexual*

Tradition, 3–8. Justin Kaplan, in "The Biographer's Problem," *Mickle Street Review* 11 (1989): 80–88, begins by observing that "the history of over a century of Whitman biography is to a large extent the history of a pussyfooting accommodation to the issue of sexuality, more specifically homosexuality. One sees biography being skewed in the interests of literary public relations." But he concludes by reconsigning the "issue" of Whitman's homosexuality to the margins when he notes that "perhaps it's time to move on to a broader focus" (83–84, 88).

4. Robert K. Martin pioneered in the field of gay studies and in the study of Whitman and homosexuality in his groundbreaking article "Whitman's *Song of Myself*: Homosexual Dream and Vision," *Partisan Review* 42 (1975): 80–96. See also Martin's chapter on Whitman in *The Homosexual Tradition*, 3–89; Cady, "Not Happy," 5–22; and Shively, *Calamus Lovers*. Myrth Jimmie Killingsworth, *Whitman's Poetry of the Body: Sexuality, Politics, and the Text* (Chapel Hill: University of North Carolina Press, 1989), and Michael Moon, *Disseminating Whitman: Revision and Corporeality in "Leaves of Grass"* (Cambridge, MA: Harvard University Press, 1991), both focus on Whitman's "sexual politics," but in emphasizing the split between the corporeal and the social self in Whitman's work, they tend to maintain the bounds between private and public, sexuality and politics, homosexuality and democracy. See also Jay Grossman, who challenges the private/public binary in critical interpretations of Whitman's work, in "'The Evangel-Poem of Comrades and Love': Revising Whitman's Republicanism," *American Transcendental Quarterly* 4 (September 1990): 201–18.

5. David Warner, "The Good G(r)ay Poet," *Philadelphia City Paper*, January 12–19, 1990.

6. Given the controversy in the early 1990s surrounding the National Endowment for the Arts and homosexuality, it cannot be entirely coincidental that the Library of Congress, which holds the largest and most substantial collection of Whitman materials in the world, sponsored no exhibit or other series of events in 1992 in commemoration of the centennial of Walt Whitman's death in 1892.

7. For a study of the relation between capitalist transformation and the male purity movement, see Carroll Smith-Rosenberg, "Sex as Symbol in Victorian Purity: An Ethnohistorical Analysis of Jacksonian America," *American Journal of Sociology* 84 (Supplement, 1987): S212–S247.

8. Jeffrey Weeks, *Sexuality and Its Discontents: Meanings, Myths, and Modern Sexualities* (London: Routledge and Kegan Paul, 1985), 6. See also Michel Foucault's comment on the emergence of the homosexual as a distinct identity in the nineteenth century: "The sodomite had been a temporary aberration; the homosexual was now a species," in *The History of Sexuality: An Introduction*, trans. Robert Hurley (New York: Random House, 1978), 43.

9. Sylvester Graham, *A Lecture to Young Men, on Chastity* (Boston: Light and Stearns, 1834); Fowler, *Amativeness*.

10. Shively, *Calamus Lovers*, 21.

11. Miller, "'Song of Myself' as an Inverted Mystical Experience."

12. Cady, "Not Happy," 15; for a similar distinction between sentimental rhetoric

and homoerotic love in Whitman's poems, see Killingsworth, *Whitman's Poetry of the Body*, 99.

13. Erkkila, *Whitman the Political Poet*, 183.

14. Michael Lynch, "'Here is Adhesiveness': From Friendship to Homosexuality," *Victorian Studies* 29 (Autumn 1985): 91, 67.

15. Joseph Cady makes a similar point in "*Drum-Taps* and Nineteenth-Century Homosexual Literature," in *Walt Whitman: Here and Now*, ed. Joann P. Krieg (Westport, CT: Greenwood Press, 1985), 49–60. But he continues to insist on a neat division between the private poet of homosexual love and the more public figure of the soldier-comrade through whom Whitman self-protectively masks his homosexual desire. What I want to stress is the inseparability of the private discourses of male homosexual desire from the more public discourses of combat and democratic nationalism in Whitman's poems of the Civil War.

16. The language of paternal and familial care is so marked in "Vigil Strange I Kept on the Field One Night" that M. Wynn Thomas, in *The Lunar Light of Whitman's Poetry*, actually reads the poems as literally about a father mourning the loss of his son during the war (208).

17. As I argue in *Whitman the Political Poet*, this representation of same-sex love between men as the ground of democracy is accompanied by an increased emphasis on the feminine and the maternal in Whitman's post–Civil War writings (261–62); see also chapter 1, "'The Federal Mother': Whitman as Revolutionary Son," in this volume.

18. For a study of the erotic bonds Whitman formed with men during the Civil War, see Charley Shively, ed. *Drum-Beats: Walt Whitman's Civil War Boy Lovers* (San Francisco: Gay Sunshine Press, 1989); see also Ed Folsom's fascinating analysis of Whitman's many photographs with his male friends—Peter Doyle (1869), Harry Stafford (late 1870s), Bill Duckett (1886), who later posed nude for Thomas Eakins, and Warren Fritzinger (1890)—in "Whitman's Calamus Photographs," in *Breaking Bounds: Whitman and American Cultural Studies*, ed. Betsy Erkkila and Jay Grossman (New York: Oxford University Press, 1996), 193–219.

19. Shively discusses Whitman's love relationship with Fred Vaughan and reprints the letters Vaughan wrote to Whitman in 1860–1862 and 1874 in *Calamus Lovers*, 36–50. Shively argues that it was Vaughan who "inspired Whitman to write the Calamus poems—perhaps the most intense and successful celebration of gay love in our language" (38).

20. Folsom, "Whitman's Calamus Photographs," 193–219.

21. In a series entitled "Suggestions for Posing," which was published in *Anthony's Photographic Bulletin* between 1870 and 1871, for example, seventy-one different examples of posing are suggested, but none shows men together; and in a section entitled "On Groups" in the popular 1883 book *About Photography and Photographers*, Henry Baden Pritchard argues that nonfamily groups are "usually a failure as an artistic work" (quoted in John Ibson, *Picturing Men: A Century of Male Relationships in*

Everyday American Photography [Washington, DC: Smithsonian Institution Press, 2002], 16). As Ibson observes, the portraits that men took together before the primarily male gaze of the studio camera in the nineteenth century reveal a world of male intimacy that "would largely disappear from view" in the late nineteenth and early twentieth centuries as taboos about male homosexuality and communality took hold in the culture.

22. Secretary of the Interior James Harlan fired Whitman from his job as a clerk in the Bureau of Indian Affairs on June 30, 1865, purportedly for his authorship of *Leaves of Grass.* Whitman's friend William Douglas O'Connor ardently defended him in *The Good Gray Poet* (1866). See the introduction to this volume, 222–23

23. Havelock Ellis and John Addington Symonds, *Sexual Inversion* (London: Wilson and Macmillan, 1897).

24. Lynch, "'Here Is Adhesiveness,'" 67.

Chapter Five

1. After completing *Whitman the Political Poet*, it was my realization that I was speaking in two very different critical voices in my work on Dickinson and Whitman—one feminist and celebratory, the other political and against the grain—that led me to write "Emily Dickinson and Class" (*American Literary History* 4 [Spring 1992]: 1–27), an essay that was described as "notorious" in the annual review *American Literary Scholarship* in 1992.

2. Emily Dickinson, *The Poems of Emily Dickinson: Reading Edition*, ed. R. W. Franklin (Cambridge, MA: Belknap Press of Harvard University Press, 1999), 656; hereafter cited in text as *Poems.*

3. Mabel Loomis Todd, ed., *Letters of Emily Dickinson* (New York: Harper & Brothers, 1931), 132; "I'm Nobody! Who are you?" (*Poems* 260).

4. Even Adrienne Rich repeats this public/private opposition in her analysis of Whitman and Dickinson as "a strange, uncoupled couple, moving together in a dialectic that the twentieth century has only begun to decipher" in "Beginners," 12.

5. See Betsy Erkkila, "Dickinson and the Art of Politics," *Oxford Historical Guide to Emily Dickinson*, ed. Vivian Pollak (New York: Oxford University Press, 2004), 138–44.

6. Erkkila, "Dickinson and Class."

7. Emily Dickinson, *The Letters of Emily Dickinson*, ed. Thomas H. Johnson and Theodora Ward (Cambridge, MA: Belknap Press of Harvard University Press, 1958), 1: 49; ellipsis mine. Hereafter cited in the text as *Letters.*

8. Charles Sumner, "Report on the War with Mexico" (April 1847); reprinted in *Old South Leaflets*, vol. 6 (Boston: Old South Work, 1902), 137–67.

9. Walt Whitman, *PW* 1: 288. According to "Emily Dickinson's Schooling: Mount Holyoke Female Seminary," "Dickinson was among eighty without hope when she entered and was among twenty-nine who remained so by the end of the year."

Emily Dickinson Museum, September 1, 2015, https://www.emilydickinsonmuseum.org/emily-dickinson/biography/special-topics/emily-dickinsons-schooling-mount-holyoke-female-seminary/.

10. "Walt Whitman and His Poems," in *Leaves of Grass: An Exact Copy of the First Edition 1855*, n. pag.

11. Betsy Erkkila, *The Wicked Sisters: Women Poets, Literary History, and Discord* (New York: Oxford University Press, 1992), 38–39; see also Martha Nell Smith, *Rowing in Eden: Rereading Emily Dickinson* (Austin: University of Texas Press, 1992).

12. In *The Poems of Emily Dickinson: Variorum Edition* (Cambridge, MA: Belknap Press of Harvard University Press, 1998), R. W. Franklin identifies 557 poems that Dickinson sent to family and friends, but there may have been many more poems sent and many other unidentified recipients (see Appendix 7, "Recipients," 1547). According to Mabel Loomis Todd, Lavinia told her that while she preserved Dickinson's poems, "She had burned without examination hundreds of manuscripts, and letters to Emily, many of them from nationally known persons," in "Emily Dickinson's Literary Début," *Harper's Monthly Magazine* (March 1930): 463.

13. For classic readings of Whitman as a mystical poet, see Miller, "'Song of Myself' as an Inverted Mystical Experience"; and Cowley, "Introduction" (*LG* 1855, xii); for readings that challenge this more transcendental Whitman, see Martin, "Whitman's *Song of Myself*"; Grossman, "'Evangel-Poem of Comrades and Love'"; Moon, *Disseminating Whitman*; and chapter 4, "Whitman and the Homosexual Republic," in this volume.

14. On Dickinson's love relationship with Susan Gilbert, see Lillian Faderman, "Emily Dickinson's Letters to Susan Gilbert," *Massachusetts Review* 18 (1978): 197–225; on the formative presence of this love relationship in Dickinson's life and work, see Erkkila, *Wicked Sisters*, 27–42; and Smith, *Rowing in Eden*, which also includes a discussion of Austin's "work" in attempting to erase the specifically lesbian dimensions of this relationship.

15. For a discussion of the more negative, guilt-ridden homosexual dimension of Dickinson's love relationships with women, especially Susan Gilbert, see Vivian Pollak, *Dickinson: The Anxiety of Gender* (Ithaca, NY: Cornell University Press, 1984).

16. Charley Shively was the first to identify Fred Vaughan as the inspiration of the "Calamus" poems, in *Calamus Lovers*, 114, 36–50. See also Gary Schmidgall, *Walt Whitman: A Gay Life* (New York: Dutton, 1997); Jonathan Ned Katz, *Love Stories: Sex between Men before Homosexuality* (Chicago: University of Chicago Press, 2001); and Betsy Erkkila, "Songs of Male Intimacy and Love: An Afterword," in *Walt Whitman's Songs of Male Intimacy and Love: "Live Oak, with Moss" and "Calamus,"* ed. Betsy Erkkila (Iowa City: University of Iowa Press, 2011), 99–162.

17. It was not until after the Civil War in the 1871 edition of *Leaves of Grass* that Whitman first used the title "Out of the Cradle Endlessly Rocking."

18. Of the ten poems that Dickinson is known to have published during her lifetime, seven of these were published during the Civil War, including her manifesto poem "I taste a liquor never brewed –," which was published as "The May-Wine" in

the *Republican* a few weeks after the war began. In 1864, she published four poems, three of which appeared in *Drum Beat*, a fund-raising magazine for the US Sanitary Commission, which was founded in 1861 to provide medical supplies and help for the Union Army. Karen Dandurand has argued importantly that these poems "must be seen as [Dickinson's] contribution to the Union cause," in "New Dickinson Civil War Publications," *American Literature* 56 (1984): 17. However, if she did contribute these poems voluntarily, and there is no evidence for this, they were more likely sent to support the sick, wounded, and dying who were sacrificing their lives in support of a cause that was—in Dickinson's view—at best questionable. For a detailed discussion of Dickinson's poems in relation to the Civil War, see Thomas Ford, "Emily Dickinson and the Civil War," *University of Kansas City Review* 31 (Spring 1965), 199–203; and especially Shira Wolosky, *Emily Dickinson: A Voice of War* (New Haven, CT: Yale University Press, 1984), and Shira Wolosky, "Public and Private in Dickinson's War Poetry," in *Oxford Historical Guide to Emily Dickinson*, ed. Vivian Pollak (New York: Oxford University Press, 2004), 103–32.

19. Abraham Lincoln, *The Collected Works of Abraham Lincoln*, ed. Roy P. Basler (New Brunswick: Rutgers University Press, 1953–1955), 7: 23, 8: 333.

20. *The Education of Henry Adams* (Boston: Houghton Mifflin, 1961), 34.

21. On Dickinson as an admirer of George Washington and a witty and articulate spokesperson for a conservative tradition, which has not been legible within the primarily textual and/or national democratic frames of American literary studies, see Erkkila, "Dickinson and the Art of Politics," 134–38. See also Lionel Trilling, who at the very moment American literary studies was being constituted as a distinct national field, observed: "In the United States at this time liberalism is not only the only dominant but even the sole intellectual tradition. For it is a plain fact that nowadays there are no conservative or reactionary ideas in general circulation," in his preface to *The Liberal Imagination: Essays on Literature and Society* (New York: Harcourt Brace Jovanovich, 1950), n. pag.

Chapter Six

1. It is Marx (*EPM*, 328; my ellipsis); Whitman ("Philosophy of Ferries," Brooklyn *Daily Eagle*, August 13, 1847 [*WJ*, 2: 308]); Whitman ("Morbid Appetite for Money," Brooklyn *Daily Eagle*, November 5, 1846 [*WJ*, 2: 103]); Marx (Karl Marx to Arnold Ruge, March 1843, in Karl Marx, *Early Writings*, ed. Lucio Colletti, trans. Rodney Livingston and Gregor Benton [London: Penguin, 1992], 206).

2. See Kateb, "Whitman and the Culture of Democracy," 545–71, and *The Inner Ocean: Individualism and Democratic Culture* (Ithaca, NY: Cornell University Press, 1992). For a discussion of the ways Kateb's model leaves out the more collective, communal, and homoerotic dimensions of Whitman's democratic theory, see chapter 9, "Public Love: Whitman and Political Theory," in this volume, 201–24.

3. The absence of any sustained comparative analysis of Whitman and Marx seems particularly revealing given the fact that Gay Wilson Allen, Whitman's major

biographer and a founding figure in the field of Whitman studies, argued in 1937 that Whitman's real roots were not in America at all but in the international proletarian movement, in *English Journal* 26 (1937), 48–52. I was brought to a realization of the ways Whitman and Marx continue to function as the demonized others of each other by a course I taught on Whitman and Marx. When I asked students the difference between Marx's *Communist Manifesto* and Whitman's "Resurgemus," which were both published in the context of the European Revolutions of 1848, one student (to my utter surprise) described "Resurgemus" as "versified Marx"; but others hastened to add that while Whitman and Marx might "sound alike," they were in fact very different because Whitman was a "Democrat" (big D) and Marx was a "Communist" (big C). What struck me about this class was first, how quickly the seemingly stable boundaries of Whitman/Marx and Democracy/Communism began to collapse; and second, how invested the students were in keeping Whitman and Marx, and especially Democracy and Communism, ideologically distinct and self-evident. In other words, almost three decades after the putative end of the Cold War, the term *Communism* remains so ideologically charged, even for a new post–Cold War generation of American students, that it is difficult to read the word *communism* within the more fluid contexts of nineteenth-century political debate without bringing to it the whole pack of demons and bugaboos with which our culture continues to invest it.

4. Karl Marx, "Letter to His Father," November 10, 1837, in *SW* 11.

5. Whitman's father was a friend of Thomas Paine, and he may have been among the freethinkers who on January 29, 1825, began to gather annually to celebrate Paine's birthday. Copies of the major freethinking texts—Volney's *The Ruins* (1791), Paine's *The Age of Reason* (1794), and Frances Wright's *A Few Days in Athens* (1822)—were cherished books in the Whitman household. For a more detailed discussion of Whitman's political roots, see Erkkila, *Whitman the Political Poet.*

6. *WWC* 3: 205.

7. Walt Whitman, "Sun-Down Papers," no. 7, September 29, 1840 (*WJ* 1: 21–22).

8. Whitman, "Our Future Lot," *Long Island Democrat*, October 31, 1838 (*EPF*, 28).

9. My argument in this essay is not about influence. It is about the transatlantic dialogue between Whitman and Marx across similarity and difference.

10. Frances Wright, *A Few Days in Athens* (1822; New York: Arno, 1972), 205; Whitman, *LGC* 644.

11. Rubin, "Whitman in 1840: A Discovery," *American Literature* (May 1937): 239–42.

12. The 1844 Paris manuscripts represent the first draft of the "Economics" that became Marx's life's work. They were not published until 1932. While critics have debated the relation between the early "humanist" and later "scientific" Marx, I follow Raya Dunayevskaya (*Marxism and Freedom: From 1776 to Today* [1958; reprint, New York: Humanity, 2000]), Erich Fromm (*Marx's Concept of Man*, trans. T. B. Bottomore [New York: Frederick Ungar, 1961]), Shlomo Avineri (*The Social and Political Thought of Karl Marx* [Cambridge: Cambridge University Press, 1968]), and David

McLellan, (*Karl Marx: The Life and Thought* [New York: Harper & Row, 1973]), who have emphasized the continuity between early and late Marx and the simultaneously economic, political, and ethical dimensions of Marxist thought.

13. In an autobiographical statement in the preface to *A Critique of Political Economy*, Marx described these articles as "the first occasions for occupying myself with economic questions" (*SW*, 424–25).

14. Karl Marx to Arnold Ruge, May 1843, in Karl Marx, *Early Writings*, 206.

15. For an eloquent examination of Whitman's labor radicalism, see also M. Wynn Thomas, *The Lunar Light*, 11–32. For an historical examination of working-class radicalism, see Sean Wilentz, *Chants Democratic: New York City and the Rise of the Working Class, 1788–1850* (New York: Oxford University Press, 1984).

16. See Edward Pessen, *Jacksonian America: Society, Personality, Politics* (Homewood, IL: Dorsey, 1969), and *Riches, Class, and Power before the Civil War* (Lexington, MA: Heath, 1973); and Wilentz, *Chants Democratic.*

17. As early as 1847 in "American Workingmen, versus Slavery," Whitman began to emphasize the disjunction between the will of "the working farmers and mechanics of the free states—the nine-tenths of the population of the republic" and the determination of southern aristocracy and the American state to impose slavery rather than freedom as the law of the land (*WJ*, 2: 320). Similarly, in his *Critique of Hegel's 'Philosophy of Right'* (1843), Marx criticized the Hegelian notion of the monarchical state as the embodiment of the will of the people and asserted: "[I]n a true democracy the political state disappears" (*SW*, 35). In the *Communist Manifesto* and "Resurgemus," respectively, Marx and Whitman represent a popular will toward liberty that exists apart from the state and will eventually defeat its oppressive power. Despite the apparent triumph of the forces of reaction in both Europe and the United States—a repetition of the monarchical past that Marx evokes in the spectral return of Napoleon in *The Eighteenth Brumaire of Louis Bonaparte* (1852) and Whitman evokes in the spectral return of King George III in one of the twelve untitled poems of *Leaves of Grass* 1855 (later entitled "A Boston Ballad" [1854])—both continue to appeal to the ultimate sovereignty of the people and forms of social solidarity outside the state—Whitman in "The Eighteenth-Presidency!" (1856 manuscript), the 1860 *Leaves of Grass*, and *Democratic Vistas* (1871), and Marx in *The Class Struggles in France* (1852), the *Grundrisse* (1857 manuscript), *Capital* (1867), and *The Civil War in France* (1871).

18. Frederick Engels, "On the History of the Communist League," in Karl Marx and Frederick Engels, *Selected Works* (London: Lawrence and Wishart, 1968), 431.

19. The office of the *Freeman* was destroyed by fire after the first issue. Although Whitman was able to resume publication in September 1849, the only extant copy of the *Freeman*, dated September 9, 1848, is in the Trent Collection of Duke University. See Joseph Jay Rubin, *The Historic Whitman* (University Park: Pennsylvania State University Press, 1973), 211. For a more extensive discussion of Whitman's involvement in the political struggles of the 1840s, see Erkkila, *Whitman the Political Poet*, 25–67.

20. Michael Paul Rogin, *Subversive Genealogy: The Politics and Art of Herman Melville* (New York: Knopf, 1983), ix.

21. See also Karl Marx and Frederick Engels, "The Economics of the *Volks-Tribun* and Its Attitude Toward Young America" (1846), reprinted as "American Soil and Communism" in *On America and the Civil War*, vol. 2 of *The Karl Marx Library*, ed. Saul K. Padover (New York: McGraw Hill, 1972), 3–6.

22. Both Whitman and Marx looked at the struggle over slavery in America as part of a larger struggle between the forces of freedom and oppression throughout the world. See Whitman, "American Workingmen, versus Slavery," in *WJ* 2: 318; and Marx, *Die Press*, Vienna, October 25, 1862, reprinted in Karl Marx and Frederick Engels, *The Civil War in the United States*, ed. Richard Enmale (New York: International Publishers, 1937).

23. Marx's weekly columns for the New York *Daily Tribune*, which was the most widely read newspaper in the United States, became his main source of income between 1852 and 1862. As contributors to the *Tribune*, Whitman and Marx shared many of the reformist ideals of its editor, Horace Greeley, whose newspaper was known for its support of labor radicalism, antislavery, free soil, feminism, socialism, and the experiments in communal living advocated by the utopian French socialist Charles Fourier and his American student Albert Brisbane, one of the founders of Brook Farm, who also contributed a regular column to the *Tribune*.

24. Brooklyn *Advertiser*, June 23, 1848, cited in Rubin, *Historic Whitman*, 206; ellipsis mine.

25. Whitman makes this point more explicitly in the 1855 *Leaves of Grass* when he replaces the more immediate visceral thrill of his original lines with the following lines on the revolutions of 1848 as an ongoing source of personal and political renewal: "O hope and faith! O aching close of lives! O many a sickened heart! / Turn back unto this day, and make yourselves afresh" (*EPF*, 40).

26. Engels, preface to the 1888 edition of the *Communist Manifesto*, in Marx, *Political Writings*, vol. 1, *The Revolutions of 1848*, ed. David Fernbach (Harmondsworth: Penguin, 1972), 62.

27. "Millet's Pictures—Last Items," *Specimen Days and Collect* (1882), in *PW* 1: 268; ellipses mine.

28. At their most politically impassioned, Marx and Whitman converge in a kind of political and prose poetics. Both make use of a densely metaphoric, embodied, political vernacular that is well worth literary study.

29. As Engels notes, after members of the Communist League were tried and sentenced to prison by the Prussian state in 1852, "the League was formally dissolved by the remaining members" and the *Communist Manifesto* seemed "doomed to oblivion." It was not until the formation of the First International in 1864 that the *Manifesto* began to make "considerable headway among the working men of all countries" (*CM*, 63, 64).

30. David Fernbach, "Introduction," in Karl Marx, *Political Writings*, vol. 1, *The Revolutions of 1848*, ed. David Fernbach (Harmondsworth: Penguin, 1972): 33n56. See

also G. D. H. Cole, who writes of "[t]he impossibility of defining Socialism": "Who can satisfactorily define democracy, or liberty, or virtue, or happiness, or the State, or, for that matter, individualism any more than Socialism?" (*Socialist Thought: The Forerunners 1789–1850*, vol. 1 of *A History of Socialist Thought* [London: Macmillan, 1953], 1).

31. In the section of the *Communist Manifesto* entitled "Bourgeois and Proletarians," Marx describes "[t]he lower middle class, the small manufacturer, the shopkeeper, the artisan, the peasant" as "not revolutionary, but conservative"; he dismisses day laborers and the unemployed as the *lumpenproletariat*, "the social scum, that passively rotting mass thrown off by the lowest layers of old society" who are likely to be "a bribed tool of reactionary intrigue" (*CM*, 77). Whitman's more inclusive vision of the people, anticipates the neo-Marxist work of Michael Hardt and Antonio Negri, who envision the possibility of a global revolution led by the multitude of oppressed everywhere (see *Empire* [Cambridge, MA: Harvard University Press, 2000]).

Chapter Seven

1. Walt Whitman, *Democratic Vistas, The Original Edition in Facsimile*, ed. Ed Folsom (Iowa City: University of Iowa Press, 2010), 11, 12, 73, 74.

2. Whitman, "Prospects of War," New Orleans *Daily Crescent*, April 17, 1848, 2, reprinted in Chronicling America, https://chroniclingamerica.loc.gov/lccn/sn82015378/1848-04-17/ed-1/seq-2/. See also Larry Reynolds, who emphasizes the role played by the "heroism and martyrdom of the European revolutionaries" of 1848 in shaping the poetic persona and major themes of the 1855 *Leaves of Grass*, in *European Revolutions and the American Literary Renaissance*, 135.

3. Brooklyn *Evening Star*, November 18, 1845, cited in Gay Wilson Allen, *The Solitary Singer: A Critical Biography of Walt Whitman* (New York: New York University Press, 1955), 72.

4. *WWC* 3: 360; ellipsis mine.

5. My translation of the following words: "La démocratie naît précisement de cette fraternité qui n'est pas dans la *Déclaration d'Indépendence* mais qui doit en permanence être mise en action: prendre la main de son voisin, l'embrasser, lui passer le bras autour du cou, dans une attitude qu'on pourrait dire christique"; in Jacques Darras, "Walt Whitman, poète de l'utopie américaine: Entretien avec Jacques Darras," *Esprit* (October 2002): 58.

6. For a discussion of Abraham Lincoln and the American Civil War in the context of the revolutions in France and elsewhere in Europe in the nineteenth century, see Betsy Erkkila, "Lincoln in International Memory," in *The Cambridge Companion to Abraham Lincoln*, ed. Shirley Samuels (New York: Cambridge University Press, 2012), 155–82.

7. Robert Tombs, *The Paris Commune 1871* (London: Longman, 1999), 12; David Harvey, *Consciousness and the Urban Experience: Studies in the History and Theory of Capitalist Urbanization* (Baltimore: Johns Hopkins University Press, 1986), 154.

8. *Galaxy* 11 (June 1871): 817, reprinted in *The Walt Whitman Archive*, ed. Ed Folsom and Kenneth M. Price, https://whitmanarchive.org/published/periodical/poems/per.00008.

9. *WWC* 1: 7.

10. Erkkila, *Whitman Among the French*, 169.

Chapter Eight

1. From Thomas Jefferson to James Breckenridge, 15 February 1821, *Founders Online*, National Archives, https://founders.archives.gov/documents/Jefferson/98-01-02-1839.

2. Rogin, *Subversive Genealogy*, 53.

3. Walt Whitman, *Faint Clues and Indirections: Manuscripts of Walt Whitman and His Family*, ed. Clarence Gohdes and Rollo G. Silver (Durham, NC: Duke University Press, 1949), 46.

4. Arthur M. Schlesinger, Jr., *The Age of Jackson* (Boston: Little, Brown, 1945), 183.

5. Moon, *Disseminating Whitman*, 26–36; Michael Warner, "Whitman Drunk," in *Breaking Bounds: Walt Whitman and American Cultural Studies*, ed. Betsy Erkkila and Jay Grossman (New York: Oxford University Press, 1996), 30–43.

6. For years critics have assumed that the lack of a final period at the end of the poem later entitled "Song of Myself" was intentional. But as Ed Folsom notes, the first census of the 1855 edition of *Leaves of Grass* conducted in 2005 reveals that at least two copies of the book have the period and thus it appears to have broken off in an "early stage of the print run," in *Whitman Making Books, Books Making Whitman: A Catalog and Commentary* (Iowa City: Obermann Center for Advanced Studies, University of Iowa, 2005), 13.

7. Melville, *The Confidence-Man: His Masquerade* (1857; Evanston, IL: Northwestern University Press, 1984), 133.

8. Whitman, *Memoranda During the War* (Camden, NJ: New Republic Print, 1875–1876), 59.

9. See, for example, Phillis Wheatley's poem "America," in which she writes: "Thy Power, O Liberty, makes strong the weak /And (wond'rous instinct) Ethiopians speak / Sometimes by Simile, a victory's won," in *Poems of Phillis Wheatley*, 125; Frederick Douglass, "What to the Slave Is the Fourth of July?" in *The Oxford Frederick Douglass Reader*, ed. William L. Andrews (New York: Oxford University Press, 1996), 129.

10. Lincoln, *Collected Works*, 8: 333.

Chapter Nine

1. Alexander Hamilton, James Madison, and John Jay, *The Federalist Papers,* ed. Clinton Rossiter (New York: New American Library, 1999), no. 37, 194.

2. Beer, "Liberty and Union," 365, 377.

3. Others who have turned to Whitman as a model in contemporary debates about

the politics of democracy include the philosophers Richard Rorty and Martha C. Nussbaum. In *Achieving Our Country: Leftist Thought in Twentieth-Century America* (Cambridge, MA: Harvard University Press, 1998), Rorty urges Americans to return to the nationalist tradition of Whitman and John Dewey as prophets of a "new, quasi-communitarian rhetoric" that "was at the heart of the Progressive Movement and the New Deal" and "set the tone for the American Left during the first six decades of the twentieth century" (8–9); in *Poetic Justice: The Literary Imagination and Public Life* (Boston: Beacon Press, 1995), Nussbaum presents Whitman's democratic poet as a model of the role that the literary imagination and sympathetic identification might play in public rationality, legal judgment, and "political relations among citizens" (xii).

4. See chapter 4, "Whitman and the Homosexual Republic"; Erkkila, *Whitman the Political Poet*; and Erkkila, "Introduction," in Erkkila and Grossman, *Breaking Bounds*, 1–20.

5. Jürgen Habermas, *The Structural Transformation of the Public Sphere: An Inquiry into a Category of Bourgeois Society*, trans. Thomas Burger (Cambridge, MA: MIT Press, 1989), 49.

6. See, for example, Mary P. Ryan's study of the multiple counterpublics constituted by women in the nineteenth century in *Women in Public: Between Banners and Ballots, 1825–1880* (Baltimore: Johns Hopkins University Press, 1990); see also Nancy Fraser, who uses the term *subaltern counterpublics* to describe the ways "members of subordinated social groups—women, workers, peoples of color, and gays and lesbians—have repeatedly found it advantageous to constitute alternative publics" ("Rethinking the Public Sphere: A Contribution to the Critique of Actually Existing Democracy," in *Habermas and the Public Sphere*, ed. Craig Calhoun [Cambridge, MA: MIT Press, 1992], 123); and Peter Coviello, who emphasizes the role of sexual intimacy in congealing American nationality in Whitman's work, in "Intimate Nationality: Anonymity and Attachment in Whitman," *American Literature* 73 (March 2001): 85–119.

7. Moon, *Disseminating Whitman*, 53–58; Warner, "Whitman Drunk," 30–43.

8. Martin, *Homosexual Tradition*, 3–89; Schmidgall, *Walt Whitman: A Gay Life.*

9. The quotation marks around the term "homosexual" are meant to signal the fact that this term did not come into general usage until later in the nineteenth century, and thus it is not an adequate descriptor of Whitman's experience and self-representation as a man who loved other men.

10. For a daring enactment of the influence of the queer working-class voice of Whitman's mother, Louisa Van Velsor Whitman, on Whitman's poetry, see Michael Moon and Eve Sedgwick, "Confusion of Tongues," in Erkkila and Grossman, *Breaking Bounds*, 23–29.

11. Whitman, *The Complete Writings*, ed. Bucke et al., 10: 18.

12. See "The Eighteenth Presidency!" in *NUPM* 6: 2120–35.

13. *Whitman's Manuscripts: Leaves of Grass (1860): A Parallel Text*, ed. Fredson Bowers (Chicago: University of Chicago Press, 1955), 12; *LOM*, 7.

14. Not coincidentally, John Stuart Mill's important essay *On Liberty* was published in 1859. Although Whitman was an admirer of Mill (he cites him at the beginning

of *Democratic Vistas*), as Habermas notes in *The Structural Transformation of the Public Sphere* (132–38), Mill's essay marks an increasing distinction between liberal privacy and the public sphere of politics, as the administrative state assumes increasing responsibility.

15. Alan Helms, Whitman's 'Live Oak with Moss,'" in *The Continuing Presence of Walt Whitman*, ed. Robert K. Martin (Iowa City: University of Iowa Press, 1992), 185–205; and Parker, "The Real 'Live Oak, with Moss,'" 145–60. For a contemporary critical attack on Whitman's "public onanism," his "public performance of what most of us would only do in private," see Robert S. Frederickson, "Public Onanism: Whitman's 'Song of Himself,'" *MLQ* 2 (June 1985): 143–60. See also my discussion of the ongoing national policing of Whitman's homosexuality in the introduction to *Breaking Bounds*, 5–8.

16. For a discussion of the struggles in the 1790s over the conflicting claims of natal, national, and international family, see Jay Fliegelman, *Prodigals and Pilgrims: The American Revolt against Patriarchal Authority, 1750–1800* (New York: Cambridge University Press, 1982), 227–30.

17. Cited in Fliegelman, *Prodigals and Pilgrims*, 230–31.

18. Adam Smith, *The Theory of Moral Sentiments*, ed. D. D. Raphael and A. L. Macfie (Indianapolis: Liberty Fund, 1984), 9. As Garry Wills writes of Adam Smith, and other Scottish moral sense philosophers, including Francis Hutcheson and David Hume: "For them, the heart was often another word for the moral sense (as was benevolence, humanity, or sociability). . . . The moral sense is not only man's *highest* faculty, but the one that is *equal* in all men"; *Inventing America: Jefferson's Declaration of Independence* (New York: Vintage, 1979), 224–25. See also Edmund Burke, who writes of the new age of reason, self-interest, and law: "Nothing is left which engages the affections on the part of the commonwealth. On the principles of this mechanick philosophy our institutions can never be embodied . . . in persons; so as to create in us love, veneration, admiration or attachment. But that sort of reason which banishes the affections is incapable of filling their place. These public affections, combined with manners, are required sometimes as supplements, sometimes as correctives, always as aids to law" (Edmund Burke, *Reflections on the French Revolution*, ed. W. Alison Phillips and Catherine Beatrice Phillips [Cambridge: Cambridge University Press, 1912], 78).

19. For an extended defense of the role that sympathetic identification associated with the literary imagination might play in public reason and democratic life, see Nussbaum, *Poetic Justice*.

20. Jan Lewis, "The Republican Wife: Virtue and Seduction in the Early Republic," *William and Mary Quarterly* 44 (October 1987): 689–721.

21. "From the Genius of Liberty," *The Key*, April 14, 1798, 105–6; cited in Jan Lewis, "Motherhood and the Construction of the Male Citizen in the United States, 1750–1850" in *Constructions of the Self*, ed. George Levine (New Brunswick, NJ: Rutgers University Press, 1992), 147.

22. "[O]nly when sex is properly treated, talked, avowed, accepted," he wrote in

a notebook of the time, "will the woman be equal with the man, and pass where the man passes, and meet his words with her words, and his rights with her rights" (Walt Whitman, *Notes and Fragments*, ed. Richard Maurice Bucke [London, Canada: A. Talbot, 1899], 33n).

23. See, for example, Drs. Jordan and Beck, who represent onanists as the living dead on the margins of society: "They drivel away their existence on the outskirts of society . . . they are at once a dead weight, a sluggish, inert mass in the paths of this busy, blustering life, having neither the will nor the capacity to take part in the general matters of life" (*Happiness or Misery? Being Four Lectures on the Functions and Disorders of the Nervous System and Reproductive Organs* [New York: Barton & Son, 1861], 39, cited in Charles E. Rosenberg, "Sexuality, Class and Role in 19th-Century America," *American Quarterly* 25 [May 1973]: 146).

24. In *Self-Preservation. Manhood, and Causes of Its Premature Decline* (New York: n.p., 1830), R. J. Culverwell writes of the male onanist: "All the intellectual faculties are weakened. The man becomes a coward: sighs and weeps like a hysterical woman. He loses all decision and dignity of character" (cited in Rosenberg, "Sexuality," 146).

25. Seyla Benhabib, "Models of the Public Space: Hannah Arendt, the Liberal Tradition, and Jürgen Habermas," in Calhoun, *Habermas*, 84.

26. Here the distinction that Michael Warner and Lauren Berlant make between *heterosexuality* as a way of organizing sexual relations and *heteronormativity* as a way of ordering the world is useful. Whereas heterosexuality was put in place in the late nineteenth century as a way of organizing sexual relations and male and female identity, "heteronormativity" is a whole set of relations, structures, and assumptions that pervade every aspect of American life. See Lauren Berlant and Michael Warner, "Sex in Public," *Critical Inquiry* 24 (Winter 1998): 548.

27. Gay Wilson Allen argues that "The Base of All Metaphysics" moves "toward sublimation and reinterpretation of the original personal confessions" of "Calamus" (*The New Walt Whitman Handbook* [New York: New York University Press, 1975], 133); Martin argues that the poem represents "a descent" from "honest statement" to "increasing vagueness" ("Whitman's *Song of Myself*," 88); and Helms argues that after 1860, Whitman "remained silent on the subject of homosexual love" ("Whitman's 'Live Oak,'" 197). See also David Oates's reading of "The Base of All Metaphysics" in *Walt Whitman: An Encyclopedia*, ed. J. R. LeMaster and Donald D. Kummings (New York: Garland, 1998), 49–50.

28. Whitman cites Plato's *Phaedrus*, in vol. 1 of Bohn's six-volume edition of Plato, first published in 1854 (*NUPM*, 5: 1881). Robert K. Martin (*Homosexual Tradition*, 46) suggests that Whitman may also have read Plato's *Symposium* in a text called "The Banquet, or on Love" in *Works of Plato: A New and Literal Version*, trans. George Burges (London: Henry G. Bohn, 1848–1852), 3: 493. Pausanias, in "The Banquet" (3: 512), uses the term "manly" love to refer to men who "associate through the whole of life together": "they are the most manly in their disposition" and have "a manly temper and manly look" (512; cited in Martin, *Homosexual Tradition*, 226).

29. Although Whitman's inclusion of "the well-married husband and wife, of

children and parents" as part of his vision of comradely love might appear to dilute or silence his emphasis on "manly love" in other "Calamus" poems, it is important to note the slipperiness of the terms "husband," "wife," "child," and "parent" in Whitman's homoerotic metaphysics. Describing himself as "the new husband" to his male lovers in his "Calamus" poems, Whitman fluidly assumes the roles of mother, brother, husband, father, and bride in representing his love relationships with men in his poems. As Ed Folsom has argued, Whitman also left a small cache of "marital" photographs taken with his boyfriends Peter Doyle (in the 1860s [Figure 7]), Harry Stafford (in the 1870s [Figure 8]), Bill Duckett (in the 1880s [Figure 9]), and Warren (Warry) Fritzinger (in the 1890s [Figure 10]). These revisionary portraits stage new identities and new versions of the family, marriage, and social relationships that blur the traditional roles of mother, father, husband, wife, brother, lover, friend. See Folsom, "Whitman's Calamus Photographs," in Erkkila and Grossman, *Breaking Bounds*, 193–219.

30. Hannah Arendt, *The Human Condition* (Chicago: University of Chicago Press, 1958).

31. The dialectic between individualism and "the ancient virtue of Patriotism" that Whitman describes anticipates the ongoing *liberal* versus *communitarian* debates within democratic theory. Whereas liberals such as John Rawls and Ronald Dworkin emphasize the sanctity of the individual person, communitarians such as Alasdair MacIntyre, Michael Sandel, and Michael Walzer emphasize the need for social virtue and community. Although parts of Whitman's *Democratic Vistas* accord with both liberals and communitarians in equating democracy with America and the American nation-state, in their most visionary dimension, Whitman's democratic vistas—like such poems as "Song of the Open Road"—imagine democracy as an *eroticized transnationalism* that links "all nations, all men" in an international community of freedom, sympathy, and love.

32. Whitman's main knowledge of Hegel came from Joseph Gostick's *German Literature* (1854) and *Prose Writers of Germany* (1855), edited by Frederick H. Hedge, which he read in the late 1860s and early 1870s, and perhaps as early as the 1850s. In addition to his references to Hegel in *Democratic Vistas* and "The Base of All Metaphysics," Whitman referred to Hegel in his 1881 poem "Roaming in Thought. (*After reading* Hegel)." See also the series of notes "Sunday Evening Lectures," in which Whitman declares: "Only Hegel is fit for America—is large enough and free enough" (*NUPM*, 6: 2011). For a discussion of the importance of Hegelian dialectics to Whitman's effort to resolve the problems and contradictions of democracy in *Democratic Vistas*, see Erkkila, *Whitman the Political Poet*, 246–59.

33. For a recent discussion of the need to distinguish among state apparatuses, economic markets, and democratic associations in democratic theory, see Fraser, "Rethinking the Public Sphere," 109–42.

BIBLIOGRAPHY

Adams, Henry. *The Education of Henry Adams*. Boston: Houghton Mifflin, 1961.

Allen, Gay Wilson. *The New Walt Whitman Handbook*. New York: New York University Press, 1975.

———. *The Solitary Singer: A Critical Biography of Walt Whitman*. New York: New York University Press, 1955.

———. "Walt Whitman—Nationalist or Proletarian?" *English Journal* 26 (1937): 48–52.

Arendt, Hannah. *The Human Condition*. Chicago: University of Chicago Press, 1958.

Arthur, Gavin. *Gay Sunshine* 35 (Winter 1975): 29.

Aspiz, Harold. *Walt Whitman and the Body Beautiful*. Urbana: University of Illinois Press, 1980.

Asselineau, Roger. *The Evolution of Walt Whitman: The Creation of a Book*. Cambridge, MA: Belknap Press of Harvard University Press, 1962.

Athenot, Éric, and Cristanne Miller, eds. *Whitman and Dickinson: A Colloquy*. Iowa City: University of Iowa Press, 2018.

Avineri, Shlomo. *The Social and Political Thought of Karl Marx*. Cambridge: Cambridge University Press, 1968.

Beer, Samuel H. "Liberty and Union: Walt Whitman's Idea of the Nation." *Political Theory* 12 (August 1984): 361–86.

Belasco, Susan, Ed Folsom, and Kenneth Price, eds. *Leaves of Grass: The Sesquicentennial Essays*. Lincoln: University of Nebraska Press, 2007.

Benhabib, Seyla. "Models of Public Space: Hannah Arendt, the Liberal Tradition, and Jürgen Habermas." In *Habermas and the Public Sphere*. Ed. Craig Calhoun. Cambridge, MA: MIT Press, 1992. 73–98.

Berlant, Lauren, and Michael Warner. "Sex in Public." *Critical Inquiry* 24 (Winter 1998): 547–66.

Bertz, Eduard. *Walt Whitman: Ein Charakterbild*. Leipzig: Max Spohr, 1905.

Burke, Edmund. *Reflections on the French Revolution*. Ed. W. Alison Phillips and Catherine Beatrice Phillips. Cambridge: Cambridge University Press, 1912.

Cady, Joseph. "*Drum-Taps* and Nineteenth-Century Male Homosexual Literature." In *Walt Whitman: Here and Now*. Ed. Joann P. Krieg. Westport, CT: Greenwood Press, 1985. 49–60.

———. "Not Happy in the Capitol: Homosexuality and the 'Calamus' Poems." *American Studies* 19 (Fall 1978): 5–22.

Cole, G. D. H. *Socialist Thought: The Forerunners 1789–1850*. Vol. 1 of *A History of Socialist Thought*. London: Macmillan, 1953.

Covielo, Peter. "Intimate Nationality: Anonymity and Attachment in Whitman." *American Literature* 73 (March 2001): 85–119.

Cowley, Malcolm. "Introduction." In *Leaves of Grass: The First (1855) Edition*. Ed. Malcolm Cowley. New York: Penguin, 1986. vii–xxxvi.

Craigie, William A. *The Study of American English*. Oxford: Clarendon Press, 1927.

Croft, Herbert. *A Letter, From Germany, to the Princess Royal of England; on the English and German Languages*. Hamburg: Fauche, 1797.

Culverwell, R. J. *Self-Preservation, Manhood, and Causes of Its Premature Decline*. New York: n.p., 1830.

Dandurand, Karen. "New Dickinson Civil War Publications." *American Literature* 56 (March 1984): 17–27.

Darras, Jacques. "Walt Whitman, poète de l'utopie américaine: Entretien avec Jacques Darras." *Esprit* (October 2002): 55–64.

Dickinson, Emily. *Letters of Emily Dickinson*. Ed Mabel Loomis Todd. New York: Harper & Brothers, 1931.

———. *The Letters of Emily Dickinson*. Ed. Thomas H. Johnson and Theodora Ward. 3 vols. Cambridge, MA: Belknap Press of Harvard University Press, 1958.

———. *The Poems of Emily Dickinson: Reading Edition*. Ed. R. W. Franklin. Cambridge, MA: Belknap Press of Harvard University Press, 1999.

———. *The Poems of Emily Dickinson: Variorum Edition*. Ed. R. W. Franklin. 3 vols. Cambridge, MA: Belknap Press of Harvard University Press, 1998.

Douglass, Frederick. "What to the Slave Is the Fourth of July?" In *The Oxford Frederick Douglass Reader*. Ed. William L. Andrews. New York: Oxford University Press, 1996.

Dressman, Michael. "Whitman, Chaucer, and French Words." *Walt Whitman Review* 23 (June 1977): 77–82.

Dunayevskaya, Raya. *Marxism and Freedom: From 1776 to Today*. 1958. Reprint, New York: Humanity, 2000.

Durkheim, Émile. *The Division of Labor in Society*. 1893. Trans. George Simpson. New York: Free Press, 2014.

Ellis, Havelock, and John Addington Symonds. *Sexual Inversion*. London: Wilson and Macmillan, 1897.

Ellmann, Richard. "Oscar Meets Walt." *New York Review of Books* (December 3, 1987): 43–44.

Emerson, Ralph Waldo. *Emerson: Essays and Lectures*. Ed. Joel Porte. New York: Library of America, 1983.

"Emily Dickinson's Schooling: Mount Holyoke Female Seminary." Emily Dickinson Museum, September 1, 2015. https://www.emilydickinsonmuseum.org/emily-dickinson/biography/special-topics/emily-dickinsons-schooling-mount-holyoke-female-seminary/.

Engels, Frederick. "On the History of the Communist League." In Karl Marx and Frederick Engels, *Selected Works*. London: Lawrence and Wishart, 1968.

Erkkila, Betsy. "Dickinson and the Art of Politics." In *Oxford Historical Guide to Emily Dickinson*. Ed. Vivian Pollak. New York: Oxford University Press, 2004. 133–74.

———. "Emily Dickinson and Class." *American Literary History* 4 (Spring 1992): 1–27.

———. "Introduction." In *Breaking Bounds: Whitman and American Cultural Studies*. Ed. Betsy Erkkila and Jay Grossman. New York: Oxford University Press, 1996. 1–20.

———. "Lincoln in International Memory." In *The Cambridge Companion to Abraham Lincoln*. Ed. Shirley Samuels. New York: Cambridge University Press, 2012. 155–82.

———. "Live Oak, with Moss." In *Walt Whitman's Songs of Male Intimacy and Love: "Live Oak, with Moss" and "Calamus."* Ed. Betsy Erkkila. Iowa City: University of Iowa Press, 2011. 1–37.

———. "Songs of Male Intimacy and Love: An Afterword." In *Walt Whitman's Songs of Male Intimacy and Love: "Live Oak, with Moss" and "Calamus."* Ed. Betsy Erkkila. Iowa City: University of Iowa Press, 2011. 99–162.

———. *Walt Whitman Among the French: Poet and Myth*. Princeton, NJ: Princeton University Press, 1980.

———. "Whitman, Melville, and the Tribulations of Democracy." In *A Companion to American Literature and Culture*. Ed. Paul Lauter. Malden, MA: Blackwell, 2010. 250–84.

———. *Whitman the Political Poet*. New York: Oxford University Press, 1989.

———. *The Wicked Sisters: Women Poets, Literary History, and Discord*. New York: Oxford University Press, 1992.

Erkkila, Betsy, and Jay Grossman, eds. *Breaking Bounds: Whitman and American Cultural Studies*. New York: Oxford University Press, 1996.

Faderman, Lillian. "Emily Dickinson's Letters to Susan Gilbert." *Massachusetts Review* 18 (1977): 197–225.

Fernbach, David. "Introduction." In Karl Marx, *Political Writings*. Vol. 1, *The Revolutions of 1848*. Ed. David Fernbach. Harmondsworth: Penguin, 1972.

Fliegelman, Jay. *Prodigals and Pilgrims: The American Revolt against Patriarchal Authority, 1750–1800*. New York: Cambridge University Press, 1982.

Folsom, Ed. "Talking Back to Walt Whitman: An Introduction." In *Walt Whitman: The Measure of His Song*. Ed. Jim Perlman, Ed Folsom, and Dan Campion. Duluth, MN: Holy Cow! Press, 2019. 1–63.

———. *Whitman Making Books, Books Making Whitman: A Catalog and Commentary*. Iowa City: Obermann Center for Advanced Studies, University of Iowa, 2005.

———. "The Whitman Recording." *Walt Whitman Quarterly Review* 9 (Spring 1992): 214–16.

———. "Whitman's Calamus Photographs." In *Breaking Bounds: Whitman and American Cultural Studies*. Ed. Betsy Erkkila and Jay Grossman. New York: Oxford University Press, 1996. 193–219.

———. "'A Yet More Terrible and More Deeply Complicated Problem': Walt Whitman, Race, Reconstruction, and American Democracy." *American Literary History* 30 (Fall 2018): 531–58.

Folsom, Ed, and Kenneth M. Price, eds. *The Walt Whitman Archive*. https://whitmanarchive.org.

Ford, Thomas. "Emily Dickinson and the Civil War." *University of Kansas City Review* 31 (Spring 1965): 199–203.

Foucault, Michel. *The History of Sexuality: An Introduction*. Trans. Robert Hurley. New York: Random House, 1978.

Fowler, O. S. *Amativeness: Or, Evils and Remedies of Excessive and Perverted Sexuality: Including Warning and Advice to the Married and Single*. New York: Fowler and Wells, 1844.

Francis, K. H. "Walt Whitman's French." *Modern Language Review* 51 (October 1956): 493–506.

Fraser, Nancy. "Rethinking the Public Sphere: A Contribution to the Critique of Actually Existing Democracy." In *Habermas and the Public Sphere*. Ed. Craig Calhoun. Cambridge, MA: MIT Press, 1992. 109–42.

Frederickson, Robert S. "Public Onanism: Whitman's 'Song of Himself.'" *MLQ* 2 (June 1985): 143–60.

Freneau, Philip. *Poems of Freneau*. Ed. Harry Hayden Clark. New York: Harcourt, Brace, 1960.

Fromm, Erich. *Marx's Concept of Man*. Trans. T. B. Bottomore. New York: Frederick Ungar, 1961.

Genoways, Ted. "'One Goodshaped and Wellhung Man': Accentuated Sexuality and the Uncertain Authorship of the Frontispiece to the 1855 Edition of *Leaves of Grass*." In *Leaves of Grass: The Sesquicentennial Essays*. Ed. Susan Belasco, Ed Folsom, and Kenneth M. Price. Lincoln: University of Nebraska Press, 2007. 87–123.

Gilman, Charlotte Perkins. *Herland and Related Writings*. Ed. Beth Sutton-Ramspeck. Peterborough, Canada: Broadview Press, 2012.

Ginsberg, Allen. *Howl and Other Poems*. San Francisco: City Lights Books, 1956.

Graham, Sylvester. *A Lecture to Young Men, on Chastity*. Boston: Light and Stearns, 1834.

Grossman, Jay. "'The Evangel-Poem of Comrades and Love': Revising Whitman's Republicanism." *American Transcendental Quarterly* 4 (September 1990): 201–18.

Grünzweig, Walter. "Noble Ethics and Loving Aggressiveness: The Imperialist Walt Whitman." In *An American Empire: Expansionist Cultures and Policies, 1881–1917*. Ed. Serge Ricard. Aix-en-Provence: Université de Provence, 1990. 151–65.

Habermas, Jürgen. *The Structural Transformation of the Public Sphere: An Inquiry into a Category of Bourgeois Society.* Trans. Thomas Burger. Cambridge, MA: MIT Press, 1989.

Hamilton, Alexander, James Madison, and John Jay. *The Federalist Papers.* Ed. Clinton Rossiter. New York: New American Library, 1999.

Hardt, Michael, and Antonio Negri. *Empire.* Cambridge, MA: Harvard University Press, 2000.

Harvey, David. *Consciousness and the Urban Experience: Studies in the History and Theory of Capitalist Urbanization.* Baltimore: Johns Hopkins University Press, 1986.

Hedge, Frederick H. *The Prose Writers of Germany.* 1870. Philadelphia: Porter & Coates, 1870.

Helms, Alan. "Whitman's 'Live Oak with Moss.'" In *The Continuing Presence of Walt Whitman.* Ed. Robert K. Martin. Iowa City: University of Iowa Press, 1992. 185–205.

Hollis, C. Carroll. "Whitman and Swinton: A Cooperative Friendship." *American Literature* 30 (January 1959): 425–49.

Holmes, Oliver Wendell. *Works.* Boston: Houghton Mifflin, 1892.

Ibson, John. *Picturing Men: A Century of Male Relationships in Everyday American Photography.* Washington, DC: Smithsonian Institution Press, 2002.

Jay, Paul, ed. *Selected Correspondence of Kenneth Burke and Malcolm Cowley, 1915–1981.* New York: Viking, 1988.

Jefferson, Thomas. *Selected Writings.* Ed. Harvey C. Mansfield, Jr. Arlington Heights, IL: AHM Publishing, 1979.

———. *Writings.* Ed. Merrill D. Paterson. New York: Library of America, 1984.

Jones, Howard Mumford. *America and French Culture, 1750–1848.* Chapel Hill: University of North Carolina Press, 1927.

Jordan, H. J. *Happiness or Misery? Being Four Lectures on the Functions and Disorders of the Nervous System and Reproductive Organs.* New York: Barton & Son, 1861.

Kaplan, Justin. "The Biographer's Problem." *Mickle Street Review* 11 (1989): 80–88.

Kateb, George. *The Inner Ocean: Individualism and Democratic Culture.* Ithaca, NY: Cornell University Press, 1992.

———. "Walt Whitman and the Culture of Democracy." *Political Theory* 18 (November 1990): 545–71.

Katz, Jonathan Ned. *Love Stories: Sex between Men before Homosexuality.* Chicago: University of Chicago Press, 2001.

Killingsworth, Myrth Jimmie. "Whitman and Motherhood: A Historical View." *American Literature* 54 (March 1982): 28–43.

———. *Whitman's Poetry of the Body: Sexuality, Politics, and the Text.* Chapel Hill: University of North Carolina Press, 1989.

Kolodny, Annette. *The Lay of the Land: Metaphor as Experience and History in*

American Life and Letters. Chapel Hill: University of North Carolina Press, 1975.

Lewis, Jan. "Motherhood and the Construction of the Male Citizen in the United States, 1750–1850." In *Constructions of the Self.* Ed. George Levine. New Brunswick, NJ: Rutgers University Press, 1992.

———. "The Republican Wife: Virtue and Seduction in the Early Republic." *William and Mary Quarterly* 44 (October 1987): 689–721.

Lincoln, Abraham. *The Collected Works of Abraham Lincoln.* Ed. Roy P. Basler. 9 vols. New Brunswick: Rutgers University Press, 1953–1955.

Lynch, Michael. "'Here Is Adhesiveness': From Friendship to Homosexuality." *Victorian Studies* 29 (Autumn 1985): 67–96.

Martin, Robert K. *The Homosexual Tradition in American Poetry.* Austin: University of Texas Press, 1979.

———. "Whitman's *Song of Myself*: Homosexual Dream and Vision." *Partisan Review* 42 (1975): 80–96.

Marx, Karl. *Capital.* 1867. In Karl Marx, *Political Writings.* Vol. 1, *The Revolutions of 1848.* Ed. David Fernbach. 2 vols. Harmondsworth: Penguin, 1973.

———. *The Civil War in France: The Paris Commune.* 1870–1871. New York: International Publishers, 1968.

———. *The Class Struggles in France.* 1848–1850. London: Martin Lawrence, 1895.

———. *Communist Manifesto.* In Karl Marx, *Political Writings.* Vol. 1, *The Revolutions of 1848.* Ed. David Fernbach. 2 vols. Harmondsworth: Penguin, 1973. 67–98.

———. *Early Writings.* Ed. Lucio Colletti. Trans. Rodney Livingston and Gregor Benton. London: Penguin, 1992.

———. *Economic and Philosophical Manuscripts.* 1844. In Karl Marx, *Early Writings.* Ed. Lucio Colletti. Trans. Rodney Livingston and Gregor Benton. London: Penguin, 1992. 279–400.

———. *Grundrisse: Foundations of Political Economy.* 1857–1858. Trans. Martin Nicholas. London: Penguin, 1993.

———. *Karl Marx: Selected Writings.* Ed. David McLellan. New York: Oxford University Press, 2000.

Marx, Karl, and Frederick Engels. *The Civil War in the United States.* Ed. Richard Enmale. New York: International Publishers, 1937.

———. "The Economics of the Volks-Tribun and Its Attitude Toward Young America." 1846. Reprinted as "American Soil and Communism" in *On America and the Civil War*, vol. 2 of *The Karl Marx Library*, ed. Saul K. Padover. New York: McGraw Hill, 1972. 3–6.

———. *Selected Works.* London: Lawrence and Wishart, 1968.

Mathews, M. M., ed. *The Beginnings of American English.* Chicago: University of Chicago Press, 1931.

Matthiessen, F. O. *American Renaissance: Art and Expression in the Age of Emerson and Whitman.* New York: Oxford University Press, 1941.

McLellan, David. *Karl Marx: The Life and Thought.* New York: Harper & Row, 1973.

Melville, Herman. *Battle-Pieces and Aspects of the War.* In Herman Melville, *Published Poems.* Ed. Robert C. Ryan et al. Evanston, IL: Northwestern University Press, 2009.

———. *Billy Budd, Sailor.* In *Billy Budd, Sailor and Other Uncompleted Writings,* ed. Harrison Hayford et al. Evanston, IL: Northwestern University Press, 2017.

———. *Clarel: A Poem and Pilgrimage in the Holy Land.* 1876. Ed. Harrison Hayford, Herschel Parker, and G. Thomas Tanselle. Evanston, IL: Northwestern University Press, 1991.

———. *The Confidence-Man: His Masquerade.* 1857. Evanston, IL: Northwestern University Press, 1984.

———. *Correspondence.* Ed. Lynn Horth. Evanston, IL: Northwestern University Press, 1993.

———. *Mardi: And a Voyage Hither.* Ed. Harrison Hayford, Hershel Parker, and G. Thomas Tanselle. Evanston, IL: Northwestern University Press, 1970.

———. *Moby Dick; or, The Whale.* Ed. Harrison Hayford, Hershel Parker, and G. Thomas Tanselle. Evanston, IL: Northwestern University Press, 2001.

———. *Piazza Tales and Other Prose Pieces 1839–1860.* Evanston, IL: Northwestern University Press, 1987.

———. *Pierre; or, The Ambiguities.* New York: Harper, 1852.

———. *Redburn: His First Voyage.* Ed. Harrison Hayford, Hershel Parker, and G. Thomas Tanselle. Evanston, IL: Northwestern University Press, 1969.

———. *Typee: A Peep at Polynesian Life.* Ed. Harrison Hayford, Hershel Parker, and G. Thomas Tanselle. Evanston, IL: Northwestern University Press, 2003.

———. *White-Jacket; or, The World in a Man-of-War.* Ed. Harrison Hayford, Hershel Parker, and G. Thomas Tanselle. Evanston, IL: Northwestern University Press, 2000.

Mencken, H. L. *The American Language: An Inquiry into the Development of English in the United States.* New York: Knopf, 1936.

Mill, John Stuart. *On Liberty.* 1859. New York: Pearson Longman, 2007.

Miller, Edwin Haviland. *Walt Whitman's Poetry: A Psychological Journey.* Boston: Houghton Mifflin, 1968.

Miller, James E., Jr. "'Song of Myself' as an Inverted Mystical Experience." In *A Critical Guide to Leaves of Grass.* Chicago: University of Chicago Press, 1957. 636–61.

Miller, Perry. *The New England Mind: From Colony to Province.* Cambridge, MA: Harvard University Press, 1953.

———. *The New England Mind: The Seventeenth Century.* New York: Macmillan, 1939.

Moon, Michael. *Disseminating Whitman: Revision and Corporeality in "Leaves of Grass."* Cambridge, MA: Harvard University Press, 1991.

Moon, Michael, and Eve Kosofsky Sedgwick. "Confusion of Tongues." In *Breaking*

Bounds: Whitman and American Cultural Studies. Ed. Betsy Erkkila and Jay Grossman. New York: Oxford University Press, 1996. 23–29.

Nussbaum, Martha C. *Poetic Justice: The Literary Imagination and Public Life*. Boston: Beacon Press, 1995.

Oates, David. "The Base of all Metaphysics." In *Walt Whitman: An Encyclopedia*. Ed. J. R. LeMaster and Donald D. Kummings. New York: Garland, 1998. 49–50.

O'Connor, William Douglas. "Another Recovered Chapter in the History of 'Leaves of Grass.'" *Conservator* (September 7, 1896): 99–102.

———. *The Good Gray Poet: A Vindication*. New York: Bunce and Huntington, 1866.

Paine, Thomas. *Collected Writings*. Ed. Eric Foner. New York: Library of America, 1995.

———. Letter to the Abbé Raynal. 1782. In *Complete Writings of Thomas Paine*. Ed. Philip S. Foner. New York: Citadel Press, 1945. 2: 211–63.

Parker, Hershel. "The Real 'Live Oak, with Moss': Straight Talk about Whitman's 'Gay Manifesto.'" *Nineteenth-Century Literature* 51 (September 1996): 145–60.

Perlman, Jim, Ed Folsom, and Dan Campion, eds. *Walt Whitman: The Measure of His Song*. Duluth, MN: Holy Cow! Press, 1981.

Pessen, Edward. *Jacksonian America: Society, Personality, and Politics*. Homewood, IL: Dorsey, 1969.

———. *Riches, Class, and Power before the Civil War*. Lexington, MA: Heath, 1973.

Pickering, John. *A Vocabulary or Collection of Words and Phrases Which Have Been Supposed to Be Peculiar to the United States of America*. Boston: Cummings and Hilliard, 1816.

Poe, Edgar Allan. *Poe: Poetry, Tales, and Selected Essays*. Ed. Patrick F. Quinn and G. R. Thompson. New York: Library of America, 1984.

Pollak, Vivian. *Dickinson: The Anxiety of Gender*. Ithaca, NY: Cornell University Press, 1984.

Pound, Ezra. *Personae*. New York: New Directions, 1926.

Pound, Louise. "Walt Whitman and the French Language." *American Speech* 1 (May 1926): 421–30.

Reynolds, Larry J. *European Revolutions and the American Literary Renaissance*. New Haven, CT: Yale University Press, 1988.

Rich, Adrienne. "Beginners." *The Kenyon Review* 15 (Summer 1993): 12–19.

Rimbaud, Arthur. *Correspondance inédite*. 1870–1875. Ed. Roger Gilbert-Lecomte. Paris: Éditions des Cahiers Libres, 1929.

Robertson, W. Graham. *Time Was: Rossetti, Oscar Wilde, Ellen Terry*. Philadelphia: R. West, 1931.

Rogin, Michael Paul. *Subversive Genealogy: The Politics and Art of Herman Melville*. New York: Knopf, 1983.

Rorty, Richard. *Achieving Our Country: Leftist Thought in Twentieth-Century America*. Cambridge, MA: Harvard University Press, 1998.

Rosenberg, Charles E. "Sexuality, Class and Role in 19th-Century America." *American Quarterly* 25 (May 1973): 131–53.

Rubin, Joseph. *The Historic Whitman.* University Park: Pennsylvania State University Press, 1973.

———. "Whitman in 1840: A Discovery." *American Literature* 9 (May 1937): 239–42.

Ryan, Mary P. *Women in Public: Between Banners and Ballots, 1825–1880.* Baltimore: Johns Hopkins University Press, 1990.

Sandburg, Carl. "Introduction." *Leaves of Grass.* Ed. Carl Sandburg. New York: Modern Library, 1921. iii–xi.

Schiller, Friedrich. *On the Aesthetic Education of Man, in a Series of Letters.* 1795. Oxford: Clarendon Press, 1986.

Schlesinger, Arthur M., Jr. *The Age of Jackson.* Boston: Little, Brown, 1945.

Schmidgall, Gary. *Walt Whitman: A Gay Life.* New York: Dutton, 1997.

Seery, John E., ed. *A Political Companion to Walt Whitman.* Lexington: University Press of Kentucky, 2011.

Shively, Charley, ed. *Calamus Lovers: Walt Whitman's Working Class Camerados.* San Francisco: Gay Sunshine Press, 1987.

———. *Drum-Beats: Walt Whitman's Civil War Boy Lovers.* San Francisco: Gay Sunshine Press, 1989.

Silverman, Kenneth. *A Cultural History of the American Revolution.* New York: T. Y. Crowell, 1976.

Smith, Adam. *The Theory of Moral Sentiments.* Ed. D. D. Raphael and A. L. Macfie. Indianapolis: Liberty Fund, 1984.

Smith, Martha Nell. *Rowing in Eden: Rereading Emily Dickinson.* Austin: University of Texas Press, 1992.

Smith-Rosenberg, Carroll. *Disorderly Conduct: Visions of Gender in Victorian America.* New York: Knopf, 1985.

———. "Sex as Symbol in Victorian Purity: An Ethnohistorical Analysis of Jacksonian America." *American Journal of Sociology* 84 (Supplement, 1987): S212–S247.

Sommer, Doris. "The Bard of Both Americas." In *Approaches to Teaching Whitman's Leaves of Grass.* Ed. Donald D. Kummings. New York: MLA, 1990. 159–67.

Spiller, Robert E. "The Cycle and the Roots: National Identity in American Literature." In *Toward a New American Literary History.* Ed. Louis J. Budd, Edwin H. Cady, and Carl L. Anderson. Durham, NC: Duke University Press, 1980.

Spiller, Robert E., et al., eds. *A Literary History of the United States.* New York: Macmillan, 1948.

Sumner, Charles. "Report on the War with Mexico." April 1847. Reprinted in *Old South Leaflets*, vol. 6. Boston: Old South Work, 1902. 137–67.

Swinton, William. *Rambles among Words: Their Poetry, History, and Wisdom.* New York: Scribner, 1859.

Symonds, John Addington. *Walt Whitman: A Study*. London: J. C. Nimmo, 1893.

Thomas, M. Wynn. *The Lunar Light of Whitman's Poetry*. Cambridge, MA: Harvard University Press, 1987.

Todd, Mabel Loomis. "Emily Dickinson's Literary Début." *Harper's Monthly Magazine* (March 1930): 463–64.

Tombs, Robert. *The Paris Commune 1871*. London: Longman, 1999.

Traubel, Horace. *With Walt Whitman in Camden*. Vol. 1: Boston: Small, Maynard, 1906; Vol. 2: New York: D. Appleton, 1908; Vol. 3: New York: Mitchell Kennerley, 1914; Vol. 4: Philadelphia: University of Pennsylvania Press, 1953; Vol. 6: Carbondale: Southern Illinois University Press, 1982.

Trilling, Lionel. *The Liberal Imagination: Essays on Literature and Society*. New York: Harcourt Brace Jovanovich, 1950.

Volney, C. F. *The Ruins, or Meditation on the Revolutions of Empire: and The Law of Nature*. 1791. Baltimore: Black Classic Press, 1991.

Warner, David. "The Good G(r)ay Poet," *Philadelphia City Paper*, January 12–19, 1990.

Warner, Michael. "Whitman Drunk." In *Breaking Bounds: Whitman and American Cultural Studies*. Ed. Betsy Erkkila and Jay Grossman. New York: Oxford University Press, 1996. 30–43.

Webster, Noah. *An American Dictionary of the English Language*. New York: S. Converse, 1828.

———. *Dissertations on the English Language*. 1789. Gainesville, FL: Scholars' Facsimiles and Reprints, 1951.

Weeks, Jeffrey. *Sexuality and Its Discontents: Meanings, Myths, and Modern Sexualities*. London: Routledge and Kegan Paul, 1985.

Wharton, Edith. *A Backward Glance*. New York: Appleton-Century, 1934.

Wheatley, Phillis. *The Poems of Phillis Wheatley*. Ed. Julian D. Mason, Jr. Chapel Hill: University of North Carolina Press, 1989.

Whitman, Walt. *An American Primer. With Facsimiles of the Original Manuscript*. Ed. Horace Traubel. Boston: Small, Maynard, and Company, 1904.

———. "The Child's Champion." Reprinted as "The Child and the Profligate" in *The Early Poems and the Fiction*. Ed. Thomas L. Brasher. New York University Press, 1963. 68–79.

———. *The Complete Writings of Walt Whitman*. Ed. Richard Maurice Bucke, Thomas B. Harned, and Horace L. Traubel. 10 vols. New York: G. P. Putnam's Sons, 1902.

———. *The Correspondence*. Vol. 7. Ed. Ted Genoways. Iowa City: University of Iowa Press, 2004.

———. *The Correspondence*. Ed. Edwin Haviland Miller. 6 vols. New York: New York University Press, 1961–1977.

———. *Daybooks and Notebooks*. Ed. William White. 3 vols. New York: New York University Press, 1978.

———. *Democratic Vistas: The Original Edition in Facsimile*. Ed. Ed Folsom. Iowa City: University of Iowa Press, 2010.

———. *The Early Poems and Fiction*. Ed. Thomas L. Brasher. New York: New York University Press, 1963.

———. *Faint Clues and Indirections: Manuscripts of Walt Whitman and His Family*. Ed. Clarence Gohdes and Rollo G. Silver. Durham, NC: Duke University Press, 1949.

———. *The Journalism*. Ed. Herbert Bergman. 2 vols. New York: Peter Lang, 1998–2003.

———. *Leaves of Grass: An Exact Copy of the First Edition 1855*. New York: Eakins Press, 1966.

———. *Leaves of Grass*. Brooklyn, NY: n.p., 1856. Reprinted in Ed Folsom and Kenneth M. Price, eds., *The Walt Whitman Archive*, https://whitmanarchive.org.

———. *Leaves of Grass: Facsimile of the 1860 Text*. Ed. Roy Harvey Pearce. Ithaca, NY: Cornell University Press, 1961.

———. *Leaves of Grass*. Washington, DC: n.p., 1871. Reprinted in Ed Folsom and Kenneth M. Price, eds., *The Walt Whitman Archive*, https://whitmanarchive.org.

———. *Leaves of Grass: Comprehensive Reader's Edition*. Ed. Harold W. Blodgett and Sculley Bradley. New York: New York University Press, 1965.

———. *Leaves of Grass: A Textual Variorum of the Printed Poems*. Ed. Sculley Bradley et al. 3 vols. New York: New York University Press, 1980.

———. *Memoranda During the War*. Camden, NJ: New Republic Print, 1875–1876.

———. *New York Dissected*. Ed. Emory Holloway and Ralph Adimari. New York: R. R. Wilson, 1936.

———. *Notebooks and Unpublished Prose Manuscripts*. Ed. Edward F. Grier. 6 vols. New York: New York University Press, 1984.

———. *Notes and Fragments*. Ed. Richard Maurice Bucke. London, Canada: A. Talbot, 1899.

———. "O Star of France!" *Galaxy* 11 (June 1871): 817. Reprinted in Ed Folsom and Kenneth M. Price, eds., *The Walt Whitman Archive*, https://whitmanarchive.org/published/periodical/poems/per.00008.

———. *Prose Works 1892*. Ed. Floyd Stovall. 2 vols. New York: New York University Press, 1963–1964.

———. "Prospects of War." New Orleans *Daily Crescent*, April 17, 1848, 2. In Chronicling America, https://chroniclingamerica.loc.gov/lccn/sn82015378/1848-04-17/ed-1/seq-2/.

———. *The Uncollected Poetry and Prose*. Ed. Emory Holloway. 2 vols. Garden City, NY: Doubleday, Page, 1921.

———. *Walt Whitman of the New York Aurora*. Ed. Joseph J. Rubin and Charles H. Brown. State College, PA: Bald Eagle Press, 1950.

———. *Walt Whitman's Memoranda during the War and Death of Abraham Lincoln*. Ed. Roy P. Basler. Bloomington: Indiana University Press, 1962.

———. *Walt Whitman's Songs of Male Intimacy and Love: "Live Oak, with Moss" and "Calamus."* Ed. Betsy Erkkila. Iowa City: University of Iowa Press, 2011.

———. *Whitman's Manuscripts: Leaves of Grass (1860): A Parallel Text.* Ed. Fredson Bowers. Chicago: University of Chicago Press, 1955.

Wilentz, Sean. *Chants Democratic: New York City and the Rise of the Working Class, 1788–1850.* New York: Oxford University Press, 1984.

Wills, Garry. *Inventing America: Jefferson's Declaration of Independence.* New York: Vintage, 1979.

Wolosky, Shira. *Emily Dickinson: A Voice of War.* New Haven, CT: Yale University Press, 1984.

———. "Public and Private in Dickinson's War Poetry." In *Oxford Historical Guide to Emily Dickinson.* Ed. Vivian Pollak. New York: Oxford University Press, 2004. 103–32.

Wright, Frances. *A Few Days in Athens.* 1822. New York: Arno, 1972.

Ziff, Larzer. *Literary Democracy: The Declaration of Cultural Independence in America.* New York: Viking Press, 1981.

INDEX

Adams, Henry, 50, 118
Adams, John, 52–53, 55; American language academy, 52–53
adhesiveness, 21, 63–64; central to Whitman's democratic theory, 80–81, 98, 203–204, 208–209, 211, 214; threat to democratic individualism, 203
"Adieu to a Soldier" (Whitman), 155
African Americans, 66, 189, 190–91
Age of Jackson, 164, 166; antimasturbation tracts, 166; increased gap between labor and capital, 166; Indian Removal Policy, 164, 166; male purity movement, 166; temperance movement, 166; theories of innate racial and sexual difference, 164, 166; white male republic, 164, 166
Allen, Gay Wilson, 4
amativeness, 19, 22, 63–64, 87–89
"America" (Whitman), 31, 49
"America's Mightiest Inheritance" (Whitman), 58, 62
American 1848, the, 132–43, 168
American language policy, 52–56, 66; American language and democratic culture, 53, 61–62, 66
American republic, 182, 191, 209; male and female couple as metaphysics, 215–16; republican myth, 182; role of homoeroticism and love, 203; and slavery, 182, 209
American Revolution, 4, 6, 31–35, 52, 57, 126, 152, 170, 181, 182, 201, 207, 215; antislavery struggle, 43; Battle of Brooklyn, 207; challenge to patriarchal authority, 215; and George Washington, 207; *Leaves of Grass* (1855), 4; Melville's critique of, 170, 181–82; proposal to adopt French as national language, 56–57; Whitman's embrace of, 138, 181
"American Workingmen, versus Slavery" (Whitman), 147; attack on slavery in America, 147; revolutionary form of *Leaves of Grass*, 147; Revolutions of 1848, 147
antimasturbation tracts, 166; and the Age of Jackson, 166
antislavery struggle, 5, 35, 36, 43, 110; Whitman's notes on "Slavery," 45
"Apostroph" (Whitman), 63
"Appendant for Working-People, Young Men and Women, and for Boys and Girls" (Whitman), 58–59; and "*A few Foreign Words, mostly French, put down Suggestively*, 58–59
Arendt, Hannah, 203; individualism as resistance to statism, 203
Armoury Square Hospital (Washington, DC), 190
"An Army Corps on the March" (Whitman), 187; and Winslow Homer's *Infantry Column on the March*, 187
Arthur, Chester, 24–25
Arthur, Gavin, 24–25; *The Circle of Sex*, 24–25; grandson of President Chester Arthur, 24

"As I Ebb'd with the Ocean of Life" (Whitman), 12, 43
"As I Lay with My Head in Your Lap, Camerado" (Whitman), 91–92; Whitman's renewed dedication to same-sex love among men, 92
Asselineau, Roger, 13, 51; *The Evolution of Walt Whitman*, 51
Athénot, Eric, 17
Austria, 136, 137; revolutions of 1848, 136–38, 147–48

Barlow, Joel, 10, 32, 33, 57, 126; *The Columbiad*, 53; rising-glory rhetoric, 32
Barnburners, 168; and Melville's *Moby-Dick*, 168; and Whitman's *Leaves of Grass* (1855), 168
"The Base of All Metaphysics" (Whitman), 213
"Bathed in War's Perfumes" (Whitman), 155
Battle-Pieces and Aspects of the War (Melville), 185–91, 193; "A Meditation," 190–91; "Supplement," 189–90, 197
Beer, Samuel H., 202–203
"Benito Cereno" (Melville), 181–82; Toussaint L'Ouverture's slave insurrection, 181
Béranger, Pierre Jean de, 63, 150; influence of his *chansons* on Whitman's songs, 63, 150
Bertz, Edouard, 95; *Walt Whitman: Ein Charakterbild*, 95
Bible, the, 185, 191; Ethiopia in Psalms, 191; Melville's *Battle-Pieces*, 185
Billy-Budd, Sailor (Melville), 21, 183, 193, 195–99; black Handsome Sailor, 196–97; future of democracy, 193, 195; Haitian Revolution, 195; homoerotic love, 197–99
Blanc, Louis, 129
"Blood Money" (Whitman), 36, 135, 169; early free-verse poem, 169; and slavery, 169
"A Boston Ballad" (Whitman), 6, 38, 43, 88
Bowles, Samuel, 109; Dickinson, 109; editor of *Springfield Republican*, 109
Braquehais, Bruno, 157; photograph of *Voltaire Lenoir Barricade of the Paris Commune*, 157
"Bravo, Paris Exposition!" (Whitman), 159; Paris Exposition of 1889, 159
Brooklyn *Daily Eagle*, 5, 70, 75, 107, 131, 168; "American Workingmen, versus Slavery" (Whitman), 75, 137, 147; Whitman as editor, 5, 107, 133, 147
Brooklyn *Weekly Freeman*, 133; and antislavery, 133; Whitman as editor, 133
Brown, Lewis, 99; and Whitman, 99
Bucke, Richard Maurice, 95; and *Calamus*, 95
Burke, Edmund, 203; erotic bonds between individuals and the state, 203
Burke, Kenneth, 17, 79
Burns, Anthony, 6, 177; "A Boston Ballad," 177; capture and return, 177

Cady, Joseph, 85
"Calamus" (Whitman), 21, 24–25, 42, 45–46, 64, 85–87, 90, 97–98, 103, 183, 211–13; addition of "The Base of All Metaphysics" to *Leaves of Grass* (1871), 98; democracy and manly love, 7, 21–22, 24, 85–86, 183, 211–12; "Live Oak, with Moss," 85–86; "political significance," 80–81, 212; Whitman's response to John Addington Symonds, 98–99
"Calamus" 5 (Whitman), 45, 64, 85, 213,

216; bonds of comradeship and love, 213, 216; manly love as force for political union, 217. *See also* "Over the Carnage Rose Prophetic a Voice"
"Calamus" 15 (Whitman): attempt to publicize the private, 217–18. *See also* "Trickle Drops"
"Calamus" 34 (Whitman), 85. *See also* "I Dreamed in a Dream"
capitalism, 4–5, 8, 15, 18, 20, 49, 70, 74, 123–26, 129–32, 153, 155, 170, 171; capitalism and democracy, 29–32; Marx's critique of, 124–25, 127, 129–32; social love, 135
Carlyle, Thomas, 193; "Shooting Niagara: And After?," 193
Carpenter, Edward, 24; visits to Whitman in 1877 and 1884, 24
"Champagne in Ice" (Whitman), 159
"Chants Democratic and Native American" (Whitman), 19, 63, 151; French title of, 151
Chaucer, Geoffrey, 59
"The Child and the Profligate" (Whitman), 21, 165, 204–205, 216; male love, 82, 166, 205, 216
"The Child's Champion." *See* "The Child and the Profligate"
"Children of Adam" (Whitman), 22, 63, 87; amative love, 87; companion piece to "Calamus" poems, 87; "obscene literature," 23; sexual radicalism of, 86–87
Civil War, 19, 20, 39, 41, 46–48, 61, 65, 70, 72, 74, 89–92, 114–18, 146, 151–53, 164, 165, 168, 183–93; America as "armed woman and warrior," 46–48; Battle of Fredericksburg, 184; Battle of Gettysburg, 116; figure of amputation in Whitman and Dickinson, 118, 184; French Reign of Terror, 151–53; "manly love," 21–22, 89–92; and Melville, 184–89; and Whitman, 184–89; Whitman as wound-dresser, 184
Clarel: A Poem and Pilgrimage in the Holy Land (Melville), 21, 194
Clay, Henry, 168; compromise resolutions of, 168
Cloots, Anarcharsis, 196; and the French Revolution, 196
Cold War, 4, 18, 66, 123–24, 141; communism and, 141
"The Columbian's Song" (Whitman), 31–32
communism, 18, 124, 131, 134, 135; Cold War, 134, 143; Soviet state, 134
Communist League, 133, 135; international workers' movement, 133
The Communist Manifesto, 133, 136; Free Soil Party, 136; revolutions of 1848, 133
Compromise of 1850, 5, 36, 106, 133, 134, 168; Daniel Webster's support, 168; Whitman's break into free-verse, 106, 168
comradeship, 21, 165, 170–71; base of democracy in Whitman, 21, 26, 81, 98–99, 190; "Calamus" poems, 151, 183, 203–204, 213; *Democratic Vistas*, 98, 198–99, 221–22; *Drum-Taps* poems, 118; France, 151, 158, 209; global union, 27, 149, 222; John Addington Symonds on "semi-sexual" relations between men, 98–99; Melville and erotic comradeship, 20–21, 198–99; Melville's *Moby-Dick,* 175–76; Melville's *White Jacket*, 170–71; Smith Adam and *The Theory of Moral Sentiments*, 214; Transatlantic Walt Whitman Association, 146; Whitman's "Democratic Nationality," 158; Whitman's erotic feeling for men, 81, 85, 89; Whitman's "A March

comradeship (*continued*)
in the Ranks," 189; Whitman's "O Star of France!," 158; Whitman's "Over the Carnage Rose Prophetic a Voice," 213; Whitman's "Poem of the Road," 209; Whitman's "The Sleepers," 26, 175; Whitman's theory of democracy, 15, 98, 194, 214; Whitman as wound-dresser during the Civil War, 89, 92
Comstock, Anthony, 23; prosecution of *Leaves of Grass* as "obscene literature," 23
Comstock Law, 23
Confederate States of America, 183
The Confidence Man: His Masquerade (Melville), 182–83
"The Conflict of Convictions" (Melville), 193; new power state, 193
Constitution of the United States, 36, 167, 170, 201, 213, 215; defended by Hamilton, Madison, and Jay, 202, 213; Madison's fear of "the public passions," 213, 215; paradox of liberty and union, 202, 213; Shays's rebellion in 1786–87, 202
Constitutional founders, 215; control of the passions and, 215
Cowley, Malcolm, 17, 79, 84, 99; on homosexuality and democracy, 17, 79, 84, 99–100
Crane, Hart, 17
Crane, Stephen, 58; *Maggie: A Girl of the Streets*, 58
"Crossing Brooklyn Ferry" (Whitman), 24, 40, 41, 182; self-doubt of poet, 40

"The Dalliance of the Eagles" (Whitman), 23; "obscene literature," 23
Darras, Jacques, 154; fraternité and *Leaves of Grass*, 154
Declaration of Independence, 14, 32, 36, 38, 75, 154, 163, 170, 177; absence of fraternité in, 154; bodily freedom, 170; Melville on, 163, 170, 190; "Song of Myself" and, 75
Democratic Party, 128, 135, 137, 164; Compromise of 1850, 135; election of Jackson, 164; Whitman's disillusionment with, 137
democratic theory, 202–204, 207–209, 215; adhesiveness and, 203–204, 208–209; democratic individuality and, 202–203; role of homoeroticism and love in, 202–203, 207–20; Whitman on, 202–23
Democratic Vistas (1871), 6, 21, 26–27, 50, 147, 193–94; democracy and "loving comradeship," 21, 98, 194; dialectics of individual and community, 195; French revolutions of 1870–71 and, 145–47; future of democracy, 193; Hegelian idealism of, 127, 194, 195; King Louis Napoléon, 145–46; modern Individualism, 193–94, 195; response to Thomas Carlyle's "Shooting Niagara," 193, 195; self-regulation as the "*sine qua non* to democracy," 75
Dickinson, Austin, 111; mutilation of Dickinson's letters to Susan Gilbert, 111
Dickinson, Edward, 103–104; conservative Whig, 103; Massachusetts state representative, 103
Dickinson, Emily, 16, 101–20; "Bloom" of creativity during Civil War, 107, 115–16; criticism of Lincoln, 116, 117; daguerreotype at Mt. Holyoke, 105; fear of Jacksonian democracy, 104; Federalist country values, 119; hand-sewn booklets of poems, 109; love crisis and "Master" letters, 111–14; love of Susan Gilbert, 111–14; at Mt. Holyoke College, 104–106; photograph of Dickinson home in

Amherst, Massachusetts, 104; poetic intercourse with Whitman, 101–20; politics, 103–106; publication of Dickinson's poems, 109–10; radical imaginary, 101–20; resistance to marketplace, 108–10; sexual revolution of, 103, 106–107; split with Mt. Holyoke Seminary, 18; Whitman and, 101–20; withdrawal into Dickinson Homestead, 119
Doolittle, Hilda (H. D.), 50; woman-centered quest myths, 50
Douglass, Frederick, 192; Ethiopia in "What to the Slave Is the Fourth of July?," 192; slavery as Egyptian captivity, 192; Whitman's "Ethiopia Saluting the Colors," 192
Doyle, Peter, 92–95, 99; photograph of Whitman and Doyle, 93
Drum-Taps and Sequel (1865), 46, 89–92, 117–18, 155–56, 185–89, 192; affection between men, 65, 89, 92; Civil War as reaffirmation of founding ideals, 187; criticism of unreason of Civil War, 117–18; Homer Winslow's sketches of the Civil War, 186–87; ordinary soldiers as heroes, 186–87; underlying melancholia, 187
Du Bois, W. E. B., 196; Black Reconstruction, 196
Duckett, Bill, 96; photograph of Whitman and Duckett, 96
Duncan, Robert, 17
Durkheim, Émile, 203; erotic bonds between individuals and the state, 203

The Eighteenth Presidency! (Whitman), 210
Eliot, T. S., 16; woman-centered quest myths, 50
Ellis, Havelock, 99; medicalization of homosexuality, 99
Emancipation Proclamation, 191
Emerson, Ralph Waldo, 36, 54–55, 170; fear of the body, 170; influence on Whitman, 5, 13–14, 16–17; Melville on, 170; sexual radicalism of "Children of Adam," 86; Whitman's letter in 1856 *Leaves of Grass*, 63
"Emerson's Books" (Whitman), 54–55
"Enfans d'Adam" (Whitman), 19, 63, 87–88, 151; French title, 151; sexual revolution and France, 151. *See also* "Children of Adam"
Engels, Friedrich, 127, 130; Communist League, 133; *Manifesto of the Communist Party*, 133, 135, 148
Enlightenment, 126; theories of human liberty and natural law, 139
Epicurus, 127
Erkkila, Betsy, 86, 103; "Emily Dickinson and Class," 103–104; *Whitman the Political Poet*, 86
"Ethiopia Saluting the Colors," 56, 191–92
Europe, 137; revolutions of 1848, 136–37, 147, 156
"Europe, the 72d and 73d Years of These States" (Whitman), 4, 19, 38, 150

"Faces" (Whitman) 60; French language in, 60
The Federalist Papers, 202, 213; *Federalist* No. 37 (Madison), 202; *Federalist* No. 49 (Madison) on control of "the passions" by "the government," 213, 215
Fernbach, David, 141; on democracy as rule by the people, 141
Field, George B., 190; calling card presented to Whitman in Armoury Square Hospital, 190
"First O Songs for a Prelude" (Whitman), 89
Folsom, Ed, 95–96

Ford, Emily Fowler, 102
formalism, 16–17
Fourier, Charles, 140; "Critical Utopian Socialism and Communism," 140
Fowler, Orson, 83; *Amativeness: Or, Evils and Remedies of Excessive and Perverted Sexuality*, 83
France, 64, 124, 137, 145–60; Bloody Week in, 157–58; French language and adhesiveness, 63–64; French Reign of Terror and American Civil War, 151–53; French Revolution of 1789, 124, 126, 152–55, 209; *Leaves of Grass*, 145–60; *Leaves of Grass* (1860), 151–53; Paris Commune and *Leaves of Grass* (1870–71), 145–60; Revolutions of 1792–93, 19, 61, 124, 153; Revolutions of 1848, 147–49, 209; Revolutions of 1848 and *Leaves of Grass* (1855), 61, 124, 126, 127, 137–38, 147–51; Revolution of 1870–71, 19, 124, 145–46, 153–57; sexual openness and, 60–64, 151–52; Whitman, 145–60
"France, the 18th Year of These States," 64, 152, 156; France as fantasy lover, 153; French Reign of Terror, 152, 156; justification in advance of American Civil War, 153; Whitman's address "to Paris, with my love," 152
Franklin, Benjamin, 31, 41, 53; American language policy, 53
Franklin Evans; or The Inebriate, 21, 82, 165–66, 216; counter-model of male affection and love, 216; male cruising, 110, 166; temperance reform, 166
Franklin, R. W., 116; *The Poems of Emily Dickinson*, 116
Free Enquirer, 126; Whitman and, 126
French Reign of Terror, 57, 214; American Civil War, 151–53; Washington's Farewell Address in 1796, 214; Whitman's longing for similar "red birth and baptism" in America, 152
French Revolution of 1789, 4, 6, 14, 32, 61, 126, 196, 209, 214, 215; Anacharsis Cloots, 196; Federalist fear of, 214; ideals of *liberté, egalité*, and *fraternité*, 196, 214; origins of 1855 *Leaves of Grass*, 4, 6, 14; Whitman, 138, 214
Freneau, Philip, 32–36, 57; "On Mr. Paine's Rights of Man," 34; pro-French, 57; rising-glory rhetoric, 32; "To an Author," 36
Fritzinger, Warren, 95; photograph with Whitman, 97
"From the Genius of Liberty," 215
"From Pent-Up Aching Rivers" (Whitman), 87
Fugitive Slave Law (1850), 36, 38, 135, 168, 171
Fuller, Margaret, 137; dispatches on Revolutions of 1848 in New York *Tribune*, 137

Gansevoort, Peter, 164; brother of Herman Melville, 164; embrace of western expansion and Texas annexation, 164; supporter of Democratic presidential candidate James Polk, 164
George III of England, 32–33, 38
German philosophy, 124; German idealism, 126, 130
Germany, 126, 146; democratic struggles, 146; Revolutions of 1848, 126, 133, 136–37, 147
Gilbert, Susan, 111–14; Dickinson's love affair with, 111–14
Ginsberg, Allen, 16; *Howl and Other Poems*, 16; the "line of transmission," 24–25; "A Supermarket in California," 16
Graham, Sylvester, 83; *A Lecture to Young Men, on Chastity*, 83

Greeley, Horace, 4
Guizot, François, 138

Habermas, Jürgen, 21, 204, 217; public sphere, 204, 217; *The Structural Transformation of the Public Sphere*, 204, 217; Whitman's theory of democracy, 204
Haitian Revolution, 215
Hamilton, 147
Harlan, James, 22–23; fired Whitman as a "Free Lover," 22
Hawthorne, Nathaniel, 17, 172, 176–77; Melville and, 177; Melville review of, 172
Hegel, Georg, 127, 128, 130; Hegelian dialectics, 138
Helms, Alan, 212
Hemingway, Ernest, 50; woman-centered quest myths, 50
Heywood, Ezra, 23, 24; arrest for publishing "To a Common Prostitute" and "A Woman Waits for Me," 24; president of New England Free-Love League, 24
Higginson, Thomas Wentworth, 110; Dickinson and, 110
Holland, Josiah Gilbert, 110; *Life of Abraham Lincoln*, 110
Hollis, C. Carroll, 62
Homer, Winslow, 186–87; *Infantry Column on the March* drawing, 187
homosexuality, 79–100, 110, 205–207, 216–19; American union, 80–81; democracy, 79–100, 201–23; Dickinson, 110; pathology, 81; practice of everyday life, 99, 216; Whitman, 21, 79–100, 201–23; Whitman as democratic theorist of, 207
"The House of Friends" (Whitman), 36, 169; early free-verse poem, 169; and slavery, 169
Hungary, 136; revolutions of 1848, 136–37, 147

"I Dreamed in a Dream" (Whitman), 85–86, 91–92
"I Sing the Body Electric" (Whitman), 25, 26
imperialism, 167, 170, 180; American democracy, 180; Melville, 167; *Redburn*, 170
Indigenous Americans. *See* Native Americans
"Inscriptions" (Whitman), 154
Irving, Washington, 54
Italy, 137, 146; democratic struggles in, 146; revolutions of 1848, 136–37, 147–48

Jackson, Andrew, 4, 103–104, 164, 166; defeat of British in War of 1812, 164; elected president in 1828, 164; Indian Removal Act, 164; Melville, 170; rhetoric of equality, 164; states' rights, 164; subjugation of Native Americans, 164, 166, 173; westward expansion, 164; Whitman, 4, 103; Whitman's brother named after, 103–104
Jackson, Helen Hunt, 110
James, Henry, 51; Whitman, 51
Jay Z, 66
Jefferson, Thomas, 32, 103; American Revolution, 32–33; Declaration of Independence, 32; Talmadge Amendment, 163; translator of Volney's *The Ruins, or Meditation on the Revolutions of Empires*, 126; Whitman's brother named after, 103
Jewish immigrants, 66
Jones, Howard Mumford, 57; *America and French Culture*, 57
Jones, John Paul, 6

Kant, Immanuel, 127
Kateb, George, 13, 202–203, 208–209; "Song of Myself" as "work of political theory," 202–203; "Walt Whitman and the Culture of Democracy," 202; Whitman and "democratic individuality," 202–203; Whitman as "greatest philosopher of democratic culture," 202
Kock, Paul de, 57

labor, 4–5, 6, 27, 124–25, 128, 129–32, 133, 135–43; capitalism and labor, 4–5, 15, 26, 70; Communist League, 133, 135; *Communist Manifesto* of Marx and Friedrich Engels, 132–33, 135; Dickinson's resistance to wage labor, 108–109; Free Soil Party, 133, 135; Karl Marx, 18, 124–25, 129–32; laborer poet of *Leaves of Grass* 1855, 107, 131–32, 137; Revolutions of 1848, 135–37; Thomas Paine, 6; Whitman's democratic songs, 7; Whitman's early political poems, 137–38; Whitman's editorials, 106, 128, 129–31, 137; Whitman's "Lively Frank," 129
Lamartine, Alphonse de, 147; Whitman, 147
"The Last of Lively Frank" (Whitman), 129
"The Last of the Loyalists" (Whitman), 32
Lauter, Paul, 20; *Companion to American Literature and Culture*, 20
Leaves of Grass (1855), 1–13, 20, 21, 37–40, 53, 60–61, 69, 71–77, 79, 106, 107–108, 110–11, 124–25, 127, 137, 142, 146–49, 154, 168, 169, 172, 177–80, 181, 205–208, 214–15, 217; American Revolution, 4, 31–36, 177; critique of capitalism, 4, 8, 15, 142–43; declaration of literary independence, 4, 36, 38, 107–10; democratic poetics, 9–10, 15–16, 132, 135; design, 1–3, 41, 107–108; Emerson, 5, 13–14, 16; engraved frontispiece of Whitman, 3, 107; experimental form, 5, 8–9, 36, 83, 148; homosexual love, 72, 110, 177–79; mystical vision, 83–84, 205–206; national and global focus, 3–4, 124–25, 137; origins in antislavery struggle, 36, 106, 169; preface, 3–4, 8, 14, 16, 37, 69, 76–77, 107, 172; "Resurgemus" as earliest free-verse poem, 6, 106, 137; Revolutions of 1848, 4, 137, 146–51; same-sex love and democracy, 83–84, 113, 177–79, 205–206; sex and the body, 60–61, 127, 205–206; Whitman's self-reviews, 5–7, 108; world proletarian movement, 3–5, 137, 148
Leaves of Grass (1856), 19, 21, 40–41, 61, 89, 150–51, 182, 201, 208–209, 216; dark "patches," 40–41; first use of term *adhesiveness*, 89, 151, 208–209; French communality and affection, 61, 63–64; French language, 59, 61, 63, 150; international focus, 150; "manly love," 216; Revolutions of 1848, 150
Leaves of Grass (1860), 19, 21–22, 41–46, 79, 85–89, 114–15, 151–53, 210–19; adhesiveness, 63–64, 85; amativeness, 63; "Chants Democratic," 41, 43, 62–63, 151; "full of indecent passages," 22; homosexual love and political crisis of democracy, 183, 210; intimate addresses to men, 63–65, 84–89; "New Bible" of American republic, 211; sexual radicalism of "Children of Adam," 86; Whitman as "evangel poet" of "manly love," 211–212, 216; Whitman's love crisis, 114
Leaves of Grass (1867), 65, 155; chaos of,

155; France, 146; French language, 65; "Inscription," 65; Whitman's revisions to "Calamus" poems, 97–98
Leaves of Grass (1871), 65, 153–57, 191, 213; anticipates final form of *Leaves of Grass*, 154; begins with "Inscriptions," 154; "Ethiopia Saluting the Colors," 191–92; France, 65, 145–60, 192; new clusters on Civil War, 155; "One's-Self I Sing" as opening inscription, 65, 153–57; "Songs of Insurrection" as new cluster inspired by insurrections in France, 146, 155, 192; "Songs of Parting" as concluding cluster, 156; "Still Though the One I Sing," 155
Leaves of Grass (1876), 214; preface to, 214
Leaves of Grass (1881), 6, 12–13, 25, 76, 88, 134, 156, 158–59; black dialect, 56; epic of democracy, 20; figure of mother, 40, 47–50; French language, 59, 61, 65; inspiration of Millet's *The Sower*, 139, 159; "language experiment," 51, 52, 56; Paris Commune, 145–60; politics of language, 51–66; sexual relations between men, 81, 98–99; "Songs of Parting" as concluding cluster, 156; teaching *Leaves of Grass*, 16
"Leaves of Grass," Poem 1. *See* "As I Ebb'd with the Ocean of Life"
"Leaves of Grass," Poem 20. *See* "So Far, and So Far, and On Toward the End"
Lebesgue, Philéas, 159; Whitman and modern French poetry, 159
Leroux, Pierre, 129
Levée en Masse, 154
Lewis, Jan, 215
"Liberty Poem for Asia, Africa, Europe, America, Australia, Cuba, and the Archipelagoes of the Sea" (Whitman), 150. *See also* "To a Foil'd European Revolutionaire"
Lincoln, Abraham, 65, 70, 110, 117, 177, 183, 188–89, 191; Whitman's annual Lincoln lecture, 158–59; Whitman's "comrade lustrous" and lover, 65; "When Lilacs Last in The Dooryard Bloom'd," 65
"Live Oak, with Moss" (Whitman), 85–87, 112, 183, 209–10, 212; "gay manifesto," 112; relation between "manly love" and democratic theory, 213, 214; Whitman renounces role as democratic poet, 112, 183, 210; Whitman's love affair with a man in late 1850s, 112, 209, 212
Locke, John, 174–75
Long Island Democrat, 31, 127; Whitman's poems in, 127
Longfellow, Henry Wadsworth, 54
Lord, Judge Otis P., 110; Dickinson and, 110
Lynch, Michael, 89, 99; homosexuality as "distinct" identity, 99

Madison, James, 213; *Federalist* No. 49 on government control of "the passions," 213–14
"Magnanimity Baffled" (Melville), 189; enemy as corpse, 189; Whitman's "Reconciliation," 189
male purity tracts, 82–83, 166
manifest destiny, 82, 104–105
The Manifesto of the Communist Party, 18, 125, 135, 138; Whitman's "Resurgemus," 138
"A March in the Ranks Hard-Prest, and the Road Unknown" (Whitman), 90, 189
Marcuse, Herbert, 203; erotic bonds between individuals and the state, 203

Martin, Robert K., 17, 206; *The Homosexual Tradition in American Poetry* (1979), 17, 206
Marx, Karl, 4, 18, 123–43, 148, 158, 174, 180; *Capital*, 125, 127–32, 143, 180; communism, 143, 148; *Economic and Philosophical Manuscripts*, 18, 123; *German Ideology*, 158; *Grundrisse*, 127; *The Manifesto of the Communist Party*, 4, 18, 125, 133, 135, 140, 148; Paris manuscripts of 1844, 129–30, 141, 143; photograph by Richard Beard, 134; revolutions of 1848, 125, 135–38, 148; "Theses on Feuerbach," 128; Whitman, 4, 18–19, 123–43; working class, 124, 129, 140
Matthiessen, F. O., 16–17, 51, 66, 171–72; *American Renaissance*, 16–17, 20, 51, 171
McCarthyism, 124
McKay, David, 24; publisher of *Leaves of Grass*, 24
"A Meditation" (Melville), 190–91
Melville, Alan, 164; father of Herman Melville, 164; Federalist, 164; depression and madness, 165; loss of import business, 165; sudden death, 165
Melville, Herman, 17, 20, 163–99, 185; and abolition, 165; and African Americans, 189, 191; American Revolution, 164, 170, 181–82; "Bartleby, the Scrivener," 181; the body, 165–67, 170; Civil War, 165, 183–89; conflict capital and labor, 163–65, 167, 170, 171, 172; critique of American imperialism, 167, 180; Declaration of Independence, 170, 199; elegy "On Sherman's Men," 185; George Washington, 177; homoerotic comradeship, 165, 170, 171; *Mardi and a Voyage Hither* as allegory of Revolutions of 1848, 169, 172; marketplace, 165, 167, 170–72, 180; *Omoo: A Narrative of Adventures in the South*, 169; oppression of women, 170, 181; political crisis over labor and slavery in *Moby-Dick*, 168; *Redburn: His First Voyage*, 169–70; slavery, 20, 171, 181, 191; "Tartaress of Maids," 181; tribulations of democracy, 163–99; *Typee: A Peep at Polynesian Life*, 166–67, 169, 172; war with Mexico, 1846–47, 167–68; *White-Jacket; or, the World in a Man-of-War*, 21, 169–70; Whitman, 20–22, 163–99; Young America movement, 169, 172
Melville, Thomas, 164: member of Boston Tea Party, 164; paternal grandfather of Herman Melville, 164
Metternich, Klemens von, 138
Mexican War, 1846–47, 104–106, 167; Civil War, 167; class, 167; debate on extension of slavery, 167; as second American Revolution, 167; Treaty of Guadalupe Hidalgo, 168
Mill, John Stuart, 217; *On Liberty*, 217
Miller, James E., 84
Miller, Perry, 66
Millet, Jean-François, 139, 159; *The Sower*, 139, 159; Whitman, 139–40, 159
Missouri Compromise, 20
Moby-Dick; or, The Whale (1851), 20, 168–77, 180; Ahab as heroic and tragic figure, 173–74; epic of democracy, 171–77; global revolution, 173; Ishmael as first-person narrator, 172; Jacksonian democracy, 173; labor radicalism, 173; literary nationalism, 173; same-sex marriage of Ishmael and Queequeg, 175; whaling adventure and metaphysical quest, 172
Moon, Michael, 82, 166, 205
Mt. Holyoke College, 104–106; daguerreotype of Dickinson, 105

Napoléon, King Louis of France, 145–46, 153–58, 173
Native Americans, 164, 165, 166–67; Melville's *Pierre*, 181; Melville's *Typee*, 166–67
New England, 63, 105–106; origin of American literature, 66; Puritanism, 63
New Orleans, 18, 57–58, 110, 137
New Orleans *Daily Crescent*, 18, 58, 137, 147; Revolutions of 1848, 147; "Sketches of the Sidewalks and Levees," 58; Whitman as writer for, 137, 147; Whitman's use of French in articles for, 57–58
"New Orleans in 1848," 58; and Latin contributions to American nationality, 58
The New World, 82, 165, 205; *Franklin Evans*, 205; mass circulation newspaper, 205
New York, 165; and party politics, 165
New York *Aurora*, 57, 75, 128, 163; Whitman's use of French in editorials, 5
New York *Galaxy*, 158; publication of "O Star of France!" in, 157–58
New York *Tribune*, 4, 137; Fuller's dispatches from Rome in, 137; Marx's weekly columns on Europe in, 137; publication of Whitman's "Resurgemus" in, 137, 147–48
Niles, Thomas, 110

"O Star of France! 1870–71" (Whitman), 19, 62, 145, 157–58; defeat of Paris Commune, 157; France as symbol of Whitman's hopes for future of democracy, 158
O'Connor, William Douglas, 22; *The Good Gray Poet: A Vindication* (1866), 22–23
"On Sherman's Men" (Melville), 184
"One's Self I Sing" (Whitman), 13, 65, 69, 102; dialectics of individual and "En-Masse" in, 154; French "Inscription" of, 65, 154
Osgood, James, 23
"Out of the Cradle Endlessly Rocking" (Whitman), 44, 114, 115–16; Civil War, 115–16; fractured union, 44; "Over the Carnage Rose Prophetic a Voice" (Whitman), 45, 64, 85, 213; Whitman's love crisis, 114; Whitman's terror, 115. *See also* "Calamus" 5; "A Word Out of the Sea"
Owen, Robert Dale, 126; "Critical Utopian Socialism and Communism," 140

Paine, Thomas, 6, 25–26, 103, 126; *The Age of Reason*, 126; *Common Sense*, 6, 25–26
Palmetto Guard of South Carolina, 183; firing on Fort Sumter, 183–84
Panic of 1819, 163; conflict between capital and labor, 163; conflict between North and South, 163; conflict between rich and poor, 163
Paris Commune, 19, 156–57; 1872 preface to *As a Strong Bird on Pinions Free*, 157; formation and bloody suppression in 1871, 156–57; greatest "popular insurrection in modern European history," 157; *Leaves of Grass*, 19, 145–60; *le Temps de Cerises*, 157; "O Star of France!," 157; photograph of *Voltaire Lenoir Barricade of the Paris Commune* by Bruno Braquehais, 157; Whitman's turn toward new volume of poems focused on "Democratic Nationality," 157
Paris Exposition of 1889, 159; exhibition of Eiffel Tower, 159; Whitman's "Bravo, Paris Exposition!," 159
Parker, Herschel, 212

"Passage to India" (Whitman), 65; Hegelian idealism of, 127
"In Paths Untrodden" (Whitman), 16, 212
Philadelphia Lesbian and Gay Task Force, 79–80
Philippe, King Louis, 136, 168; dethroned, 136; Second French Republic declared, 136, 168; Revolutions of 1848, 168
phrenology, 22
Pickering, John, 53; American language policy, 53, 66
"Pictures" (Whitman), 128; Epicurus in, 127–28; scene from Wright's *A Few Days in Athens*, 127–28
Pierre; or, the Ambiguities (Melville), 181
Plato, 203; erotic bonds between individuals and the state, 203
Poe, Edgar Allan, 54; and pure poetry, 54
"Poem of the Propositions of Nakedness" (Whitman), 182. *See also* "Respondez!"
"Poem of Remembrance for a Girl or a Boy of These States" (Whitman), 182
"Poem of the Road" (Whitman), 208–209; first use of word adhesiveness in, 208. *See also* "Song of the Open Road"
"Poem of Salutation" (Whitman), 182. *See also* "Salut au Monde!"
"Poem of the Sayers of the Words of the Earth" (Whitman). *See* "Song of the Rolling Earth"
"Poem of Women" (Whitman). *See* "Unfolded Out of the Folds"
"Poets to Come" (Whitman), 24, 119–20; Dickinson and, 120
political theory, 201–23; and Samuel H. Beer, 202–203; Whitman and, 201–23
post–Civil War years, 119, 155, 193–96; Dickinson's "Work for Immortality," 119–20; emergence of new power state, 193; failure of black equality and civil rights, 196; Melville's embrace of non-state forms of democratic affection, 194; social decline, 119; Whitman's *Democratic Vistas*, 193–94; Whitman's "Poets to Come," 119–20; Whitman's "Songs of Insurrection," 194
Pound, Ezra, 7, 66
The Primer of Words (Whitman), 10, 53–54, 62, 63
Protestant missions, 166; in Age of Jackson, 166; to Hawaiian Islands, 166; to South Pacific, 166
"Proto-Leaf" (Whitman), 64, 65, 210–11. *See also* "Starting from Paumanok"
"Proud Music of the Storm" (Whitman), 65
Proudhon, Pierre-Joseph, 129
Prussia, King of, 146
public education movement, 166; Age of Jackson, 166
public sphere, 204; Habermas and, 204; non-state forms of participation, 204; resistance to liberal privatization, 204; resistance to sexual oppression, 204; Whitman and, 204

Rambles Among Words, 62; Whitman as coauthor of, 62
Raynal, Abbé, 25
The Rebellion Record (1862–65), 184; Melville and, 184
"Reconciliation" (Whitman), 188–89; attempt to bind up wounds of nation, 188–89; Lincoln's Second Inaugural Address, 188–89; Melville's "Magnanimity Baffled" and, 189

Reconstruction, 165, 193; leviathan state and, 193
"Recorders Ages Hence" (Whitman), 212. *See also* "Live Oak, with Moss"
Rees Welsh and Company, 23
republican myth, 182
Republican Party, 110, 177
"Respondez!" (Whitman), 40–41, 150, 182–83; democratic world in negative, 150; relation of poet's crisis to political crisis of nation, 41
"Resurgemus" (Whitman), 4, 5, 6, 36, 137–38, 147–49, 169; *Communist Manifesto* and, 138; earliest free-verse poem in 1855 *Leaves of Grass*, 137, 169; revolutions of 1848 in Europe, 137, 147–49, 169. *See also* "Europe, the 72d and 73d Years of These States"
Revolutions of 1848, 125, 126, 133, 135, 137, 140, 147–51, 168, 169, 209; Europe and, 137; *Leaves of Grass*, 4, 6, 18–19, 36–37, 38, 125, 135, 137; Marx and, 123–43; Millet's *The Sower*, 139, 159; "Resurgemus," 137, 147–49; Whitman and, 123–43, 147–51
Rheinische Zeitung, 128; Marx's writings for, 128–29
Ricardo, David, 130
Rich, Adrienne, 18; "Beginners," 18
Rimbaud, Arthur, 14
"Rise O Days from your Fathomless Deeps" (Whitman), 89
Rogin, Michael, 135
Rome, Andrew, 1
Rorty, Richard, 209; *Achieving Our Country*, 209; "Whitman's image of democracy was of lovers embracing," 209
Rossetti, William Michael, 154
Ruskin, John, 54
Russia, 145; abolition of serfdom in, 145
Saint-Simon, Henri de, 140; "Critical Utopian Socialism and Communism," 140
"Salut au Monde!" (Whitman), 19, 42, 43, 61, 63, 150, 182; *chansons* of Pierre-Jean de Béranger, 150; international focus, 150, 182
Sawyer, Tom, 99; Whitman and, 99
Schiller, Friedrich: *On the Aesthetic Education of Man*, 1
Schmidgall, Gary, 206
"The Scout toward Aldie" (Melville), 184; Civil War ballad, 184; erotic camaraderie, 189
Second World War, 4
sectional conflict, 133; southern secession, 133
sentimentalism, 165; *Franklin Evans* and, 205; language of, 205
Shakespeare, William, 170; Melville on, 170
Shively, Charley, 14, 82, 84
"A Sight in Camp in the Day-break Grey and Dim" (Whitman), 90
Sismondi, Jean Charles Léonard de, 140; "petty-bourgeois socialism" of, 140
"Slang in America" (Whitman), 55
slave revolt, 181; insurrection led by Toussaint L'Ouverture's in San Domingo, 18; Melville's "Benito Cereno," 181
slavery, 4–5, 70, 103–105, 132, 133, 135, 145, 167–71, 181, 191, 210; Compromise of 1850, 135, 167–71; extension of, 135; removal in the United States, 145, 152
"The Sleepers" (Whitman), 6, 24, 25, 26, 60–61, 103, 207; French language, 60–61; "obscene literature," 23; sex and the body, 60
Smith, Adam, 130, 214; *The Theory of*

Smith, Adam (*continued*)
Moral Sentiments and Whitman's theory of democracy, 214
Smith, John, 52; *Map of Virginia*, 52
Smith-Rosenberg, Carroll, 23
"So Far, and So Far, and On Toward the End" (Whitman), 41, 43
socialism, 4, 126; Horace Greeley, 4
"Song of the Answerer" (Whitman), 8–9
"Song of the Broad-Axe" (Whitman), 61
"Song for Certain Congressmen" (Whitman), 135, 137–38
"Song of the Exposition" (Whitman), 48, 65
"Song of Myself" (Whitman, 1855), 1–4, 6–14, 16, 23, 60–61, 69–79, 100, 103, 108, 154, 177–80, 207–208; anti-masturbation tracts, 73, 83; capitalism, 15, 70, 74, 180; dialectic of *I* and *you*, 108, 180; drama of identity, 6–7, 16, 70, 74, 88; epic of democracy, 71, 178; experiment in self-government, 70–76, 178–79; homoerotic love and democracy, 177, 205–206; homosexual love in, 72, 110–11, 177, 205–23; lack of final period in 1855, 7, 76; Marx's 1844 Paris manuscripts, 141–43; masturbation and democracy in, 72–73, 179, 206–207; poet's mystical vision in, 37, 84, 177, 205–206; reader, 13, 27, 77, 108, 180
"Song of Myself" (Whitman, 1881), 24, 100, 123; as political theory, 202–203
"Song of the Open Road" (Whitman), 19, 24, 61, 64, 88, 150; adhesiveness in, 64, 150; French fraternity in, 64; French language in, 64–65, 150
"A Song of the Rolling Earth" (Whitman), 61, 88
"Songs of Insurrection" (Whitman), 155; French inscription of, 155–56; grouping added to *Leaves of Grass* (1871), 155; Revolutions in France, 156
Spain, 146; democratic struggles in, 146
"Sparkles from the Wheel" (Whitman), 119; labor as craftsmanship, 119
Specimen Days and Collect (Whitman), 152
Spiller, Robert, 65–66
Stafford, Harry, 92, 94, 95; Whitman and, 92
"Starting from Paumanok" (Whitman), 64, 210–11; confessional voice of, 22; "manly love" as source of political union, 210–11; as preface to 1860 and future editions of *Leaves of Grass*, 210; Whitman as "evangel poet" of "manly love," 211. *See also* "Proto-Leaf"
Stevens, Oliver, 23, 24
"Still Though the One I Sing" (Whitman), 155
As a Strong Bird on Pinions Free and Other Poems (Whitman), 157–58; "Democratic Nationality" as new form of affective union worldwide, 158; new volume of poems on "Democratic Nationality" announced in preface, 157–58
Sue, Eugène, 57
"Sun-Down Poem" (Whitman), 182. *See also* "Crossing Brooklyn Ferry"
Swinton, William, 62; *Rambles Among Words*, 62
Switzerland, 148; and transnational origins of *Leaves of Grass*, 148
Symonds, John Addington, 95, 99; medicalization of homosexuality, 99; "sexual inversion" as abnormal and pathological, 99; *Walt Whitman: A Study*, 95; Whitman's six children, 99

Talmadge, James Jr., 163; Missouri Compromise of 1820, 163
Talmadge Amendment, 163; Thomas Jefferson on conflict between North and South, 163
Taylor, Isaac: *Liberty Triumphs Over Tyranny*, 33–34
Taylor, Zachary, 105
temperance movement, 165–66, 205; *Franklin Evans*, 205; same-sex eroticism, 205
Tennyson, Alfred, 54
"There Was a Child Went Forth" (Whitman), 38–40
Thoreau, Henry David, 17
"Thou Mother with Thy Equal Brood" (Whitman), 65
Tobey, Edward S., 23–24
"To a Common Prostitute" (Whitman), 23; as "obscene literature," 23
"To a Foil'd European Revolutionaire" (Whitman), 150, 156; war for democracy in Europe, 156
"To Foreign Lands" (Whitman), 154
"To the Sayers of Words" (Whitman). *See* "A Song of the Rolling Earth"
"To Thee Old Cause" (Whitman), 154, 155
"To Think of Time" (Whitman), 60
Transatlantic Walt Whitman Association (TWWA), 27, 146; founded in Paris, France, in 2007, 146; founding values of international comradeship, sympathy, and love, 146
Traubel, Horace, 11, 23, 97
Treaty of Guadalupe Hidalgo, 168; Revolutions of 1848 and, 168
"Trickle Drops" (Whitman), 214
Tucker, Benjamin, 23–24

"Unfolded Out of the Folds" (Whitman), 40, 44
United States, 183, 195–96; crisis of union, 183; depression of 1857, 183; Ku Klux Klan, 196; lynching, 196; politics of Jim Crow, 196; rise of imperial state, 195–96; slavery and, 183
United States and Democratic Review, 108

Van Buren, Martin, 133
Vaughan, Fred, 99, 112; Whitman and, 99, 112
"Vigil Strange I Kept on the Field One Night" (Whitman), 90
"Virginia—the West" (Whitman), 46–48
Volney, Constantin, 126; *The Ruins, or Meditations on the Revolutions of Empires*, 126

Wadsworth, Charles, 110; and Emily Dickinson, 110
Walt Whitman Bridge, 80
Walt Whitman Poetry Center, 80
Warner, Michael, 166, 205
Washington, George, 6, 21, 31, 41, 48, 103, 201, 207, 215; as democratic comrade in "The Sleepers," 103, 201, 207; farewell to Continental army, 201, 207, 215; new forms of antipatriarchal authority, 201; Whitman's brother named after, 103
Washingtonian movement, 205
Webster, Noah, 52–53; *American Dictionary of the English Language*, 52, 59; *Dissertations on the English Language*, 53; on decline of British language, 53
Wharton, Edith, 51; *A Backward Glance*, 51
Wheatley, Phillis, 192; and Whitman's "Ethiopia Saluting the Colors," 192

"When I Heard at the Close of the Day" (Whitman), 90
"When Lilacs Last in the Dooryard Bloom'd" (Whitman), 118
Whig Party, 105–106; fear of imperialist policies of President Polk, 105–106
White-Jacket, or, The World in a Man-of-War (Melville), 21, 169–70; bonds of affection between men, 170–71; criticism of flogging in American Navy, 170; criticism of slavery, 171
Whitman, George, 95; brother of Walt Whitman, 95
Whitman, Walt: adhesiveness, 21, 63–65; African Americans, 25, 26, 56, 214; amativeness, 63, 87; American Revolution, 31–50, 164; antislavery of, 4–5, 20, 35, 36, 106, 133, 145, 149, 163–64, 167–69, 171–72, 177; Bill Duckett, 95, 96; the body, 1, 7–8, 11–12, 26, 69–77, 165–67; Chaucer, 59; Christ-likeness photograph of, 142; "chum" photographs, 93, 94, 95–97; Civil War, 46–48, 65, 89–92, 116–18, 163–64, 183–89; clerk in Attorney General's office, 23; clerk in Bureau of Indian Affairs, 22–23; Compromise of 1850, 135; critic of capitalism, 4–5, 8, 15, 18, 20, 49, 70, 74, 124–32, 149, 163–64, 171, 180; democratic individualism, 4, 13, 123; Democratic Party, 126, 128, 137, 164; Dickinson, 17–18, 101–20, 210; editor of *Aurora*, 57; Edmond Burke, 214; Emerson, 5, 13–14, 16–17; fired for moral turpitude by Department of Interior, 97; France, 62, 124, 130, 136, 145–60, 209; French language, 51, 56–66, 209; foreign language, 51–52, 56–66; Fred Vaughan, 99; Free Soil Party, 133; French champagne, 159; French language, 57–59, 151–52, 209; French Reign of Terror, 151–53; Freneau, 35–36; global democratic struggle, 124, 136, 141, 145–60; global union, 125, 179–80; "good gray" poet, 65, 89, 92, 95–97; Harry Stafford, 92, 94–95, 99; Henry James, 51; homoerotic comradeship, 165–67, 215; homosexuality, 4, 7, 13–14, 16, 17, 79–100, 112, 123, 177–79, 199; homosexuality and democracy, 21, 79–100, 177–79, 215; "illegitimate sons," 99; "immense problem" of "Labor" and "Capital," 158, 163–64, 167, 180; international vision, 4–5, 7, 124–25; John O'Sullivan, 167; journalist and editor, 126, 128, 165; labor, 124–25, 128, 129–32, 133, 163, 214; *Leaves of Grass* (1855) as epic of democracy, 171–72, 177–81; Lebesque, 159; Lincoln as "comrade lustrous" and lover, 65; Marx, 4, 18–19, 21, 123–43, 158; materialist philosophy of Epicurus, 127–28; Melville, 163–99; Millet's *The Sower*, 139, 159; move to Camden, New Jersey, 95, 119; "mystical" poet, 17, 79; national language policy, 53–54, 66; Native Americans, 25, 26; New Orleans romance, 110, 137; notebooks on language, 10–11; Paine, 126; paralytic stroke, 95, 119, 158; Paris Commune, 153–60; personal crisis and crisis of the union, 40–44; Peter Doyle, 92–95; Philéas Lebesque, 159; political theory, 21, 201–23; politics of language, 51–66; post–Civil War years, 65, 95, 97–98; the public sphere, 204–205; race, 25, 26, 36; relation democratic language and American polity, 53–66; relation with reader, 13, 27, 180; revolutions of 1848, 4, 6, 18–19, 36–37, 123–43, 147–50; "set-tos with the state,"

22–24; support for expansionist politics of President Polk, 167; tribulations of democracy, 163–99; trip to New Orleans and French language, 57–58; on U.S. imperialism, 25, 167; victory of Union as triumph of comradeship and love, 189; Volney, 126; war with Mexico, 1846–47, 167; Warren Fritzinger, 95, 97; Washington, DC hospitals, 65, 89–92, 116, 184, 186; Whitman and Scottish moral sense philosophy of Adam Smith, 214; Whitman's "boys," 92–98, 119; women, 25, 31–50, 214; worker revolution, 4, 141, 147–49; working-class roots, 6, 125–26, 165; wound-dresser, 48, 89–90, 96, 184; Young America movement, 172
Whitman, Walter Sr., 103, 164; anticapitalist and anticlerical platform of, 165; carpenter, 165; free thinker, 164; subscriber to *Free Enquirer*, 164–65; supporter of socialists Frances Wright and Robert Dale Owen, 164–65; Thomas Paine radical, 103, 164
Wilde, Oscar, 24; visit with Whitman, 24; Whitman's kiss, 24
Wilmot, David, 168; the Wilmot Proviso, 168
Witherspoon, John, 52, 54, 66
Wolosky, Shira, 116
"A Woman Waits for Me" (Whitman), 23, 24, 101–103; amative love in, 87; censorship of, 87; as "obscene literature," 23; phallic male sexuality in, 87–88
women's suffrage, 110
"A Word Out of the Sea" (Whitman). *See* "Out of the Cradle Endlessly Rocking"
World War I, 50
"The Wound-Dresser" (Whitman), 89–90
Wright, Frances, 126; *A Few Days in Athens*, 126, 127–28

"Years of the Modern" (Whitman), 156; American Civil War as global democratic war, 156; formation and bloody suppression of the Paris Commune in 1871, 157; uprisings in France in 1868 and 1871, 156
"Years of the Unperform'd" (Whitman), 192; "solidarity of the races" in, 192
Young America movement, 169; and Melville, 169

Ziff, Larzer, 51; *Literary Democracy*, 51; Whitman's use of foreign terms, 51

THE IOWA WHITMAN SERIES

The Afterlives of Specimens: Science, Mourning, and Whitman's Civil War
by Lindsay Tuggle

Conserving Walt Whitman's Fame: Selections from Horace Traubel's "Conservator," 1890–1919
edited by Gary Schmidgall

Constructing the German Walt Whitman
by Walter Grünzweig

Democratic Vistas: The Original Edition in Facsimile
by Walt Whitman, edited by Ed Folsom

Every Hour, Every Atom: A Collection of Walt Whitman's Early Notebooks and Fragments
edited by Zachary Turpin and Matt Miller

The Evolution of Walt Whitman
by Roger Asselineau

Intimate with Walt: Selections from Whitman's Conversations with Horace Traubel, 1888–1892
edited by Gary Schmidgall

Leaves of Grass, 1860: The 150th Anniversary Facsimile Edition
by Walt Whitman, edited by Jason Stacy

Life and Adventures of Jack Engle
by Walt Whitman, introduction by Zachary Turpin

"The Million Dead, Too, Summ'd Up": Walt Whitman's Civil War Writings: A Selection with Commentary
by Ed Folsom and Christopher Merrill

A Place for Humility: Whitman, Dickinson, and the Natural World
by Christine Gerhardt

The Pragmatic Whitman: Reimagining American Democracy
by Stephen John Mack

Selected Letters of Walt Whitman
edited by Edwin Haviland Miller

Song of Myself: With a Complete Commentary
by Walt Whitman, introduction and commentary by Ed Folsom and Christopher Merrill

Supplement to "Walt Whitman: A Descriptive Bibliography"
by Joel Myerson

"This Mighty Convulsion": Whitman and Melville Write the Civil War
edited by Christopher Sten and Tyler Hoffman

Transatlantic Connections: Whitman U.S., Whitman U.K.
by M. Wynn Thomas

Visiting Walt: Poems Inspired by the Life and Work of Walt Whitman
edited by Sheila Coghill and Thom Tammaro

Walt Whitman: The Centennial Essays
edited by Ed Folsom

Walt Whitman: The Correspondence, Volume VII
edited by Ted Genoways

Walt Whitman and the Class Struggle
by Andrew Lawson

Walt Whitman and the Earth: A Study in Ecopoetics
by M. Jimmie Killingsworth

Walt Whitman and the World
edited by Gay Wilson Allen and Ed Folsom

Walt Whitman, Where the Future Becomes Present
edited by David Haven Blake and Michael Robertson

Walt Whitman's Reconstruction: Poetry and Publishing between Memory and History
by Martin T. Buinicki

Walt Whitman's Selected Journalism
edited by Douglas A. Noverr and Jason Stacy

Walt Whitman's "Song of Myself": A Mosaic of Interpretations
by Edwin Haviland Miller

Walt Whitman's Songs of Male Intimacy and Love: "Live Oak, with Moss" and "Calamus"
edited by Betsy Erkkila

Whitman & Dickinson: A Colloquy
edited by Éric Athenot and Cristanne Miller

Whitman among the Bohemians
edited by Joanna Levin and Edward Whitley

Whitman and the Irish
by Joann P. Krieg

A Whitman Chronology
by Joann P. Krieg

Whitman East and West: New Contexts for Reading Walt Whitman
edited by Ed Folsom

Whitman Noir: Black America and the Good Gray Poet
edited by Ivy G. Wilson

Whitman in Poland: The Reception and Role of the American Poet in Polish National Culture
by Marta A. Skwara, translated by John Merchant

The Whitman Revolution: Sex, Poetry, and Politics
by Betsy Erkkila

Whitman's Drift: Imagining Literary Distribution
by Matt Cohen